ANTHROPOLOGY, DEVELOPMENT AND NATION BUILDING

About the Editors

A.K. Kalla (*b*.1942) is a Reader in the Department of Anthropology of the University of Delhi, and has succeeded late Prof. L.P. Vidyarthi, as President of Indian Anthropological Association (Regd.). Dr. Kalla is the author of the book "Kashmiri Pandits and their Diversity" and about 40 research articles published in Indian and international journals. He has directed U.G.C. sponsored research projects, and is presently directing an Indo-German research project on "Anthropological Study of Variation in Cranlo Spinal Fusion".

Dr. Kalla was invited by the Seventh International Congress of Human Genetics (Berlin - Sept. 21-26, 1986) to present an invited paper.

K.S. Singh (*b*.1935) has spent many years serving and studying backward communities in middle India. He was fellow, Indian Institute of Advanced Study, Shimla (1970) and Jawaharlal Nehru Fellow (1970-72). As Director of the Anthropological Survey of India (1976-77), he planned and organised many all-India surveys to generate the profiles of tribal society. He has written about 200 papers and reports and three books: Birsa Munda and His Movement in Chotanagpur, (1983). The Indian Famine 1967: A study in Crisis and Change (1975), and Tribal Society of India (1985). He edited Tribal Situation in India (1976) for the Indian Institute of Advanced Study and two volumes on Tribal Movements and Economies of the Tribes and thier Transformation. He has also introduced W.G. Archer's Santal Laws and Justice (Concept 1983). Currently, he is Director-General of the Anthropological Survey of India.

ANTHROPOLOGY, DEVELOPMENT AND NATION BUILDING

Edited by
A.K. KALLA and K.S. SINGH

CONCEPT PUBLISHING COMPANY PVT. LTD.
NEW DELHI-110059

(Based on the National Seminar on 'Anthropology in the service of nation' November 19-21, 1986, jointly organised by the Indian Anthropological Association and the Anthropological Survey of India)

ISBN: 978-81-7022-001-5

First Edition 1987

Published and Printed by

Concept
Since 1974

Concept Publishing Company Pvt. Ltd.
A/15-16, Commercial Block, Mohan Garden,
New Delhi-110059 (India)
T: 91-11-41101460
E: publishing@conceptpub.com, *W*: www.conceptpub.com

PREFACE

Sometime ago the Indian Anthropological Association (IAA) and the Anthropological Survey of India (ASI) decided to collaborate in a number of ways to promote the cause of anthropological research and explore its relevance to the task of nation building. The seminar on "Anthropology in the Service of Nation" is the first tangible result of this institutional collaboration.

Few disciplines are as close to people and provide such a holistic picture of society as anthropology does. The forte of an anthropologist has been his many years of exposure to people. Even though the compulsions of a fast moving age such as ours have robbed an anthropologist's adventures of much of their romance, the imperatives of the field work considerably aided by the new technology of investigation still hold. In the colonial period, ethnographers generated information about people and their coustoms for the benefit of the raj. Some of them also spoke up for the primitive communities and suggested measures for their welfare. After Independence, anthropologists have got together frequently to explore the relevance of their studies to the growing challenge of development. In recent years, path-breaking researches have been undertaken in the field of physical anthropology, which are immensely relevant to the task of upgrading the status of health and nutrition for a vast number of our people living below the level of poverty. Similarly, in the area of social and cultural anthropology a good deal of work has been done that offers a valuable insight into our people's traditions, attitude and bahaviour which are now considered an essential social input in planning and development process.

Therefore, the Indian Anthropological Association and the Anthropological Survey of India decided to explore together the latest trends of research which have significant implications for the urgent task of nation building in all its aspects. The papers generated with this objective in view fall into five major concerns. These relate to health and nutrition, genetic structure and well-being of weaker sections, problems of women and children, development of backward areas and backward communities, conservation of ecology and environment and intervi relationship of ethnicity, secularism, communal harmony and national integration. The first two papers promote a general perspective. Taken together, the papers are fairly representative of the work being done in various sub-disciplines of anthropology. Today these researches are symbolic of the Indian anthropologist's commitment to nation building.

Our thanks are many. First, we would like to express our gratitude to the funding agencies such as Ministry of Welfare, Govt. of India, Anthropological Survey of India, Indian Council of Social Science Research and World University Service (Delhi Unit). We also thank Lok Kalyan Simiti (Delhi) for their help. Prof. S.C. Tiwari, Head of the department of Anthropology, University of Delhi, and his colleagues deserve a very special thanks for all the help they have rendered to us. We are thankful to Dr. S.L. Malik, Reader, in the department of Anthropology, University of Delhi for helping us in the final preparation of the manuscript. We would particularly like to thank the young and enthusiastic scholars Sunil Khanna, Mohinder Prakash and Miss Saraswati Sharma of the department of Anthropology, University of Delhi for their valuable contribution in the preparation of the manuscript and for the enormous work they did to organise the seminar. The Concept Publishing Company has already established its reputation as the publisher of works on Anthropology which have been widely welcomed.

A. K.KALLA K. S. SINGH

CONTENTS

Preface v
List of Contributors ix

1. Physical Anthropology—Its Relevance in Nation Building **A. K. Kalla** 1

2. Anthropology, Culture and Development **K. S. Singh** 13

3. Mother, Child and Family in West Bengal : A Study of Some Correlates Influencing their Welfare **Kanti Pakrasi, P. Dasgupta** and **I. Dasgupta** 37

4. People—the Missing Link of the National Health and Family Welfare Programme **A. Bardhan** and **D. C. Dubey** 49

5. Ethnic Identity and Nation - Building in North-East India **A. C. Sinha** 61

6. Survival and Revival of Ethnic Identities of Chakmas and Mizos of Mizoram **B. B. Goswami** 77

7. Genetic, Socio-cultural and Health Care among Tribal Groups of Jagdalpur and Konta tehsils of Bastar district (Madhya Pradesh) **Salil Basu** 87

8. Genetics and Health of Weaker Section : An Anthropological Insight **R. K. Gulati** 107

9. Genetic Differentiation among the Tribal Populations of Orissa, India **A. K. Kapoor** 117

10. Genetic Structure Studies and Well-being of Weaker Sections : An Over View With some New Thoughts for Biological Anthropologists **Lalit K. Kashyap** 127

11. Promoting Occupational Mobility among Scheduled Castes : Problems and Prospects **R. R. Prasad** 147

12. Development and Anthropology : Rebuilding Rural and Tribal India **P. K. Bhowmick** 157

13. Hunter - Gatherers of the Bay Islands : Problems and Nature of Culture Contact **T. N. Pandit** 165

14. Role of Nutrition in Physical Growth and Development **J. C. Sharma** 175

15. Physique and Body Composition of Indian Female Players **L. S. Sidhu** and **R. Mokha** 189

16. Auxological Anthropometry in Monitoring Population Health and Nutrition **S. Prakash** 201

17. Health Care in Rural India : Problems and Challenges **S. Srinivasan** 211

18. Communal Harmony in India : Reflections in a Secular Context **Shalina Mehta** 221

19. Political Anthropology of Displacement, Relocation and Future of Transfer of Technology : An Overview and Issues **B. K. Roy Burman** 233

20. Anthropology of Displaced : Problems of Resettlement and Development Alternatives **P. K. Nayak** 247

21. Ecology, Environment and Population : Some Basic Issues **M. R. Chakravartti** 261

22. Man-Tree Relationship in an Urban Setting: a Socio-ecological Study **Kailash C. Malhotra** and **M. Vijaya Kumar** 273

LIST OF CONTRIBUTORS

BARDHAN, S (Assoc. Professor) and DUBEY DC (Professor), Department of Social Sciences, National Institute of Health and Family Welfare, New Mahrauli Road, Munirka, New Delhi-110067.

BASU, SALIL (Assoc. Professor), Head, Department of Population Genetics and Human Development, National Institute of Health and Family Welfare, New Mahrauli Road, Munirka, New Delhi-110067.

BHOWMICK, PK (Professor), Department of Anthropology, University of Calcutta, Calcutta-700019.

CHAKRAVARTTI, MR (Professor), Department of Anthropology, Manipur University, Kanchipur-705003, Imphal, Manipur.

GOSWAMI, BB (Joint Director), Anthropological Survey of India, Indian museum, 27 Jawahar Lal Nehru Road, Calcutta 700016.

GULATI, RK (Deputy Director), Anthropological Survey of India, North West region, Kaulagarh Road, Dehradun-248195.

KALLA, AK (Reader) Department of Anthropology, University of Delhi, Delhi-110007.

KAPOOR, ANOOP (Lecturer) Department of Anthropology, University of Delhi, Delhi-110007.

KASHYAP, LALIT K (Asstt. Director), Commission for Scheduled Castes and Scheduled Tribes, Ministry of Welfare, Government of India, Lok Nayak Bhawan, New Delhi-110003.

MALHOTRA, KAILASH C (Professor), KUMAR M VIJAYA (Asstt. Professor), Anthropometry and Human Genetics Unit, Biological Sciences Division, Indian Statistical Institute, 203, B.T. Road, Calcutta-700035.

MEHTA, SHALINA (Lecturer), Department of Anthropology, Punjab University, Chandigarh-160014.

NAYAK, PK (Reader), Post Graduate Department of Anthropology, Utkal University, Vani Vihar, Bhubaneswar-751004. Orissa.

PAKRASI, KANTI (Professor), DAS GUPTA P (Assoc. Professor), DAS GUPTA I (Asstt. Professor), Anthropometry and Human Genetics Unit, Biological Sciences Division, Indian Statistical Institute, 203, B.T. Road, Calcutta-700035.

PANDIT, TN (Deputy Director), Anthropological Survey of India, Indian museum, 27, Jawahar Lal Nehru Road, Calcutta-700016.

PRAKASH, S (Reader), Department of Anthropology Punjab University, Chandigarh-160014.

PRASAD, RR (Deputy Director), Faculty of Cultural Anthropology, National Institute of Human Development, Rajendra Nagar, Hyderabad-500030, A.P.

ROY, BURMAN, BK (Professor) Centre for Studies of Developing Society, 29, Rajpur Road, Delhi-110054.

SHARMA, JC (Professor) Department of Anthropology, Panjab University, Chandigarh-160014.

SIDHU, LS (Professor), MOKHA R (Lecturer) Department of Human Biology, Panjabi University, Patiala-147002.

SINGH, KS (Director General) Anthropological Survey of India, West Block—2, First Floor, 6th Wing, R.K. Puram, Sect. I, New Delhi-110022.

SINHA, AC (Professor), Department of Sociology, North Eastern Hill University, Shillong.

SRINIVASAN, S (Asstt. Director), Faculty of Human Resource Development, National Institute of Rural Development, Rajendra Nagar, Hyderabad-500030.

ONE

PHYSICAL ANTHROPOLOGY - ITS RELEVANCE IN NATION BUILDING

A.K. Kalla

Power may come through the barrel of the gun but need not necessarily be retained through this Maoist device - a fact so clearly understood by the imperialist adventurists in India; they started working on an alternative formulation for retention of their stranglehod over this rich and beautiful land. There could be only two alternatives - one, mass co-operation, and two, mass-division and selective patronization. To the British rulers, mass co-operation looked like an ever-distant thing, and rightly so. Their ultimate choice fell on 'mass-division' for sustaining their mighty rule in India. It was not the passion of the Britishers to understand the people of this great nation that brought an administration anthropologist of the rank of Sir Herbert Risley on the scene, but it was their subtle move to initiate such studies through him so that the first generation of Indian anthropologists may in their own ways, transcribe the message of Risley's studies - i.e., of the striking diversity of the Indian masses, giving full hog credibility to the caste system, the system of 'superior' and 'inferior' groups of people of India. Grierson's linguistic survey of India was further misused to project a highly divided nation on this ground. But for their misuse, these two studies, even with their shortcomings, can be rated as monumental anthropological studies in a country in which anthropology had yet to make a regular formal beginning.

Fortunately for us, the very first generation of Indian anthropologists belonging to the Calcutta School, did not fall into the trap of the Britishers and, as in any other field, started thinking on their own. The existing paradigms were difficult to dispense with; no wonder that R. P. Chanda sounded like another Risley in his work on Indo-Aryan Races. But soon the lead was taken by the anthropologists influenced by the indigenous traditions of 'taking a look from within'. Sarat Chandra Roy, B. S. Guha, and N. K. Bose, ensured through their varied anthropological studies that the Indian masses exhibit a unity in diversity - whether physical, social or cultural - a message more relevant today than ever before.

B.S. Guha can be considered the pioneer physical anthropologist of India; his 'Racial Elements in the Population' publsihed in 1944 remains a masterpiece work, albeit its major criticism was that it was based on too small samples to allow generalizations of the nature attempted in it. Guha's sixfold classification of Indian population, based on morphological diversity, richly imbibed the knowledge of racial history, palaeoanthropology, cultural anthropology and human geography; its distinctive feature has been the establishment of relevance of physical anthropology in the Indian context.

Schools of anthropology led by Majumdar (D.N.), Biswas (P.C.) and Karve (I.) further revealed the significance of physical anthropological studies in India. While Majumdar propagated a healthy combination of physical anthropology and social anthropology, Biswas cultivated the expertise on the applied aspects of physical anthropology, and Iravati Karve worked for the synthesis of physical anthropology with archaeology and socio-cultural dynamics. One generation later, the Chandigarh school of physical anthropologists, led by S. R. K. Chopra, distinctively re-established the significance of physical anthropology in palaeoanthropological studies dealing with search for early hominids in the country (Chopra and Simmons 1969). His work in the Sivalik region received international recognition.

All these efforts highlighted in the multifacted usefulness of physical anthropology in nation building; while on the one hand formally trained anthropologists continued in their endeavour, on the other hand experts from medicine, zoology, genetics and statistics got attracted by the meaningfulness of these studies and started making their own contributions towards physical anthropological researches - mostly in collaboration with trained anthroplogists and sometimes independently; nevertheless, it invariably furthered physical anthropological knowledge about our people with its consequentially increased applied scope. The pragmatism of the founders of physcial anthroplogy in India posed an exciting and challenging situation before Indian physical anthropologists with a number of channels open for them for their pursuit to be able to serve the nation; but this could occur only if they applied proper discretion of their own and caught the right wave, ignoring avoidable counter currents. The various channels made available to the Indian physical anthroplogists ranged in their contents from the classic Evolutionary studies to the biological welfare of the people; these are search for early hominids and reconstructing the histroy of evolution of man in India; understanding Indian population structure, bio-demographic genetic, and morphological; and understanding adaption of Indian population. While works of Sankalia (1969), Sankalia and Karve (1949), Chopra (1979), and Malhotra (1967) have provided sound foundation for the evolutionary studies in India, the studies conducted by Tiwari (1972), Kumar and Ghosh (1967), Chakravartti (1967), Sharma (1970), Das et al (1975), Bhatia and Sanghvi (1962), Balakrishnan and Sanghvi (1965), Kaur and Srivastava (1982 and 1983), Seth et al. (1983), Seth and Seth (1978), Tara Devi (1979), Ghosh et al. (1979) are the indicators of a reasonably high level of achievement in understanding genetic (whether population genetic or biochemical genetic, or medical genetic or serological genetic or cytogenetic) structure and variability of the Indian populations. Morphological structure of Indian castes, communities and tribes is rather widely studied by various anthropologists; these studies attempted to understand variation.

Sanghvi (1953), provided the basic analytical tool for comparing genetical and morphological differences between various populations. Studies have been conducted on variations in growth and development patterns of various caste/community/tribal groups (Singh 1966; Singh and Raja 1980; Kaur and Singh 1983; Sharma and Sharma 1984; Prakash and Pattimanathan 1984), dermatoglyphic variations (Biswas 1936; Singh 1959; Sarkar 1961; Sharma 1966; Mukharjee 1967; Sharma and Taneja 1968; Datta 1969; Bali and Chaube 1971; Kumbnani 1978 etc.), variations in Dental morphology, (Sharma and Kaul 1977; Kaul and Prakash 1984; Rami Reddy 1985; Bhasin et al. 1985), and skin colour variations (Tiwari 1963; Kalla 1985; Jaiswal 1977; Das and Mukherhjee 1963), Banerjee, (1979).

The bio-demographic structure of Indian population has been studied by various physical anthroplogists but the in-depth studies have been attempted by few (Chakravartti 1968, 1978; Chakravartti and Chakravartti 1977; Bhowmick 1969; Malhotra 1974; Basu 1982; Kalla 1985; Fernandez 1985; Gupta 1985 etc.). Such micro studies need to be further strengthened and improved in order to be of better consequence in the population planning schemes of the nation. To be of greater use to the nation, anthroplogists need to work out a blue print of the plan of research of such studies at the regional level, identifying continuity and or contrasts in nation's approach for population planning within a region. An appropriate co-ordination with the planning commission and other allied agencies will be inevitable and must be sought. Let it be remembered that population planning may as radically be changed as now done in China (Bongaarts and Greenhalgh 1985), the most populated nation in the world which, in terms of population, is followed by no other country than India.

Choose and pick policy in anthropological studies needs to be abandoned. Indian physical anthroplogists, in general, have somehow come to adhere themselves to what I may call 'phototranscribing research' - theses after theses and paper after paper on the same pattern with variation in the noun parts of it. Even such theses and papers could be of use if contemplated in the format of regional planning; but unfortunately it is not so. Without having the obsession of the pioneer Indian physical anthropologist, namely, B.S. Guha, his vision and research planning must always be borne in mind by each and every physical anthropologist on the Indian scene-whether an entrepreneur or an experienced one, if one intends to seriously serve the nation through one's anthroplogical endeavour.

Some 'leading' and some 'not so leading' Indian physical anthroplogists working in the field of bio-chemical genetics or serological genetics have unfortunately cultivated a habit of sending blood samples of different Indian caste/community/tribal groups to various foreign laboratories; this ominous trend must stop if we seriously want to play a more constructive part in the development of the nation. As in any other science, we may import the technology from abroad but we must practise it ourselves. Despite lots of financial restrains, our nation is in a position to provide us sufficient research grants for anthropological researches and for developing indegenous technology or for borrowing foreign technology, provided that the research plans are well conceived. Surprisingly the sort of analysis of the blood samples sought from foreign laboratories is invariably indegenously obtainable and practised. Besides depriving the nation of developing or importing the needed technology for the present and the future needs of the nation, the above, none-too-happy trend, may also lead to expose our population to a covert risk in times of international crisis involving India. How can one be sure whether the blood samples of some of our strategically important populations, like the tribal populations of sensitive areas, will only be analysed for a particular blood group or enzyme system and not tested for some other chemical warfare purpose? While the Indian physical anthropolgists are thinking of entering the phase of genetic engineering or welfare of the nation, it should not elude their imagination that the serum or the cells of blood can also be tested to render the information, so gathered, useful in the times of subtle chemical warefare. Shall we, then, do some rethinking about it, lest the Indian Physical anthropologists fail in serving the nation and instead harm her cause?

However, it does not undermine the usefulness of the study of genetic structures by the physical anthroplogists of the nation. As India is a nation with the largest genetic and morphological diversity of her people, living in the most diversified geographical locales. Therefore, the physical anthroplogists here are better poised than perhaps in any other nation to serve her through their studies of bio-demographic-genetic-morphological structure of the people. This compact structure will provide a comprehensive scale for measuring the biological well-being of a population and for planning for its improvement.

Closely linked with it is the aspect of population adaptation. 'Adaptive processes operate to maintain physiological, behavioural and developmental homeostasis. If the capacity for adaptation is inadequate to obviate environmental change, some loss in homeostasis will ensue. Examples of this have usually been sought in extreme environmental conditions causing loss of homeostasis as is evident in mortality and clear morbidity. But, the success of adaptability is one of the infinite degree and apprently minor but persistent and every day environmental threats will also eventually cause homeostasic failure' (Harrison 1985).

Physical anthroploogists of India have started proving their worth by studying the population adaptation processes through the studies of bio-demographic structure, genetic structure and morphological structure in the specific environmental context (Sarkar 1960; Aggarwal 1967; Ganguly 1975; Malik 1976; Bhardwaj et al. 1977; Ganguly and Pal 1984; Bhardwaj et al. 1985). The usefulness of their studies could be enhanced if they were to seek the collaboration of physiologist environmentalists and social anthroplogists. One such attempt was recently made by Singh and Bhasin (Personal communication) through a MAB research project, but the precise outcome of their study is yet to be published. If not properly planned, such a study may have tendency to become unwieldy and dispersed and it, therefore, needs to be pursued with greater caution.

Physical anthropologists find a more explicit utility in serving the nation through aviation anthropometry to nutritional anthropometry, forensic application and genetic counselling; yet the impact of these is still to be realised. Even after so many years of stint with physical anthroplogy, the Indian physical anthroplogists are sitting almost on the periphery with respect to these so very obvious applied aspects of the subdisciplines. What prompts such a situation, is a matter of grave concern. Is it the fear of paucity of job opportunities or the lack of efforts in cultivating adequate talent for such jobs ? In any case the Indian physical anthroplogists have not contributed as much as they could in these spheres of nation building, partly because it called for greater entrepreneurship. Though forensic anthropologists have been able to receive some patronage from the state, the role of physical anthropologists in genetic counselling and in designing equipments, aircrafts, and various other items that need the application of Kineanthropometry (Malik et al. 1984), is yet to be properly recognized by the state agencies. Mere token services rendered by some anthroplogists in these fields can not deliver goods. Of late, the physical anthroplogists engaged in systematic growth and developmental studies have made their influence felt in the field of sports at national level (see Sidhu and Grewal, 1983; 1984) and this endeavour needs to be cautiously furthered because herein they face challenging competition from the physiologists and men of medicine.

The physical anthropoligists need to press for their recognition boldly at the right quarters. The largest corporate body of anthropologists of the country, namely, the Anthropological Survey of India, and the Rashtriya Manav Sangrahalaya, in collaboration with the three important associations of Indian Anthropologists, with widely overlapping memberships from universities and other institutions, must makė an attempt in this direction, irrespective of the field of specialization of the anthropologists at the helm of the affairs.

Biological heritage of India is surely of no less importance to be understood than her cultural heritage. It is a well attested fact that the problem of ethnicity or race has inadvertently centred around the biological heritage, though sociopolitical in manifestation. Now that we have the Rashtriya Manav Sangrahalaya, it can be hoped that under its aegis the biological heritage of India will also be properly attested like her cultural heritage. In order to obtain this national objective more meaningfully, a two pronged strategy needs to be adopted - (i) for understanding pre and proto historic biological heritage and (ii) for understanding contemporary biological heritage. Palaeoanthropological exacavations, conceived through joint efforts of physcial anthropologists and archaeologists be carried out under a long drawn plan to discover the pre and proto-historic biological heritage of the country, besides systematically analysing and putting on record the material of palaeoanthropoligical interest, discovered by Archaeological Survey of India. While Rashtriya Manav Sanghralaya can exclusively undertake this responsibility in collaboration with some university departments of Anthropology, especially those of Chandigarh and Pune, studies on the historic and contemporary biological heritage can be co-ordinated and conducted by the Anthroplogical Survey of India which can compile the existing information and has the largest manpower to generate systematic data required for this purpose. Photo mapping of Indian population could achieve this goal more demonstratively for the Rashtriya Manav Sangrahalaya or the National Museum of Man.

What must be borne in mind while searching for the earliest hominid in India, after Ramapithecus from Sivalik hills having been finally relegated to the status of Sivapithecus, is the fact that our endeavour must be guided with more knowledge than zeal.

While Sivalik ranges may provide promising sites for the search of early hominids, earliest man in India is more likely to be found from Narmada basin because of the following reasons:

(i) there is an audible similarity between the Sivalik fauna and the fauna associated with the pithecanthropus from Trinil beds of Java, (ii) there occurred a south and south- eastward shift in the tropical belt during miocene period, which would have resulted in the migration of the warmth loving animals south and south-eastwards, (iii) the Sivalik hominids at that time were at critical stage in evoluation, (iv) Sivalik fauna is found in plently from the early pliestocene period in Narmada basin.

Hitherto, the above expectation appears to have been realised to some extent by the discovery of pleistocene human fossil remains from Hathnora (Delumley H and Sonakia 1985; De Lumley Marie - Antoinette and Sonakia 1985) in the Narmada region.

In spite of the notable usefulness of physical anthropology in India, with its given and much improvable standards, it has so far not found its due place in nation building; this may be, primarily due to two reasons: (I) domination of social anthropologists on the national scene because of more easily appreciable immediate relevance of their sub-discipline by the averagely educated but highly posted and glorified IAS breed that has been and will continue to govern this nation, yielding no grounds to the technocrats and other professionals, notwithstanding a few who have attained specific professional expertise; (ii) an undeclared, yet practised cold war against physical anthropology by some well connected anthropologists who did not miss the opportunity of drastically slicing down the physical anthroplogical contents even in the syllabi for the most prestigious national competitive examinations; thanks to the blissful ignorance of the U.P.S.C. officials in this matter. Indeed this is an unfortunate state of affairs which must be corrected not only by physical anthroplogists but by the whole breed of Indian anthropologists, notwithstanding their sub-disciplines of specialization; this will enhance the role of physical anthroplogy in nation building but in no way at the cost of other sub-disciplines of anthroplogy. This should not be misconstrued as propagating the sharp divisions of anthropological pursuits; one must be clear in one's mind that physical anthropological studies devoid of social anthropological inputs will be as less useful as social anthropological studies undermining biological realities. Yet, the two retain their special identity.

However, the purpose is there, and the goal is there; it is for the Indian physical anthropologists to strive and achieve it in an ever snowballing manner to be of increasing relevance to nation building.

Reference List

Aggarwal HN (1967) Reproductive life of Onge women. Vanyajati 15:139-149

Balakrishnan V, Sanghvi LD (1965) Use of digital computer in the estimation of blood group gene frequencies. Acta Genet 5:345

Bali RS, Chaube R (1971) On the formulation of palmar creases. Z Morph Anthrop 63:121-130

Banerjee S (1979) Genetics of skin pigmentation. Ind Anthrop 9:139

Basu SK (1982) Inbreeding in India, its genetic consequences and implications in health care. In : Roy S, Basu S, Jindal A (ed) Population genetics and health care issues and future strategies. National Institute of Health and Family welfare, New Delhi, pp71-77

Bhalla V (1961) Blood groups of Kinnar Kanets of Chini Valley : Proceedings of Ind Sci Cong part 3, p441

Bhalla V, Roy S (1979) Specific binding activity of some plant agglutinins with red cells of leukaemic and myeloid leukaemic patients. IRCS Medical Science 7:563

Bhalla V, Bhatia K, Gaur V (1977) Anti H type haemagglutinins in six plant species from North India. Acta Anthropgenet 1:

3-8

Bhardwaj H, Verma SS, Zachariah T, Bhatia MR, Krishnan S, Malhotra MS (1977) Estimation of body density and lean body weight from body measurements at high altitude. Eur J Appl Physiol 36:141-150

Bhardwaj H, Jain SC, Chakraborty KP, Satwanti (1984) Body composition in relation to high altitude acclimatization. In:Basu A, Malhotra KC (ed) Human Adaptation, vol2. ISI, Calcutta, p.70-80

Bhasin MK, Sharma A, Singh IP, Walter H (1985) Morphological and metric dental study on Indians. Z Morph Anthrop 76:77-90

Bhatia HM, Sanghvi LD (1962) Rare blood groups and consanguinity Bombay phenotype. Voxsang 7:245-248

Bhande YM, Deshpande CK, Bhatia HM, Senger R, Race RR, Morgan WTG, Watkins WM (1952) A new blood group character related to the ABO system. Lancet 1:903-904

Bhowmick KL (1969) Some aspects of reproductive life of Angami women in a Nagaland village. Res Bul of the Inst of Soc Studies, Calcutta.

Biswas PC (1936) Uber hand und fingeriesten von Indern. Z Morph Anthrop 35

Bongaarts J, Greenhalgh S (1985) An alternative to the one child policy in China. Pop Dev Rev 11:585-617

Chakravartti MR (1967) A statistical appraisal on the relationship between non ABO blood group system and diseases. Hum Genet 5:1-27

Chakravartti MR (1968) Consanguinity in India. Z Morph Anthrop 60:170-182

Chakravartti MR, Vogel F (1973) Topics in Human Genetics: a twin study on Leprosy. Stuttgart, Thieme, vol 1

Chakravartti MR, Chakravartti A (1977) Consanguinous marraige and genetic load. Hum Genet 36:47

Chakravartti MR, Chakravartti R (1978) ABO blood groups and fertility in an Indian population J de Genet Hum 26:133-144

Chopra SRK, Simons EL (1969) Gigantopithecus (Pongidae, Hominoidea a new species from North India). Postilla 133

Chopra SRK (1979) Palaeontological evidence bearing on the problem of human origins in northwest India. In : Chopra SRK (ed) Early man of northwest India, Allied Publishers Pvt. Ltd., Bombay

Das BM, Deka R, Flatz G (1975) Predominance of the haemoglobin E gene in a monoloid population in Assam India. Hum Genetik 30:187

Das SR, Mukherjee DP (1963) A spectrophotometric skin colour survey among four Indian castes and tribes. Z Morph Anthrop 54:190-200

Datta PK (1969) Inheritance of Hallucal dermatoglyphic configurations in human soles, The Anthrop 145-151

Henry De Lumley, Sonakia A (1985) Stratigraphical and archaeological context of the Narmada man, Hathnora MP India. L' Anthropologie 89:3-12

Lumley M, Sonakia A (1985) First discovery of a Homo erectus on the Indian subcontinent at Hathnora in the middle valley of the Narmada river. L' Anthropologie 89:13-62

Fernandez P (1985) A study of the factors influencing demographic structure of the Warli and the Kokna tribes of the union territory of Dadra and Nagar Haveli Doctoral Thesis, University of Delhi.

Ganguly P (1975) The Negritos of little Andaman Island, Ind Mus Bull 10: 727

Ganguly P, Pal A (1984) The problem of survival of the Onge of little Andaman island. In:Basu A, Malhotra KC (ed) Human Adaptation, ISI, Calcutta, 2:157:164

Ghosh PK, Rani R, Nand R (1979) Lateral asymmetry of constitutive heterochromatin in human chromosomes. Hum Genet 52: 79-84

Gupta SP (1985) A bio-demographic study of the Rajputs and the Jats of rural Haryana. Thesis, University of Delhi

Harrison GA (1985) Adaptation and well being, In:Basu A, Malhotra KC (ed) Human Adaptation, ISI, Calcutta, 2:165-171

Jaiswal IJS (1977) Skin reflectance studies with special reference to Indian populations. J Ind Anthrop Soc 12:167-174

Kalla AK (1983) Melanin pigmentation : its variation and genetics studied through Indian population. Ind J Phys Anthrop Hum Genet 9:171-198

Kalla AK (1985) Kashmiri Pandits and their diversity. B.K. Publishing Corporation, Delhi 244

Kaul V, Prakash S (1984) Crown dimensions of deciduous and permanent teeth of Jats from Haryana India. Ann Hum Biol 11:351-354

Kaur H, Shrivastav PK (1982) Studies on the Dd antigen antibody system I the nature of antigen Dd and its antibodies. Experimentia 38:1481-1482

Kaur H, Shrivastava PK (1983) Studies on the Dd antigen antibody system II antigen Dd reactivity in some north Indian populations, Experimentia 39:91-92

Kaur DP, Sing R (1983) Intra familial correlations and hereditability coefficient of body measurements in a rural Indian population. Ind J Med Res 78:224-232

Kumar N, Ghosh AK (1967) ABO blood groups and sickle cell investigations in Madhya Pradesh, Ujjain and Dewas districts. Acta Genet 17:55

Kumbnani HK (1978) Main line index and transversality in trisomy 21. In : Mawalvala J (ed) Dermatoglyphics and in-

ternational.perspective, Mouton publishers, Paris p351
Malhotra KC (1967) Further observations on the human skeletal remains from Piklihal. The Anthrop 14:99-111
Malhotra KC (1974) Sociobiological investigations among the Nandiwallas of Maharashtra. Bull Urgent Anthrop Ethn Sci 16:63-102
Malik SL (1976) Age changes and few biological responses at high altitude: a study among male Bodhs of Ladakh. Thesis, University of Delhi.
Malik SL, Jurgens HW, Helbig K (1984) Designing a chair a scientific perspective. Ind Anthrop 14:41-61
Mukherjee DP (1967) Quantitative genetics of dermal ridges with special reference to an Indian population. Thesis, University of London
Prakash S, Pattimanathans (1984) Age at menarche in Sri Lankan Tamil girls in Jaffna. Ann Hum Biol 11:463-466
Rami Reddy V (1985) Dental Anthroplogy. B.R. Publishing Corporation, Delhi
Sanghvi LD (1953) Comparsion of genetical and morphological methods for a study of biological differences. Amer J Phys Anthrop 22:3
Sankalia HD, Karve I (1949) Early primitive microlithic culture and people of Gujarat. Amer Anthrop 51:28-34
Sankalia HD (1969) Early man in India, IAS Bombay 173-181
Sarkar SS (1960) Onge population and settlements. Athropo 35:561-563
Sarkar SS (1961) The simian crease A Morph Anthrop 51:212-219
Seth S, Seth PK (1978) HLA and diseases revisited. Acta Anthropogenet 2:61-90
Seth S, Seth PK, Dixit VP (1983) Genetic variations in primates' red cell enzymes and serum proteins in rhesus baboons and langurs. In: Seth PK (ed) Perspective in Primate biology. Today and tommorrow's: Printers and Publishers, New Delhi, p181-187
Sharma A, Taneja (1968) A methodological study of axial angle in quantitative palmar dermatoglyphics. The East Anthrop 21:257-266
Sharma A (1966) Axial triradi formulation and certain fresh indexes giving metric expression of variable positioning of axial triradii and digital triradii c&d. In: proceedings of summer school in Anthropology Dalhousie (1964)
Sharma PD (1970) Incidence of major congenital malformations in Mysore. Ind J Pediat 36:618
Sharma JC, Kaul V (1977) Dental morphology and odontology in Punjabis. J Ind Ass Phy Anthrop 12:213-226
Sharma K, Sharma JC (1984) Familial resemblance of forehead size in Punjabi population of India. Hum Biol 11:577-580
Sidhu LS, Grewal R (1983) Effect of training on subcutaneous

and lean tissues of female volleyball players. Hung Rev Sports Med 25:85-89

Sindhu LS, Grewal R (1984) Effect of training on the cardiovascular system in Indian women hockey players J Sports Med Phys Fit 24:37-40

Singh IP (1959) Inheritance of finger ball pattern. Thesis, University of Delhi

Singh R (1966) Nutritional somatometric study of adult males with special reference to skinfold measurements and intercorrelation. In: Biswas PC, Singh IP (ed) Aspects of Indian Anthropology. University of Delhi

Singh R, Raja C (1980) Estimation of body volume and body density from leg dimensions in Panjabi girls. Anthrop kozl 24:223-239

Tara Devi S (1979) Biochemical genetics and mental retardation a study of haemoglobins Australia antigen G-6-PD. Thesis, University of Delhi

Tiwari SC (1963) Studies of crossing between Indians and Europeans. Ann Hum Genet 26:219

Tiwari SC (1972) Distribution of ABO blood groups in the population of the Himalayas, In: Mathur KS, Verma SC (ed) Man & Society, Lucknow p 137-150

TWO

ANTHROPOLOGY DEVELOPMENT AND CULTURE

K. S. Singh

Anthropology has highlighted the variety of human experience, the heterogeneity and variation of populations, the uniqueness of each social formation, and the role of ethnicity and pluralism. This paper deals with the interaction of anthropology with the development process and cultural policies and programmes with some reference to the role of the Anthropological Survey of India (ASI) and the Rashtriya Manav Sangrahalaya (RMS). The discussion in this paper is in two parts. The first takes up the role of anthropology in determining the physical status of the Indian population,the traditional preoccupation of anthropology with the generation of information about people through specific projects and enthnographic surveys, and the endogenous processes of development. The second part deals with cultural heritage, cultural pluralism policy and programme, and the role of anthropology in the dissemination of culture. It would also be pertinent to discuss the ASI projects proposed to be launched in years to come in collaboration with the university departments of anthropology and anthropological institutions, and the linkages that need to be established among all institutions concerned with anthropoligical research.

II

The ASI surveys the human surface of India, the demographic, anthropometric and genetic structure of its people, as also its society and culture. It has been described as the biggest organization of its kind, employing the largest number of professional anthropologists under one roof in the world. Since its inception in 1945 it has been engaged in the study of the physical status of Indian population, the study of various communities, and the processes of social change. It has blazed many a trail in the field of anthropological research particularly through its anthropometric and bio-anthropological surveys and the survey of the distribution of material traits. It is the sole custodian of the skeletal remains discovered at historical sites. It has explored unkown communities; it has published 100 memoirs and books and 1232 papers, besides building up five anthropological museums which hold about 5000 specimens. The ASI has considerably enlarged its perspectives in the Seventh Five Year Plan. The policy resolution of 1970 of the ASI has now been substantially amended to commit it more explicitly to the task of surveying the human surface of India, and to provide anthropological input for the study and evaluation of plan programmes relating to conservation of environment, poverty alleviation, combating malnutrition, welfare of women and children, development of weaker sections, and physical fitness. The ASI has accordingly identified 15 national projects to be taken up in collaboration with the departments of anthroplogy and institutes of anthropological research in order to generate a national profile in such areas.

In our country anthropology has expressed its concern for the tribes and has presented a charter for the welfare and development of the backward communities. The ethnographers and anthropologists were the first to raise their voice for the protection of the tribes that found an echo in the provisions of the Constitution of India for the welfare and protection of these communities. The ASI has continued to project this concern through its studies of these communities, its involvement in the formulation and evaluation of development programmes and in various other ways to articulate their fears and aspirations.

The RMS was conceived as the first national museum of anthropology as early as in 1976 in the draft report prepared by the ASI. It was designed to bring together the prespectives on evolution of man, human variation, origin and growth of material culture, and the wideranging patterns of living cultures encompassing both tribal and peasant communities to be presented in regional and national dimensions. After a great deal of discussions its character as an anthropological museum rather than as a museum of tribal art or as an ethnographic museum has been settled. It may also serve as the custodian of the fossils of the primates. The ASI and the RMS through their museums will identify such of the fast-vanishing cultural artifacts as need to be salvaged, and launch a co-ordinated programme for their collection and preservation. Both will explore the ever-fascinating dimension of the "unity in diversity". The RMS will also serve as the centre for training and research in museology of the type it represents. The visits to the RMS and various museums of the ASI , when they are built up, should be for the visitors, a living experience of the processes described above. Both also have a role to play in the dissemination of culture, and should be able to set in motion a museum movement in the country, involving larger sections of our people in the understanding of our biocultural systems and the preservation and development of our cultural heritage.

One of the major concerns of anthropology in India has been the determination of the physical status of the Indian population. It started with racial classification of the Indian populations and shifted to the study of morphological variations among them. The All India Anthropometric Survey (1961-63) was conducted in terms of thirteen anthropometric traits. While the data, collected twenty five years ago, are going to be published shortly, the survey is being extended to cover West Bengal, Sikkim and many parts of Rajasthan to make possible comparison of the data collected over years. The limitations of this kind of survey have been realised. Mere description of intra-group and inter-group variations is of little avail, particularly when the samples are drawn from a district which is not an ecological zone. There has to be a correlation of such anthropometric data to such variables as climate, ecology and nutrition. Attempts to establish relationship between anthropometric characteristics and comparable hierarchical status have failed to bring out any meaningful patterns; caste/ethnic groups or race does not seem to determine intergroup anthropometric variability. The All India Bio-anthropological Survey covered a wider spectrum and sought to explore the demographic profile in terms of fertility, food, health status, mating practices, morbidity and mortality, besides environmental factors. What makes physcial anthropology immensely relevant to the development process is its concern for the upgradation of the status of those sections of the population which suffer from genetical disorders, incidence of malnutrition and disabilites of all kinds, particularly the women and children. Therefore the need for the study of the genetic structure of the Indian populations has been felt by the ASI partly as a continuation of the study of the physical structure of Indian population it has been conducting. While such studies have brought to surface the biological diversities among Indian populations, their genetic structure has not been studied on an all India level. Therefore the ASI, in collaboration with the university departments of anthropology, has decided to undertake the study of genetic structure in terms of distribution of genetic markers, level of genetic relationship between and among different regions, genetical distances among populations, probable and discernible effects of the ongoing processes of evolution etc. The study of the nutritional status of the Indian population is another area which should be explored, even though a great deal of the ground has been already covered. The studies suggest that the diet of the low income group population is inadequate and that a large section of Indian population suffers from varying degrees of malnutrition. Therefore we propose to collect data for the assessment of nutritional status of Indian population for the country as a whole as also for various regions. This should help us to identify the geographical distribution of the incidence of malnutrition and its magnitude, variations in the body build, intake of diet and nutritional practices of various communites including tribes in different ecological zones. The survey will thus generate an all India profile of nutritional status. Most of the surveys of the kind mentioned above have been men's affairs, conducted by men for men themselves. Though the females constitute above fifty per cent of the population, few studies of females have been undertaken. Therefore the ASI proposes to fill up this information gap by undertaking the anthropometric survey of Indian women through women ahthropologists to bring out morphological variations among females of various communities and in different regions. Apart from anthropometric measures observations will be made on somatoscopic characters. This survey should help devise measures to improve further the health status of Indian female.

Social anthropologists were probably the first among the social scientists to describe man in his environment and habitat and to highlight their inter dependece. In recent years in spite of the warnings by anthropologists this relationship has come under severe stress with the sharp deterioration of soil, pollution of air and water, and reckless destruction of forest, which has led to the recurrent cycles of drought and flood. Mining has ravaged land, and together with new projects displaced indigenous communities. Their rehabilitation in their environment poses a problem. The ASI's project on environement, ecology and human population seeks to explore communities' perception of their environment, their role in its preservation and degradation, their attitude to environment and conservation programmes, and the extent of their participation in them in various parts of the country. We will also study landuse patterns, landcarrying capacities in various parts of India and in various economies such as hunting and food gathering, shifting and terrace, pastoral and settled, and various other forms of interaction of the communities and their environment. Secondly, the ASI will continue to honour its commitment to the study of tribes, particularly the most primitive among them. Their movements, customary laws and economies have already been studied through quick short surveys and their findings have been published. In the next three years, we propose to adopt the same methodology to study agrarian systems and laws, stratification and social change, religion in tribal society of India. The autonomy of tribal system and persistence of many elements of continuity in midst of change will be particularly highlighted. One of the hypotheses about tribal religion, wrongly described as animism in anthropological literature until recently, has been that it was fated to be swallowed up by major religions like Christianity and Hinduism which a good number of tribals have embraced. Recent studies suggest that the tribals have their own religion in a holisitc sense which is part of their harmonious system, and that though they have been converted to Christianity and Hinduism - and some of them to Islam and Buddhism - the elements of the old faith have not entirely disappeared but have even recreated and readapted to meet the exigencies of the new soical situation. Therefore it is proposed to take up a study of religion and tribes. This will consist in a study of tribal religion on the one hand and the impact of Hinduism, Christianity, Islam and Buddhism on the tribals, on the other. Thirdly, a distressing aspect of the tribal scenario is the disappearance of tribal artifacts and the loss of oral traditions at a rapid pace in various parts of tribal India as a result of the impact of the processes of modernisation, identity crises and migration of tribal communities. Verrier Elwin had launched a survey of tribal art and myths in middle India and elsewhere and had also documented oral traditions in tribal India. It is proposed to continue and complete this line of work, to salvage and document such specimens of tribal and folk art as they face the threat of extinction, and to document oral traditions in all tribal regions. Further, onomastics, the science of names, has emerged as an important area of study in which linguists, geographers and cultural anthropologists have been active. In our country the study of placenames is still to be pursued systematically by anthropologists as part of their study of society and culture. Placenames reflect the settlers' perception of their environment and their relationship with it. The gamut of belief, rituals and other practices is linked with personal names, the changing patterns of which also reveals the process of social change. Therefore, the Survey proposes to take up this project during the Seventh Plan period. This study will help us in understanding the various facets of the culture of our people, their origin and migration, their habitat and settlement, their relationship with environment, formation of region and subregion, and the process of linguistic and social change. Fourthly, in 1976 the ASI had drawn up a format for the study of the structure pattern and process of transformation in Tribal India. Its need had been acutely felt because while there were a number of monographs on tribes, there were few composite studies of tribal society which could present a holistic view of all its aspects. The ASI has been involved in the field of tribal studies for the past 40 years and has an admirable track record of studies in this field. Therefore the old format for the study of structure pattern and process of transformation in tribal India has been revived with some modification. The objective is to present an overview of the tribal society in India based on the existing studies as also fresh material in terms of ecology, habitat, demography, bio-anthropological characteristics, language, economy, social system, religion, politics, legal system and the processes of change in terms of urbanization, industrialization, acculturation, transfer of technology etc. Fifthly, the ASI has been involved in the study of the structure and processes of ethnicity, socio-political development in the North-East under the Area Study programme, and the regional study of electoral processes elsewhere. We have two distinct types of political processes at work in tribal India. One is centered on the issue of ethnicity like in North-East and the other is encountered elsewhere in the country whereby tribals are being assimilated into the set of regional and all-India political system, parties and politics. The tribals have also participated in the Panchayati raj institutions and elections to these bodies. There have also been survivals of "autonomous" systems in Middle India. Therefore we propose to study all these patterns and processes under this project. Sixthly, next to tribes the study of women is proposed to be taken up in terms of their role in rural development and the identification of gender bias in employment, wages, education, food distribution etc.

A question that may be asked at this stage is whether descriptive ethnography generally considered outdated now as it has been overtaken by other concerns is still relevant. Should we continue to engage in the study of communities about which we know nothing or about which our knowledge has become obsolete ? Can such communities be studied without offending the Indian Constitution which prohibits discrimination on the ground of race, caste and religion ? In our considered opinion ethnography is still relevant, because either we know little or our knowledge has become out of date about a very large number of our communities. Such communities are already being independently studied by scholars. Since H.H. Risley wrote his book, the People of India (1915) which is a collection of his papers rather than an account of various communities in India, there have been no composite studies of all communities of India. Contrary to general impressions the ethnographic surveys for different regions of the country did not cover all communities. To give an example, E. Thurston in his monumental seven-volume work on southern India covers only about 529 communities and refers to very large numbers of sub-castes (28), clans (494), sub-divisions (519), titles (153) and synonyms and which make the ethnographic picture too confused. According to our own list for the south there are 1200 communities (excluding sub-divisions etc.), which means that a large number of them have remained unstudied. This emphasises the urgent need for a study of all people of India. We have also to take note of the formation of new communities as a result of migration on a large scale of the communities since the partition and afterwards in search of a new homeland, job, business etc. It has been said since the census started that such enumeration divides people and fosters sectarian and communal influences. Experience shows that such influences arise more from ignorance of our people, and therefore if we take up the study of people and of the linkages that bring them together, we will promote an understanding that alone will act as a corrective to ignorance and divisive forces. What is required is a systematic study of the communities both at micro-and macro-level. We have to have both monographs to provide an in-depth study of a community and also an overview to yield a perspective on all communities. Therefore the ASI launched a massive project for the study of about 5000 communities under the People of India project, on 2nd October 1985, exactly 100 years later than the first 27-point format for the ethnographic survey of India had been drawn up by three British ethnographers. The objective of the project is to generate a brief anthropological profile of a community, highlight the process of change, describe inter-community linkages and reflect the community's attitude to development. It has four dimensions, historical, ethnographic and two others relating to development and integration.

Anthropology is relevant to the endogenous processes of development. It is now being realised that the development process must be initiated from below, and that the people must identify their own felt needs, that they must have a role in executing the schemes meant for their benefit and in fashioning their life in the way they like it. A consciousness is dawning that development from above or that the exogenous model of change which are not more than a bundle of schemes identified by experts does not work. There is a great deal in the people's own traditions, their indigenous ways that can be harnessed to ensure prosperity and happiness for a local community. This community must be encouraged to organize itself in order to take advantage of the programmes designed for its development. This involves conscientization, raising the level of not only people's aspirations but also of their awareness. Here anthropology can help. All projects involve social relationships, and are to be viewed against the background of universal behavioural characteristics. Anthropology provides a corrective to generalized assumptions and universal models by emphasizing the specificities, inter-relatedness of elements, and uniqueness of the local situation. This makes for better formulation of a project, its social feasibility. In this process the social anthropologist may sometimes make "unorthodox" suggestions: payment of wages in kind for rural labourers to offset the fall in real wage; or they may plead for a greater role of a sadhu or Brahmin scholar in promoting acceptance of change, but this is a different matter. There is a great deal in an anthropologist's suggestion that the village people should be approached through their own cultural frame of reference. For example in the case of effective medical aid it is necessary that scientific medical practice should divest itself of certain western cultural accretions and clothe itself in the "social homespun of the Indian village", but whether the shamans, medicine men can perform the new role is again a different matter.

Preservation and development of the endangred communities has been a major concern of anthropology. In our country on the mainland atleast many of the preagricultural, pastoral, hunting and foodgathering communities once faced with the threat of extinction appear now to have crossed the hump. The population of the Todas for example has not only stabilized, but also increased. However, the Negrito communities in our islands, like their counterparts elsewhere in South Asia, being more sensitive to change, face the real danger of survival. There is an urgent need for setting up a highlevel committee to go into the problem of the physical survival of the endangered Negrito communities of the Great Andamanese and the Onges and the Mongoloid community of the Shompens. Since 1901 their population has been declining. The decline was particularly marked during the period 1911-1931. Though in recent years a decline in this trend has been noticed, as far as the Onges are concerned, yet their number has become very small. Their preservation and development is a task of national importance. It is to the abiding credit of our country that we have preserved all communities and have never followed any policy of ethnocide that has resulted in the annihilation of primitive communities elsewhere. Therefore, the first step should be to appoint an experts' committee to go into the question of the health and medical care of these communities, and to suggest long-term strategies. There is no dearth of reports and recommendations by teams of experts from outside. A fresh look is needed and recommendations have to be put in the form of long-term strategies of growth and survival for these communities. The team should consist of a doctor specialising in the health care of primitive communities, a physical anthropologist, a geneticist, a planner, a psychologist and a cultural anthropologist. The Regional Office of the ASI which is involved in the study of these communities for the last 35 years should provide leadership in this matter. Measures should also be taken to set up a separate administrative organisation for the care of these communities. The social workers are doing a fine job, but in order to implement a long-term policy it is necessary to have a separate organisation. Therefore, to begin with, a separate organisation should be created in this Union Territory with separate branches for the communities such as the Great Andamanese, the Onge and the Shompen. The Jarawa and the Sentinelese should not be disturbed except in the slow and cautious manner in which we are trying to establish contact with them at present, unless we have demonstrated our capacity to ensure the survival of the communities who are already fully exposed to us. Various studies also reveal that one of the communities, the Onge, are facing the threat of extinction because of the rate of high infant mortality caused mainly by diarrhoea, malaria and tuberculosis. There is also the incidence of incompatible marriages which is a matter for social anthropologists and social workers to look into. Cleanliness and sanitation should receive priority. Further, unless these three communities are encouraged to eke out a living for themselves, instead of continuing to depend on doles from the government they could not be helped to survive. The will to survive must be generated. This implies that they should be trained in such crafts and encouraged to take up such avocations as come naturally to them or such as can be taken up with the least effort and easily identified to be in tune with their ecology, resource endowments and their own requirements. Lastly, if a free port is eventually established in the Great Nicobar Islands then special efforts will have to be made to preserve and protect the Shompens from the kind of fate that has overtaken the Onge and the Great Andamanese.

One of the major tasks before us is to establish linkages among various institutions engaged in the area of anthropological research. The ASI has no doubt been declared to be a clearing house of information relating to anthropology. However, a good will remain to be done to establish close and continuing relationship with the institutions of anthroplogical research under the collaborative and fellowship programmes of the ASI in terms of various national projects jointly conceived and sought to be operationalized by all of us. The ASI has to establish its own linkages with various official or semi-official bodies in an effective manner. Direcotor General is the anthropological adviser to Government of India but somehow this role has not been performed because of absence of linkages with the concerned ministries. Now that the Director General's office is functioning from Delhi, it should be possible to perform this role. The two areas in which the expertise of the ASI should be available to the appropriate ministries of the Government of India are: (a) physical anthropology and (b) tribal studies. As the ASI is conducting basic researches through anthropometric survey, bio-anthropometric survey, nutrition study etc., therefore we propose to interact closely with the Ministry of Home Affairs (tribal matters), Ministry of Women and Social Welfare (regarding the problems of women and children), Ministry of Health and Indian Council of Medical Research (regarding nutrition etc.), Ministry of Forest and Environment (tribals and forest) and the Planning Commission. At this stage we are consulted by the Planning Commission in matters of tribal welfare and associated with the preparation of tribal sub-plan, but this linkage is not on a permanent footing. Linkages have to be established through a highlevel committee with Secretary, Department of Culture, as Chairman and Secretaries of various ministries concerned as its members. This will promote coordination between ASI and other ministries. Or we could extend the scope of the Advisory Committee for ASI in the Department of Culture to include the representatives of the concerned ministries. Similarly, at the regional level the regional offices should set up local committees of the representatives of appropriate departments of state government including Planning Board, university departments, tribal research institutes etc. The ASI is represented on the committees for various Tribal Research Institutes and is trying to function as the apex body but a lot more remains to be done to establish close linkages with these organisations to give a new thrust to tribal study programmes.

III

The importance of cultural input in terms of the formation of consciousness at ethnic, community and national levels, and the promotion of culture as a tool of all round development which is intrinsic to the developmental process is universally recognized, even though it is not as well translated into a set of relevant cultural policies and programmes. Economic processes continue to prevail over the cultural; economic programmes constitute the 'core' sector that culture does not. Even so, the role of the cultural factor is now being recognized as basic to development as any other.

Of the two interrelated aspects of our cultural heritage the first is the rise of regional cultural formations including languages, literatures and life styles; the second is the overarching national system, with its unity of cultural idioms that cut across and articulate through various regional systems. Both national and regional systems have evolved together, in dynamic interaction, over time. Thus while on the one hand, the regional systems have acquired an autonomy that is their own, they have also interacted to throw up the composite cultural system encompassing our country. In the same way we have also the two streams of Indian cultural heritage, the classical and the folkloric, the tangible and the intangible aspects of our cultural property, which feed upon each other and enrich and enliven the cultural process as a whole. Our freedom struggle was accompanied by a cultural awakening in which some of our most creative minds participated in the search for our roots that could stimulate our thrust towards freedom, equality and a new way of life. In the process they drew closer to our people and their traditions, our villages, and sought to integrate the folkloric and the classical heritage, in their regional and national dimensions.

In recent years, since independence, there has been an unprecedented cultural awakening in our country, particularly in the field of revival of our classical art. At the same time we are losing a great deal too. Our priceless treasures of art are smuggled out of our country to build up or equip museums abroad. It is estimated that about one-fourth of our art objectives has already found its way out of the country. We have made our laws a little more stringent recently to protect our antiquities. Even so, a great deal remains to be done to generate an awareness of the cultural heritage of our country among our people to combat this menace through our media and by initiating suitable measures.

While the "tangible aspects" of our culture that represent the peak of our classical heritage are better known, there are some aspects of our folk heritage that deserve as close attention. A striking experience of recent years in our country has been that as in many parts of the developing world, there has been a flowering of folk culture, an explosion of interest in it with the sharpening of identity consciousness at the community and national levels. Study of folklore is becoming a part of school curricula. Researches in history and various other disciplines are drawing upon the vast reservoir of folklore. The awareness that folk traditions are the matrix of the classical heritage, of its tangible expressions, is spreading rapidly. It is being increasingly realised that dissemination of folklore has an important role to play in improving the quality of life in rural areas. Rural artisans are being assisted under poverty alleviation programmes to develop their skills. Many such groups of artisans have now come into their own. They are not only conscious of the importance of their folklore but are also consciously using it to eke out a decent living. Folk culture is active, even vibrant in its natural setting in some areas of our country. And yet with this very welcome development goes the deplorable experience of the debasement of folklore, much to the anguish not only of the purists but also the creators of the original forms. Commercialisation has provided the stimulus for both growth and vulgarisation of folklore. In recent memory atleast two traditions of folk painting, one belonging to the peasant (Madhubani) and other to the tribe (Warli) which have almost achieved the dimension of a movement, have also been comercialised. Communities working in metal are now producing for market both internal and abroad. Secret and sacred aspects of tribal and indigenous culture have been exposed in an indecent way by the foreign media. This has evoked protest.

The emphasis so far in the process seems to have been more on preservation, promotion and development of folk heritage than on its protection against commercial exploitation. Therefore, the paramount need of the hour is the application of a conscious policy to safeguard folk culture and to set up a suitable machinery for this purpose. We have to examine various modalities including the one to set up a central authority if possible in a cultural situation of continental diversity such as ours. Our Copy Right Act does not protect folk culture, because it is group-or community-oriented, and does not relate to individual artist or author. At the moment we have a number of agencies both at the government and voluntary levels engaged not only in promoting and developing facets of cultural heritage but also in affording such protection as they require against uncontrolled exploitation. We have the "traditional" institutions, the Archaeological Survey of India, safe-guarding around 6,600 of our historical monuments, the ASI dealing with the preservation of the tangible forms of folklore, and the All India Handicrafts Board which has done pioneering work in preserving our crafts and promoting their development both as an item of export and as an item of culture. This Board has been instrumental in reviving the traditions of Mithila folk painting which were almost destroyed by a famine in the 1960s by providing relief and employment for the artisans. Preservation of the folk culture of tribals has been a cardinal principle of the state policy. We could set up a National Council or National Commission on folklore to work out the modalities for safeguarding it. The second thrust of our endeavours should be to identify and salvage the artifacts faced with the threat of extinction. Our museums and universities should conceive of and undertake projects for the identification, collection and preservation of such artifacts all over the country. Such salvage operations are a crying need at present.

There is the need for building up a chain of museums, which is intrinsic to the development of our cultural heritage. Museums have served everywhere not only as the repository of culture, but also as centres of its dissemination, as a tool of education and national integration. However, instead of having single-theme museums as we have now, we should build up composite museums. There is no dearth of single-theme museums at the national/metropolitan state level, where taken together they present a composite picture of our culture, the scientific, industrial and technological on one hand, and the artistic, literary, anthropological and archaeological on the other. The experience all over the world, particularly in Western Europe, Eastern Europe and other Socialist countries has been that creation of museums has been an integral part of the development of culture and of nation-building. In fact, museums at local level in these countries are proliferating every year; in contrast, in our country, museums are being designed and expanded only at the national level. The state level museums are ill-kept and starved of funds. They have yet to be effectively integrated with our school system, and visits to them is to be part of the school curricula. Not that such national museums have not been able to promote cultural consciousness among the elite, but they have failed to generate a museum movement in the country, which is intrinsic to the dissemination and development of culture. The problem of dissemination of culture in our country therefore arises at the district (340) and subdivisions or taluq (600) levels, where, barring a few places, few museums, to say nothing of the composite kind of museums exist. In recent years, a few enterprising people have set up "archaeological museums" to preserve and protect the statues lying scattered in the countryside at the mercy of smugglers and thieves. But such efforts need to be followed up. Construction of a chain of composite and "living" museums from the district to taluq level - like a model school in every district as planned now - should be taken up as part of a state policy, and planned over next two plans, supported by both the central and state governments.

It is common knowledge that in many areas many forms of tribal art have decayed, even disappeared (pottery, basketry, weaving, ornaments etc.). The onslaught of market forces has destroyed traditional technology (such as iron-smelting); starved of resources folk artisans have forgotten their skills. There has no doubt also been the countervailing process of intervention by the state to protect artisans. As a result of this there has been a revival of tribal art in some forms in some areas. Much of the credit for it goes to the All India Handicrafts Board as mentioned above and to the "market" which has stimulated demand for tribal/folk artifacts. Surveys of tribal art and crafts were launched in the 1930s, and by the Board in recent years, and it should not be difficult to identify the areas where protection is needed. It should be remembered that revival of folk culture in many countries has been a function of the market, of the creation of demand for folk artifacts as appreciation of their beauty and usefulness has been promoted by education and media.

Protection of cultural heritage and development of culture go together. People's involvement in the protection and development of their cultural heritage is essential, but no serious attempt has been made to generate it. Therefore, all Panchayat raj institutions from the district to the village level should be involved in the protection of our cultural heritage in their respective area. The antiquities acts and other laws should be amended to provide for the cultural role of the Panchayat raj and Panchayat institutions in the protection of the "unprotected monuments" and effective protection of the protected ones. The panchayati raj acts should also be correspondingly amended to provide for the role of such bodies in the preservation of cultural heritage, and promotion of folk culture. We may also think of taking up renovation of unprotected monuments and construction of "culture huts" under various rural development programmes which now allow for construction of school buildings etc.

The ASI has been concerned more with research than with the presevation of folk or tribal art. The RMS as stated above has been designed to recreate the story of human evolution and variation, development of material culture and the range of living cultures (tribal, peasant etc.,) in all their regional variations. Our effort at this stage is also to identify and salvage the artifacts faced with the threat of extinction. Identification, collection and preservation/conservation of such artifacts is the function of all museums including those of the ASI and the RMS, as mentioned above.

There is one area of culture where action is needed immediately, i.e., preservation of the rock art heritage of India. Notionally, it falls within the area of the responsibility of the Archaeological Survey of India, but shortage of funds stands in the way of their protection. We propose to set up the nucleus for the preservation of rock art heritage in the RMS.

The ASI, and other institutions have been working over

years in their respective area to document folk artifacts. It should not be difficult to identify "soft ware" for wider dissemination. The ASI has produced ethnographic films and photographs and collected a mass of artifacts, and is in a position to identify communities and cutlural areas for which "soft ware" can be planned, produced and disseminated. The dissemination of culture could therefore be strengthened by undertaking the production of video films on various communities and facets of their culture in its regional and national setting. Effective publicity should be arranged of the laws existing or proposed and of the activities of the government and voluntary agencies such as Indian National Trust for Art and Cultural Heritage (INTACH) to preserve cultural heritage. There should be a national debate on the preservation of cultural heritage and development of culture. All this can help in inculcating respect and healthy attitude towards folk culture and appreciation of its place in national culture.

Preservation of tribal identity is crucial to tribal development which is no longer a matter only of economic growth but also of allround development with a good deal of cultural input thrown in. In the first decade of our independence, inspired by Nehruvian vision and idealism, we had the panch sheel of tribal policy, which recognised the individuality of tribes and the need to respect their autonomy, and a model of growth in it that suited their requirements without forcing the pace of their development. A great deal was achieved, atleast in the North-East, in terms of the development of an indigenous literature for tribes. However, with the rise of the "Scheduled" languages (i.e., the languages of states) the tribal languages receded in the background, and creation of a tribal literature was left to the initiative and enterprise of a new tribal scholars and missionaries, rather than pursued as a conscious tool of the state policy. The result was the decay of the tribal languages and slow growth of tribal literature. Except the Austric languages in eastern India, tribal languages are everywhere on the decline in middle India: the Gondi and the Bhili languages divided between more than one state have registered a decline. The Bhils and the Gonds and other tribes elsewhere in middle India are getting more integrated with the cultural and linguistic system of the states, losing their own identity. The thrust of a conscious tribal policy in matters of education and cultural development so evident in the fifties and early sixties which produced grammars and primers, among others, has all but disappeared today. A few tribes (such as Santals led by Pandit Raghunath Murmu who was a renaissance figure) are no doubt valiantly trying to create their own literature and their own script. There are five scripts-based movements today in tribal

India, the most famous being the ol chiki recognised by West Bengal government, but the odds are against tribes. Therefore there is an urgent need to refashion the strategy of tribal education in order to create a sense of tribal identity. This can only be done by making compulsory primary education for tribals in their own language. This will necessitate the creation of a literature which must be undertaken with full state support. This will also involve appointment of tribal teachers or training of teachers in tribal languages, which must also be undertaken. We may not, at this stage, recognize tribal scripts because various scripts including Devanagari have been in use for about 200 years in tribal areas. Devanagari rather than Roman was the script popularised by the missionaries in Middle India. The steps outlined above, if introduced, will ensure that the tribals will atleast not forget their languages and with it their rich oral traditions which are available. The universities and colleges must also be called upon to set up a department of tribal languages as has been done in the Ranchi University for the Chotanagpur group of tribal and regional languages. The state academies should also be entrusted with the task of building up a literature in tribal languages. They should encourage translation, preparation of text books, and recognise the contributions of tribal literatures by instituting a system of rewards.

A tribal is a born artist with natural grace and beauty, a sense of rhythm and felicity of movement. Nothing strikes a visitor to tribal areas of the North-East and eastern India more than the cultural revival on an unprecedented scale. The Chotanagpur festival which was first organised in 1978, and later revived on a larger scale in 1985, is a case in point. The success of the Naga team in the Festival of India is another. While political system, the planning process, and market - a highly unequal one - are bringing tribes within the national mainstream - the cultural factor is missing. There is an urgent need to harness this great potential of tribal people in national interest.

The Seven Zonal Cultural Centres (ZCC) set up to promote inter-regional cooperation in the development of culture in all its aspects, will also deal with tribal culture. However, there are some areas in the country where tribal culture is under stress, like tribal society itself, where tribal artifacts are dying away or are being smuggled out, and therefore there is need to salvage, document and preserve them. Such areas are spread all over the country. The ZCC in the North-East, which is predominantly tribal, can well look after its tribal culture and its varied manifestations. In the north-west, in Ladakh, the existing Buddhist culture centre should be able to take care of its culture. Similarly, the Allahabad and Patiala centres should be able to protect their tribal culture in such small areas as they exist. The problems of safeguarding tribal culture are formidable in Middle India, the South and the islands, where influx of the outsiders over years has created a very difficult situation for tribes and their way of life. Therefore it has been proposed by us that in order to impart a new thrust for preservation of tribal culture, we should set up the Adivasi Kala aur Sanskriti Kendra (AKASKA), or Tribal Art and Culture Centres, as adjuncts of the ZCCs. Like them, these tribal centres will include the tribal regions cutting across presentday state boundaries. Five such centres have been identified: Ranchi, Bastar, Ooty, Port Blair and Dharmapur. They will be attached to the ZCCs at Santiniketan, Allahabad, Thanjavur and Udaipur respectively. All these five places represent the nerve centre of the tribal world in our country. Ranchi is at the heart of the Munda-Oraon belt of central and eastern India, cutting across south Bihar, northern Orissa, western Bengal and eastern Madhya Pradesh, which are peopled by these tribes. It has been the centre of tribal upsurge. Bastar, similarly, is the point of confluence of tribal cultures of northern Andhra, southern Orissa, eastern Maharashtra and southern Madhya Pradesh, peopled by the largest tribal group, the Gonds (more primitive sections) etc. Dharampur or another suitable place may be recommended for the location of the centre in western India, away from Udaipur, where we have the tribes particularly the second largest tribal group of India, the Bhils, of southern Rajasthan, western Maharashtra, western Madhya Pradesh, and southern Gujarat and where a lot of good work has already been done. Port Blair is our window on our pre-historic connections with south-east Asia. Like the great museums situated on both sides of the Pacific, we may develop one of our own, considering the fact that "oceanic intrusion", particularly from the Pacific has been a significant factor in our cultural formations in terms of influence of language, and movement of people and artifacts. The Nilgiris and Wynad have been the homeland of the smallest, probably the weakest tribal communities, where there is also the need for the greatest protection for their way of life. It should be noted that while the main purpose of these centres will be to promote tribal culture they will also promote interaction between tribes and non-tribes in such areas of culture as both have shared.

The Bharat Bhawan in Bhopal is a unique experiment in the promotion and recreation of many forms of tribal culture, which also affords excellent opportunities to tribal artists for self-expression. But efforts are required to be dispersed in many parts of Middle India, and in a more modest way, to salvage tribal culture, and involve tribal people in the preservation and development of their culture. The AKASKA will function, as mentioned above, as a subsisdiary of the Zonal Cultural Centres which are registered as societies. They will function as autonomous organisations, eligible for receiving grants from the central and state governments, voluntary agencies etc. They will have their own governing councils, which will consist of representatives of the ZCCs; representatives of the state and central governments; representatives of various local bodies, artists, tribals; representatives of such research bodies as the ASI, Archaeological Survey of India, National Museum; various voluntary organisations involved in preservation and promotion of tribal art, university departments of anthropology and archaeology etc. The AKASKA may prefer to adopt tribal names for themselves such as akhara for Ranchi or maral for Bastar. The functions of AKASKA may be spelt out as follows:-

(i) Preservation of all aspects of tribal art and culture;
(ii) Promotion of all aspects of tribal art and culture with the cooperation of the tribal people;
(iii) Salvage of tribal artifacts;
(iv) Documentation of tribal art and culture;
(v) Setting up a chain of tribal cultural organisations such as akhara, cultural huts and museums at local level;
(vi) Organising tribal festivals at local, regional and national levels;
(vii) Building up tribal literature by encouraging original works in tribal languages and through translation;
(viii) Promoting tribal languages;
(ix) Integrating study of tribal art and culture with the local education curricula; and finally
(x) Building up an impressive cultural complex, designed according to tribal ethos, including cultural stadium at the five places to discharge and coordinate the functions mentioned above.

The cultural situation in the North-East is somewhat unique inasmuch as it is truly a mosaic, with each tribe having its distinct culture, particularly in matters of dress, forms of dance and music, oral traditions and crafts. The North-East has not been a melting pot in the same sense as Middle India has been. It is a young and vibrant region. Even though in some areas old forms of tribal culture are decaying under the impact of modernisation, a great deal of them can still be salvaged and recreated. This cannot be said of the large parts of Middle India where the traditions of weaving and wood carving are all but dead; on the other hand they are still very much alive in the North-East. The communities here have also enjoyed a measure of cultural and political autonomy, which has helped them to preserve their distinct ways of life. With this background the proposed ZCC in the North-East has to play a role suited to the specificities of its cultural situation. First, it will have to establish a state level centre for all the four or seven states, particularly where none exists. Similarly, sub-centres will have to be established at district level, except where these have been established as part of a conscious cultural policy, as in Arunachal Pradesh. These centres, as envisaged in our plan, will perform many roles and have a museum attached to it, which will serve as the nerve centre of the action plan for the promotion and preservation of tribal culture, not only in its traditional forms but also with its facets of change and modernisation. Thus a hierarchy of cultural centres, which will cater to the cultural needs and aspirations of each tribal community or a group of tribal communities, has to be envisaged right from now as an integral part of the ZCC project.

Archaeology has emerged as a major discipline in North-East in recent years. For the first time, the North-East appears on the archaeological map of India as a zone of transition of culture from eastern India to South Asia or vice-versa. This has been more due to the efforts of the university department of Anthropology and Archaeology in Gauhati than due to the activities of the Archaeological Survey of India. Frontiers of prehistory have now been pushed back a hundred thousand years in the North-East. Therefore, archaeology must figure as a prominent aspect of the functions of the zonal centre. The North-East has also one of the oldest departments of anthropology in the country, probably the third in terms of its establishment. Anthropology has emerged as a strong discipline in many universities in the North-East; therefore its role in the study of tribal culture has to be recognized by making an explicit reference to it in our project. Historical archives are either non-existent or are in a poor shape. One has to be established as part of the cultural centre.

This brings us to the contemporary cultural situation in the North-East. A number of organisations, literary, cultural and research-oriented exist in the region, which have to be linked up with the proposed cultural centre. In addition to the non-official organizations we have well-established departments in universities which are engaged in the investigation of the different aspects of the life and culture of the people of this region. Therefore, the organisational structure functions and activities of the ZCC have to be recast to reflect the role of existing organisations and provide for coordination among them.

Considering the diversity of the cultural formations in the North-East, our ZCC project has rightly aimed at promoting cultural interaction among various tribal communities. There should also be a provision for interaction of the North-East as a whole with the rest of the country as also with the tribes across the international border in South Asia, with which our links are spread over both prehistoric and historical periods, if it is considered appropriate, and at a later date. Therefore the proposed centre should take up particularly projects that will promote joint cultural endeavours such as organizing festivals among all states in the north-east, and the rest of the country. The North-Eastern Council should be recognized as the nodal point for coordination in matters concerning the construction and development of the proposed zonal cultural centre. It is obvious that the work plan for the North-Eastern Cultural Centre should be worked out in great detail, not only by officials but also by experts drawn from various areas of cultural activities in the North-East.

Another area to be taken care of is the Himalayas. Few mountain systems in the world have so profoundly influenced the psyche of a people as the Himalayas have done ours. Like in all mountains, a certain uniformity of cultural patterns can be seen from the north-eastern to the north-western Himalayas. The apparent unity of Himalayan culture is reinforced by the influence of Lamaism from the north and the cultural influences from the plains. However, the Himalayas have three distinct eco-cultural divisions (i) north-eastern region which consists of Arunachal Pradesh, Sikkim and the remaining states of the North-East where Himalayan culture is relatively well preserved (ii) the middle region consisting of Uttar Pradesh where the Himalayan eco-system has been severly damaged and where culture is in a shambles, and (iii) the north-western Himalayas consisting of Himachal Pradesh, Kashmir and Ladakh where both the Lama cultural traditions and the "Hindu" traditions survive but where a great deal of pilfering of art objects is going on. Therefore, when we speak of the culture of Himalayas we have to keep in mind the three distinct cultural situations and the three set of problems of preservation and development they pose. At present we have no institution for the study of Himalayan culture as a whole. The north-western regional office of the ASI, located at Dehradun, has concentrated on the studies of Himalayan communities. It has also collected artifacts of various communities in the Himalayas and is assisting the RMS in Bhopal in collection from selected communities. The Garhwal University at Srinagar has departments of anthropology and ancient history and archaeology. There are universities at Shimla, Kumaon, Srinagar and a university is coming up in Arunachal Pradesh.

They propose to have their museums. There is also the North-Eastern Hill University. Then we have museums at the district level in Arunachal Pradesh, "palace museum" (Leh, Chamba, Jammu) and local level museums in Himachal Pradesh, apart from the state level museums. At the third level, we have enterprising individuals or groups who have been collecting artifacts on their own for preservation. Therefore, our first task should be to identify and prepare a list of such institutions as exist in this region. Our second task should be to assist these museums/organisations/individuals in (a) identifying the problems of preservation of culture and of the specific aspects of it (such as temples, paintings, indigenous technology) as need immediate protection (b) promotion of folk culture in the widest sense of the term ranging from art (painting), technology (woodcarving) to oral traditions (c) strengthening existing museums and setting up new ones (d) establishing close coordination between our three zonal centres at Patiala, Allahabad, Santinikentan/Dimapur and various organisations and individuals working in Himalayan regions; and (e) locating and financing individuals or groups of individuals who are engaged in preservation of various forms of folk culture. Only after sufficient ground has been covered in the areas mentioned above that we can think of, at a later date, setting up of an institute of Himalayan culture in the same manner as we have now the Wadia Institute of Himalayan Geology located at Dehradun. Preservation of culture in the Himalayas has also to be part of the larger scheme of development, particularly in terms of generation of employment for the people at the local level and provision for education.

The third and the last line of activity should be taken up in a systematic way is setting up a composite museum at Port Blair and a small museum in the Car Nicobar Islands. The composite museum at Port Blair should display the artifacts and reflect the natural endowments and varied cultural traditions of the original inhabitants, the settlers and the recent migrants. The Andaman and Nicobar Islands have been a melting pot, an India in a miniature, where communities have discovered a new identity for themselves. It is also the homeland of the most primitive communities in India, of both the Negrito and the Mongoloid stock. The composite museum at Port Blair should consist of an anthropological section that will be built upon the existing one and will be entirely maintained by the ASI. The reason for establishing a separate museum in the Nicobar Islands is that the Mongoloid communities in the context of South Asia have probably had their farthest north-western outpost in the islands. Collection of Nicobari artifacts and their preservation is absolutely necessary not only for the RMS but also for an understanding of indigenous culture in the islands. Similarly, the collèction of artifacts from the Negrito communities at Port Blair will be important. In fact these two museums should act as mentioned earlier as India's window on South Asia. The islands lie across the great route of migration from Madagascar, South and East Africa to the Pacific islands, across which moved influences of various kinds, linguistic, cultural and ethnic. This is a story that exists in fragments. It is time that we know this story in an integrated manner. Archaeologists and anthropologists are trying to reconstruct the outlines of what is now being called Indo-Pacific archaeology and anthropology. If we are able to establish the museum we would contribute a great deal to this process.

IV

The anthropologists however must ponder over the state of anthropology today. On the one hand, since independence, departments of anthropology have multiplied; there are more students studying anthropology today than ever before; there are more practising anthropologists than was the case until sometime ago; anthropology is a paper, reportedly popular, for the competitive examinations and so more non-anthropology students are reading anthropology today. Short of inducting anthropologists into the positions of authority at the highest echelons in the country, they have been given at times, a role in the formulation and evaluation of schemes. There exists a network of the Tribal Research Institutes at the state level which are active. And yet, on the other hand, barring notable exceptions, anthropology in the country has yet to raise the quality of its research to a level that commands respect; anthropology has failed to attract the best students in many universities; the syllabus of anthropology which should reflect its possibilities leaves much to be desired. Anthropology has yet to become a vibrant discipline, ready to open up to allied disciplines such as sociology, social history and economics. Above all, it has to tolerate dissent and remain receptive to suggestions from outside. It is a matter of regret that anthropology gives the impression of having become "sectarian" while as a matter of fact there are few disciplines as eclectic, down-to-earth and holistic as anthropology's. An innocuous suggestion made by a distinguished sociologist who himself started as a social anthropologist to bring down the barriers between sociology and social anthropology caused an earthquake and raised a howl of protest. A distinguished anthropologist recently narrated his experience when his suggestion to include a paper on the culture and civilization of the people of India in the syllabus of anthropology was rejected because it was feared that it would undermine the autonomy of the discipline. The result of such an attitude has been that anthropology in India has not diversified at the same pace as it has done elsewhere, branching off into new lines of inquiry. An exposure to either the International Congress of Anthropological and Ethnological Science (ICAES) or to the American Association of Anthropologists is a revealing experience where anthropology can be seen developing as a very dynamic discipline. In our country however anthropology is not interacting with allied disciplines as vigorously as it has begun doing elsewhere. In order to produce a meaningful study of our communities and our people who have existed in the context of a culture and civilization with a time depth of 5,000 years - many communities' own time depth ranges from medieval to the colonial period and to the present times - and in a society of such complexity as ours, it is necessary to collaborate with other disciplines engaged in the study of its various facets. It does not mean that anthropology should cease to be anthropology. It means that anthropology while maintaining its identity and continuously defining it must evolve a methodology and a conceptual framework which are suited to the study of Indian society. This process has no doubt begun at the level of research by individuals but it has to be resolutely carried forward and made part of anthropological stream.

The other point that should be made before concluding this discussion is that never was the moment so opportune as now for relating anthropology more rigorously to the imperatives of change and development, for pressing the claims of anthropologists for participation in the policy-making and policy-implementation level including the formulation and evaluation of programmes from the bottom upwards. Today the Indian society is opening up as never before. Our countryside is the throes of the processes of radical change set in motion not only by the government but by non-governmental agencies including grass-roots activists. The youth is going into the countryside to study people and to serve them and is being thus exposed to the social realities of a kind much earlier in their career than was probably the case with the generation of senior anthropologists. Today no discipline is more qualified than anthropology to speak of the holistic nature of human resource development. Therefore the anthropologists should sieze upon the opportunity to assert their role sharpen the tools of their investigation and improve the quality of their research so that they serve the country still better.

Reference List

Anthropological Survey of India (April 1977) National Museum of Man A plan outlay

Office of the Director General Anthropological Survey of India 1986 Seventh Five Year Plan for Anthropological Survey of India (draft)

Madan TN (1983) Culture and Development, Oxford University Press

Mathur Hari Mohan (ed) Anthropology in the development process, Vikas Publishing House

Risley HH (1915) The People of India, Oriental Book Publishers Delhi

Singh KS Notes on Cultural projects (Ms)
People of India (Ms)

Spectra of Anthropological Progress (1979) " Identity crises in Anthropology " 217-33 Department of Anthropology University of Delhi, Delhi

THREE

MOTHER, CHILD AND FAMILY IN WEST BENGAL: A STUDY OF SOME CORRELATES INFLUENCING THEIR WELFARE

Kanti Pakrasi, P. Das gupta and I. Das gupta

Children in India account for 116 million out of a total of 683 million enumerated in 1981 Census. They constitute the 'critical human resource' that influences to a large extent national health and growth. Again, children below five and women in the reproductive age (15-45) are found to comprise 37 per cent of the total population and they form the largest vulnerable group in the country. The number of married couples per 1000 population is 170 (rural: 172/urban: 160) and a little less than one-fourth of them are in the range of 15-19 years, the higher concentration being in rural India. In West Bengal the mean age at marriage of female was 17.76 (rural: 16.78 and urban: 23.64) against all India mean age of 17.23 (rural: 16.67 and urban: 19.22) in 1971. On the other hand, the rate of married couples is 152, while the general marital fertility rate and total marital fertility rate happen to be 152 and 5.57 respectively in urban areas of the State. These two fertility rates are, of course, lower than the all urban India rates (172.9 and 6.05). From the standpoint of age specific marital fertility rate it is found that even the married women in the age-bracket 20-24 yield highest rate (300.1) in urban West Bengal. In this State 53 per cent of rural mothers experience at least 3 livebirths against 59 per cent of their urban counterparts. In contrast, the rural mothers showing 6 and more livebirths explain a little less than one-fourth cases, whereas the urban mothers with 6+ livebirths constitute slightly less than one-fifth cases in West Bengal (Govt. of India: 1976-77). This confirms that large families prevail in rural society, while small families dominate in urban society of the State. In another dimension it is known that India is one of the 40 countries of world with high infant mortality rate. High level of morbidity, widespread under-nutrition, infectious diseases are responsible for such a high rate. It is quite alarming to note that deaths under 1 month per 100 livebirths revolve round 74.8, rate of deaths within 1-6 months and 6-12 months are 42.7 and 22.4 respectively in India. Maternal mortality rate per 100,000 livebirths touches the level of 17.6. We find that the estimated crude birth rate and death rate are presently about 33.0 and 15.0 respectively in India (1980). Infant mortality rate in rural India was 129 in 1976. Neonatal mortality (rural: 63/urban: 45 per 1000 livebirths) explains a sizeable portion of the general infant mortality in the country. As a matter of fact, about 50% of neonatal deaths are reported to have occurred within the first four weeks of their birth.

To account for this miserable demographic situation it has been admitted that a large proportion of cases of child morbidity and mortality is due to infectious diseases which should really be attributed to malnutrition. A vicious circle of malnutrition-infection-further malnutrition is rampaging to snap away many lives in early childhood. Malnutrition in India is, indeed, quite severe among women and children to make them highly vulnerable. Moreover, pregnant and lactating mothers are particularly exposed more to undernourishment and this increases mortality among them. It also has an adverse effect on the health and mortality of the babies to be born. It is known that the most critical period in the life of an Indian is early childhood (0-4 years) and only 40% of our children get adequate diets to grow and survive (Health for All: 1981).

If growth retardation is considered as an indicator of nutritional status, about 60-65 per cent of the Indian children should be regarded as undernourished. It has been estimated that there are now about 45 million undernourished children in the country. It is obvious that without improving the nutritional status of the family as a whole it is not possible to improve the nutritional status of a child and thereby to ensure maximum welfare of both family and its constituent members.

Under the circumstances, a child's social, physical, mental and emotional health remains naturally exposed to a great amount of risk. In order to meet the challenge of such risk a National Policy for children has rightly emerged in 1974 and an appropriate guidance to child welfare in upholding his better growth and development is available in the country. This Policy has laid special emphasis on services to children, and expectant and nursing mothers. Eventually the much needed Integrated Child Development Service (ICDS) scheme has come to stay for more than a decade as one of the most important national programmes. In West Bengal more than 800,000 mothers and children dispersed over 110 project areas have so far been brought under ICDS scheme. Combined with the general health services under Mother-Child Health (MCH) programmes the ICDS scheme is strongly expected to bring desired welfare of the mothers and their children.

It has recently been stated by the Minister of Relief and Welfare Department, Government of West Bengal, that in the areas where the projects under ICDS scheme have been started since 1975 in the State definite improvements in the health status of children and mothers have been marked. Even the incidences of mortality, morbidity and malnutrition have considerably reduced under the impact of project linked activities which are guided by the principal objectives of the ICDS. The objectives are inter alia (i) improving health and nutritional status of children, (ii) reducing the rates of mortality, morbidity and malnutrition, (iii) laying foundation for physical, psychological and social development and welfare of the child, and (iv) enhancing mothers' capability for undertaking improved health care of the children. The nation is thus committed to improve the general state of growth and development of the children.

That physical growth and development of an individual most basically depend upon adequate food and again, that different sociocultural factors determine the pattern of nutrients in the society at large are two very wellknown human experiences. But at the same time one has to accept that biological characteristics of the individuals under diverse nutritional and environmental circumstances are also inherently responsible to cause significant effects on growth and development (Greene and Johnston 1980).

Recent researches have firmly suggested that most of the observed differences in physical characters like height (stature) and weight are the consequences of environmental stresses, especially nutritional, during the course of growth and development (Habicht et al 1974, Frisancho 1980). This is also true that while the genetic make-up of an individual sets the upper optimal limit of growth, favourable environmental conditions help to accomplish that limit. It has been found that several biosocial factors like number of children in the family, birth order, parental age, social class, parent's height and weight, birth weight, gestation period influence the growth of an invidivual significantly. Keeping these growth influencing correlates in mind a growth study of the Bengali children aged 7-16 has recently been undertaken in Calcutta. The study reveals that:

(1) effect of father's education is significant on the growth of height and weight of the children, but growth of skinfold (fat) thickness is not significantly influenced by his education level,
(2) effect of birth order of the children is also significant on weight, triceps skinfold thickness or limb fatfold indicating calorie reserves and other seven characters. Birth rank of a child has significant influence on his growth and health status,
(3) effect of higher income and standard of living as measured by per capita expenditure capacity of a family is at once observed to be significant on height, weight and triceps skinfold (limb fat) thickness and other eight characters of the children, and
(4) effect of occupation status of father is similary observed to be significant on nine different body characters including weight, calf circumference, biacrominal diameter (shoulder breadth), and triceps fatfold thickness.

From a recent study of a sample of rural children (1-5 years) of the Bengali parentage we learn that as good as 62 per cent of them suffered greatly protein energy malnutrition and the same was most acute in the 2 years old babies. Their growth pattern has been anthropometrically examined to show that they possess lesser weight, shorter height and lower circumferential measurements (head, chest and mid-arm) in comparison with the national standards given by the Indian Council of Medical Research (Banerjee et al. 1983). The study of the rural pre-school children indicates clearly how malnourishment influences growth, development and overall well-being of the Bengali children. Height of children is considered to be the most sensitive measure of inadequate nutrition and the anthropologists recommend strongly anthropometric surveys at regular intervals to check the extent of nutritional effect on health, growth and total welfare of the children and thereby to assess how changes in social circumstances affect ultimately growth (Grant 1964; Rona et al. 1978; Goldstein 1971; Mueller 1976; Smith et al 1980). In evaluating the influences of the correlates like father's social class, family size, birth order on height as a measurable sensitive indicator it is learnt that the group of Bengali children who are brought up in deprived circumstances are unlikely to grow at their maximum potential rate.

In this context we would like to refer to a longitudinal anthropometric study made in Poland in highlighting the significant role of parental age and birthrank in the child's development (Chrzastek-Spurch 1977). The study shows with respect to mother's age that (A) a slower development is evident among the offspring of the youngest teenage mothers aged under 20, (B) the highest stature is for the children of mothers aged 21-25, (C) the highest weight is achieved by the offspring of mothers aged 21-25, (D) the slowest growth rate of weight and height is registered by the children of teenage, adolescent mothers, (E) increase in height and weight is found to be highest in the children of the mothers aged 21-25. These interesting results confirm that the best child-bearing age of the mother is 21-25, whereas the age below 20 affects the growth of children adversely. On the other hand, with reference to birth rank the study reveals that (F) first-borns are lighter and shorter than second and further children, (G) the fastest growth, both of height and weight, occur in first borns, and the slowest in third and further children. The fast growth of the first borns can explain why these children achieve a higher level of physical development in spite of their lower height and weight at birth. The above facts provide, no doubt, important lessons to appreciate (1) which social and biological predictors should be given due weightage in evaluating nutritional and growth status of the Bengali children and (2) in what direction monitoring of their nutritional and over-all welfare conditions should be organized. Internationally it has already been stressed that individual monitoring of nutritional status should be by growth velocity charts for height, chiefly and weight, if interpreted correctly. Height for age and weight for height, irrespective of age, are universally recommended by the anthropometricians as monitors for the children aged 1.0 to 9.99 years (Tanner 1976).

In the first post-natal year satisfactory breast-feeding and feeding of more balanced diets after weaning have been urged for providing necessary immunological protection and growth-inducing nourishments to a child. A worldwide survey of the patterns of breast-feeding in human society has shown that the mothers of the economically advantaged urban families wean their babies much earlier than their counterparts in the economically disadvantaged rural families (WHO 1981). The differential breast-feeding practices are found to affect growth and development of the children. In this direction a study on feeding habits of the Bengali infants in their first year of life after birth has been made to examine how their growth is influenced by feeding habits (Bandopadhyay et al. 1981).

We learn that the infants of poor mothers were given mostly prolonged breast-feeding (6+months) and again, more starch food after weaning and eventually they suffered relatively greater malnutrition. Upshot is that in the process of post-natal growth during twelve months after birth the children of the poor families experience lower mean values for all the six physical characters like length (height), weight, chest girth, biacrominal (shoulder) breadth, head length and head breadth, than their coevals born to the well-off families. The finding confirms that environmental factors like socioeconomic condition and cultural practice of breast-feeding of the mothers do have significant role to influence the rate of growth and the body build of a child reflects essentially the resultant effects of both the genetical and environmental factors with necessary interactions.

Birth weight and perinatal mortality have already been accepted as two very useful measurements of reproductive efficiency of a mother. It is known that where environmental conditions are less favourable, perinatal mortality rates increase and birth weights happen to be lower at all stages of gestation. A number of unfavourable factors like malnutrition, hard labour, low economic condition, infections, bad housing, teenage marriage, repeated pregnancy etc., is shown to be highly responsible for deteriorated health and loss of reproductive efficiency of the mothers (WHO 1961; Nag and Pakrasi 1980). The variables of birth order, maternal height and social class act as a vital background to growth, development and general well-being of a growing fetus. These background variables remain on the other hand related to birth weight and gestation time (Pakrasi et al. 1985b).

Birth weight provides not only an index of individual viability but also conveys on the population level vital information on the nutritional status of a mother. Birth weight <u>per se</u> is again the most crucial factor to explain the risks of perinatal, neonatal, and late fetal mortality. The low-weight infants (2.5 kg or less) are more liable to be relatively small children with evidence of neuro-psychological impairments. Prevalence of protein-calorie malnutrition is better understood by weight deficiency in all age groups and again, by over-all growth failure. The biological factors like maternal age, sex of baby, birth order, and gestation time are known universally to exercise significant influence on the fetal growth and birth weight.

In the immediate context of the above propositions the problems of birth weight, especially low birth weight, in the Bengali infants have meanwhile been studied in a Calcutta hospital to examine how various biosocial factors like maternal age and socioeconomic condition, sex of baby, birth order, gestation time, and season of birth affect intra-uterine growth and body weight (Pakrasi 1985b, 1986). It is interesting that the babies of poor mothers living mostly in environmentally disadvantaged condition present the lowest mean birth weight and this significantly varies from that of their counterparts of the well-off mothers. Again, the infants of the teenage mothers (under 20 years) are significantly lighter than their coevals of the more aged mothers, irrespective of socioeconomic condition. Among the teenaged mothers the low weight babies (2.5 kg or less) occur significantly in highest order. Again, in poor mothers a little more than one-half of their newborns are of low-weight category whereas in the well-off mothers the low-weight infants explain only 36 per cent cases. In general, 46 per cent of all single livebirths are low in weight in the urban sample.

From the study of a rural sample of Bengali infants we have found that the babies of the teenaged adolescent mothers show also the lowest mean weight, whereas the mothers aged 30-34 possess the heaviest infants. The incidence of low weight infants account in general for 58 per cent of all single livebirths. In this respect the young mothers below 20 years are also found to possess such low-weight babies in maximum strength. The significant relationship between mother's age and intrauterine growth of the fetus is thus well confirmed among the Bengali population, irrespective of their rural or urban affiliation. In rural sample we find again that the incidences of low-weight babies fall steadily between the first and fourth birth orders and thereafter the same increases slightly.

The developing countries of the world are shown to have in general a very high incidence of low-weight babies (WHO: 1961). Among the Bengali children delivered in a Calcutta hospital the incidences of low-weight babies account for about 50 per cent of the female births, whereas in the males only 42 per cent stand for such immature infants. In contrast, in the rural sample of Bengali infants the low weight females explain as high as 62 per cent against 55 per cent among the males. Rural-urban differences in the magnitudes of low-weight babies (2.5 kg and below) confirm at once that the rural Bengali mothers are subjected to more economic and nutritional deprivements and this situation in turn acts as a strong deterrent to normal growth and development of their children.

The importance of nutritional, genetic, emotional and socioeconomic factors in the study of motor development of the child has already been emphasized (Neligan and Prudham 1969; Vauhghan and Mckay 1975; Malina 1980). Motor development means an increase in the number of physical abilities related principally to body movements like head-lifting, rolling, crawling, sitting, standing and walking under the interaction between nervous system properties and environmental experiences (Towen 1981). That adequate nutritional intake is essential to support the needs of normal growth and development (including motor development) has already been stressed. In a longitudinal study of Bengali infants classified by nutritional status the influence of environmental condition on their motor development has been examined to get some interesting results (Pakrasi et al. 1985c). The study helps to understand that those babies who are given limited breast-feeding (6 months or less) but adequate nutritious food (rich in protein and vitamins) attain necessary motor skills for performing the above mentioned body movements significantly earlier than their coevals having prolonged breast-feeding (more than 6 months) and inadequate nutritious food (rich in carbohydrate but poor in protein and vitamins). As a matter of fact, for each stage of development when 70% or a little more of the adequately nourished babies reach any one of the given stages, not even 50% of the inadequately nourished infants can achieve the same stage by the same time.

A close examination of the age norms for the developmental stages reveal that the adequately nourished Bengali infants reach each one of six stages of motor development significantly earlier than their inadequately nourished counterparts. Truly speaking, except for the stage of head-lifting in the remaining cases the inadequately nourished group lags behind the adequately nourished group by more than a month to reach the concerned stage. It is thus evident that growth in the central nervous system and motor development of the Bengali children hinge very strongly upon the nourishments given to them in their first postnatal year.

According to the World Health Organization (1977), the prevalence rate of 'persistent and socially handicaping' mental health problems among children aged 3-15 in developing countries is well comparable with that estimated for the developed countries. It has been said that the children who are in general exposed to disease, infection, malnutrition, poor health care and living condition, 'reproductive casually' (i.e., low birth weight, prematurity pregnancy, hazards, toxaemia etc), and above all, to poverty and deprivation fall victims to mental developmental disorders. The relationship of poverty and deprivation to mental retardation is accepted to be of course associative and not causal (Begab 1976).

In accordance to the above situation we have attempted to study how different biosocial factors may influence mental disorders among the Bengali children (Pakrasi et al. 1986). It is interestingly found that the incidences of mental retardation are significantly associated with (i) the age of children, (ii) the maternal age and socioeconomic condition, (iii) the family size, (iv) the birth order, (v) the tempo of motor development. We obtain that compared to non-retarded, mentally disordered children the retardates have the following significant characteristics: (a) they occur more in the age group 7+years, (b) are born more to relatively young mothers, (c) they originate more from low socioeconomic (manual) class, (d) they belong more to large families, (e) they are more of first and second birth orders and (f) they experience more delayed motor development.

Knowledge of social determinants (Davis 1978) has been stressed to appreciate better the problems of development of central nervous system and mental disorders. In our study the incidences of retardation in children are found to be more frequent in the lower socioeconomic (manual) class. When in India the families of low socio-economic class are in a large majority and very widely subject to poverty culture it is not unusal that the mentally disordered children from the poor families (manual) would generally outnumber their counterparts coming from higher socioeconomic class. In this context we note what Begab (1976) has stated in pointing out that an overwhelming majority of the retardates are no doubt poor, but only a small portion of these poor is really retarded. This small portion on the other hand is concentrated in those families which experience in general low nutrition, poor education, early and adolescent marriage, repeated pregnancy, high fertility and mortality. Our study has confirmed that larger the size of family, higher is the incidence of mentally retarded children. In this very context the importance of small family cannot but be reiterated with full conviction. For the welfare of the malnourished children the mothers have to be motivated for small family. Immediate benefits which a mother can draw from small family can convincingly be explained on the basis of those scientific facts which are available from many empirical researches.

We have discussed so far some facets of the problems of mutual welfare of mother, child and family. Some social and biological correlates which have significant role to influence nutritional status, growth and development in the Bengali children are highlighted here. We emphasise the universal truth that greater protein and calorie reserves are consistently associated with increased growth in both sexes and all age groups and again, that higher protein reserves have a significantly larger effect on growth than the increased calorie reserves

(Greene and Johnston 1980). In the highly stratified society in India where about 50 per cent of the population are said to be below poverty level the prospect of all round welfare of the children and mothers is obviously limited. But National programmes of Integrated Child Development Service and Mother-Child Health Service do ensure greatly desired welfare of the most vulnerable group in the country.

Summary and Conclusion

In the context of the National Programmes of Integrated Child Development Service and Mother-Child Service the problems and prospect of general well-being of the Bengali children have been discussed to highlight how varying biosocial characteristics of the mothers affect growth and development of their infants and children. The correlates like mother's age, socioeconomic condition and parity (birth order), breast and post-weaning feeding practice, sibship size, father's education, social class (occupation standing) and income cum per capita expenditure capacity, baby's nutritional status are found to maintain significant influence on child welfare. Surveillance of growth as a measurement of health and nutritional status is urged, especially for the economically more disadvantaged groups in which large families prevail and poverty is more common.

Reference List

Bandyopadhyay S, Pakrasi K, Banerjee J (1981) Growth of Bengali infants by feeding habit from birth to age twelve months Anthrop Kozl 25:61-80

Banerjee J, Banerjee AR, Chowdhury M (1983) Nutritional and anthropometric profile of pre school children in rural Bengal J Vivekananda Inst Med Sci 3: 56-58

Begab MJ (1976) Barriers to the application of knowledge Address to the opening session of the 4th congress of IASSMO In: Mitlle P (ed) Research to practice in mental retardation 1

Chrzastek-Spruch, Hanna M (1977) Some genetic problems in physical growth and development Acta Genet Med gamellal 26:205-219

Davis Kingsley (1938) Mental hygiene and the class structure psychiatry In: Rose AM (ed) (1950) Mental health and mental disorder Routledge & Kegan Paul Ltd 55-65

Frisancho AR (1980) Role of calorie and protein reserves on human growth during childhood and adolescence in Mestizo Peruvian population In: Greene LS, Johnstom FE (ed) Social and biological predictors of nutritional status physical growth and neurological development Academic Press New York

Goldstein H (1971) Factors influencing the height of seven year old children results from the national child development study Hum Biol 43:92-111

Government of India (1976-77) Family welfare programme in India year book Ministry of Health and Family welfare New Delhi

Grant MW (1964) Rate of growth in relation to birth rank and family size Brit J Prev Soc Med 18:35-42

Greene LS, Johnston (eds) (1980) Social and biological predictors of nutritional status physical growth and neurological development Academic Press New York

Habicht JP, Lechtig A, Yarbrough C, Klein R (1974) Maternal nutritional birth weight and infant mortality In: Elliot K, Knight J (ed) Size at birth Associated Scientific Publishers Amsterdam 353-377

ICSSR, ICMR (1981) Health for all on alternative strategy Indian Ins Edu Pune

Malina RM (1980) Biosocial correlates of motor development during infancy and early childhood In: Greene LS, Johnston FE (ed) Social and biological predictors of nutritional status physical growth and neurological development Academic Press New York

Mueller WH (1976) Parent child correlations for status and weight among school aged children a review of 24 studies Hum Biol 48:379-397

Nag RN, Pakrasi K (1980) On fast pregnancy birth pattern with special reference to teenage mothers a biosocial study from Calcutta In: Pakrasi K, Banerjee AR, Halder AK (ed) The Calcutta couples a biosocial profile Editions India Calcutta

Neligan G, Prudham D (1969) Norms for four standard developmental milestones by sex social class and place in family Develop Med Child Neurol 11:413-422

Pakrasi K, Basu Mallik T, Chowdhury S, Chakraborty M (1986) Mentally retarded children of eastern India a biosocial study Soc Biol 33 (in press)

Pakrasi K, Sil S, Das gupta P, Das gupta I (1986) Birth weight in relation to maternal age parity and gestation time among poor and well of finfants in Calcutta India Acta Medica Auxologica (in press)

Pakrasi K, Sil S, Das gupta P (1985) Body weight at birth and incidence of low weight babies in Calcutta India Anthropologie 23:81-94

Pakrasi K, Sil S, Das gupta P, Das gupta I (1985) Patterns of low birth weight in the Bengali newborns, Ind j Phy Anthrop Hum Genet (in press)

Pakrasi K, Bandyopadhyay, Banerjee J, Banerjee AR (1985) Motor development of Bengali infants by nutritional status in the first year of life Anthrop Kozl 29:46-54

Rona RJ, Swan AV, Aitman DG (1978) Social factors and height of primary school children in England and Scotland J Epidem Commu Heal 32:147-158

Smith AM, Chinu Susan, Rona RJ (1980) Social factors and height gain of primary school children in England and Scotland Ann Hum Biol 7:115-124

Tanner JM (1976) Growth as a monitor of nutritional status Proc Nutri Soc 35:315-322

Touwen B, Co L (1981) The neurological development of the infant In: Davis JA, Dobbing J (ed) Scientific foundations of Paediatrics William Heineman Medical Books Ltd London 830-842

Vaughan VC, Mckay RJ (eds) (1975) Nelson text book of pediatrics WB Saunders Co edi 10

WHO (1981) Contemporary patterns of breast feeding Geneva

WHO (1977) Child mental ealth and psychological development Technical report series no 13 Geneva

WHO (1961) Public health aspects of low birth weight Technical report series no 217 Geneva

FOUR

PEOPLE - THE MISSING LINK OF THE NATIONAL HEALTH AND FAMILY WELFARE PROGRAMME

A. Bardhan, D. C. Dubey

The Constitution of India envisages a new social order based on among other things, improvement of public health, freedom from ill health, improved level of nutrition and higher standard of living for its people. These are considered as some of the primary duties of the State. Since independence, the government is making several sincere efforts to realise the above health aspirations stated in the Constitution.

The year 1978 is of special significance to the health of the masses because in this year the country became signatory to Alma Ata declaration. The declaration aimed at attaining by 2000 AD a minimum level of health that would permit people to lead an economically productive and socially useful life. The declaration recommended that primary health care would be an effective and practical approach for reaching the goal. This concept of primary health care was considered as the control driving force for determining policies, framing strategies and developing action plans. The concept of primary health care is further defined as consisting of eight elements. These are:

- Education of the people about prevailing health problems and methods of preventing and controlling them.
- Promotion of food supply and proper nutrition.
- Adequate supply of safe water and basic sanitation.
- Maternal and child health care and family planning.
- Immunization against major infectious diseases.
- Appropriate treatment of common diseases and injuries.
- Provision of essential drugs.

These eight elements are to be operationalised through two critical processes of (a) Community involvement or making people as partners for achieving their health goals and (b) promoting intersectoral co-ordination. According to the WHO's concept health is defined as "Health is a state of complete physical, mental and social well-being which is essential for leading a productive life, and it is not merely the absence of disease or infirmity. Provision for health should be considered a fundamental human right and attainment of highest level of health is a most important social goal".

Realisation of this positive concept of health depends upon a co-ordinated action of several health-related sectors such as, education, drinking water, agriculture, rural development, social welfare, etc. Both these processes clearly identify the people as beneficiaries and people as providers of health-related services in sectors other than health, to be at the centre of the health plans, strategies and programmes. Unfortunately, our existing approach to health has not adequately recognised the crucial importance of working with people as partners. Their involvement and participation is missing. We have failed to change the health status and their health practices in the way we want them to be. We have also failed to make people responsible for their own health inspite of the sincere desire and efforts on the part of the government and health workers.

Approaches and Methods

In the above context it is worthwhile to ask and review ourselves what we had been doing in the area of health during the past several decades since independence and what is stopping the people from behaving and doing what we want them to do? While it is so obvious to the health workers what people should do why is it not obvious to them? We have a view of how we would like health care to be and we want them to share that view and act accordingly! We want them to do something, they are not doing now and we want to commit them to responsibilities they don't currently carry. In other words, we have view for their health which we want to give them without a caring for their health values, perceptions and health care practices.

We have been approaching 'health' firmly believing that our aproach is right. There is strong belief in health workers that people should do as we expect. Our policies have been developed under somewhat impractical enviable assumptions that we must protect the people from future maladies and diseases which they don't know and don't care about. We therefore, provide services which the people and the community have not necessarily asked for; nor willing to pay for. Our understanding of the health programmes to be promoted may not have the same importance and meaning to the people. This moral view of our vision may satisfy us, but it may not be so or shared by the people. To a great extent the above analysis explains why inspite of our sincere desire and substantial technical as well as financial input, we have not made any significant positive impact on the health of the people.

If we agree that the above description is largely attributable to what we have been truly doing in the field of health, the question which arises next is, Is there any alternative? And if so, what is that alternative? It is here that one finds the critical importance and relevance of primary health care approach and its goal of providing health for all. The primary health care approach is based upon proven and practical principles and action-strategies of marketing approach which keeps the values, preferences, likes and dislikes, needs and cost considerations of the buyer who is in the centre of their planning and strategies of selling goods. Like marketing approach, the primary health care approach too demands our understanding of what people are prepared to 'buy' from what we want to 'sell'. Do our health programmes and tasks offer solutions to any of their health problems? What are the likely benefits and advantages people are likely to derive from our activities? What costs or risks are involved in their accepting of our programmes and practices? Both the primary health care approach and marketing approach demand from us much local and community knowledge to understand the risks and benefits to people and to make use of local values and real benefits as possible appropriate tools for motivating them for better health. The primary health care approach is basically persuasive, information and education based, with hard labour and intensive work. To maintain partnership with people a lot of handholding and repeated reassurances are required. To maintain partnership with the people repeated reassurences are required to be given to them. Promting partnership for health with the people will require the workers to listen well. Promoting partnership in health with the people in present health system required to do much more of listening and much more of testing. The precondition for the successful operation of primary health care approach would be (a) credibility of the health worker and health system. As of now this is very low; (b) the capacity of the health system to come out with technological innovative which are useful and usable to the masses, (c) willingness on the part of the health system and health workers to work hard; persistent and persuasive and provide appropriate time span required for any change for specific health practices; and (d) demonstrating usefulness, feasibility and practicality of the primary health care approach for attaining better health in visible forms over a short period of time.

The National Institute of Health and Family Welfare as an apex body in the field of health and family welfare, in the year 1984 took up the challenge of demonstrating, operationalising and developing the methodology of this concept of primary health care particularly its basic two central processes of community involvement or developing partnership with the people and intersectoral co-ordination in the sense of locating or placing health programme within the context of total integrated development.

The Project Objective

The overall general objective of the project is "promoting the community awareness, knowledge and competence to organise and mobilise community and outside resources for meetings health goals of the community." To make the general objective more meaningful and to operationalise, the specific objectives of the study are worked out as:

- Increasing level of public awareness, knowledge and concern about health problems and programmes;
- Improving health services, image and health service presentation through a more effective action by the health personnel and a more efficient operation of the programme.
- Increasing acceptance and utilisation of health services on the part of the potential users through need-based messages and actions integrated with other development programmes.
- Participation of the community group (existing or newly formed) in the programming, implementation of control of specific health talks and activities including related communication-education aspects, and
- Promoting education and acceptance of national health programmes including MCH and family welfare.

Methodology

A simple three step methodology was evolved for the implementation of the above genesis. These three tiers are: (a) establishing credibility of the health workers while assessing the health needs of the community, (b) mobilising the individuals of the community and its resources in order to achieve the health goals jointly and (c) establishing contact with other developmental programmes in order to initiate inter-sectoral coordination and co-operation in the context of the total integrated development.

These three stages include three major components of

(i) communication-education
(ii) Community interest groups/institutions (existing or newly formed) and
(iii) community's specific health activities.

Communication-Education

In the project the communication-education component was considered to be one of the key processes. The usual conventional information-education-communication (IEC) approach as is being practised, was considered to be highly inadequate for the project as the project has the focus primarily on community involvement and partnership in order to achieve goals set for. In the usual (IEC) approach there is a major concern only for informing people about the health programmes planned outside the community on a "take it or leave it" basis. The motivation aspect of communication is very weak and inadequate as communication is oriented to the interests (targets) of the providers of services. A most crucial factor of communication process on 'feed back' is missing. And the communication is not co-ordinated as it is geared to independent health programmes. There is very little continuity and therefore no or very little learning takes place.

Thus, it was felt in the project that the communication programme should lead to a continuing dialogue among all concerned parties e.g., community members of all castes, invoke groups and social status, health workers and other development workers, voluntary organisations and block and district administrators. To strengthen the motivation force of communication, it was exclusively geared to the health felt-needs of the people. Continuity and co-ordination in the communication process was ensured by linking it to the semi-formalised community interest groups like (Village health committees, Mahila Mandals, School Health Clubs etc.). The implementation of the community specific health activities provided continuity of dialoque, which in turn provided a feed back mechanism at face to face situation. Not only that, the continuity of dialogue generated motivation maximises natural as well as specially contrived communication opportunities leading to learning and improving the competence of the people for organising, mobilizing and implementing health and family welfare programmes. It was also felt necessary that in the course of continuous contact of the health workers and the community there will be exchange of views and interaction regarding the peoples' health values perceptions and health practices. This will enable the health workers to respect in due course peoples' health values and culture. Efforts were also made to promote acceptability of communication-education with the help of local media, individual contact and through group discussions and personal visits.

Community Interest Groups/Institutions

These are the second important components of the strategy. From the very beginning it was decided that the project will be so implemented that it gradually develops capacities of its own existing and new institutions to identify immediate actions and implement decisions. However, at the initial stages help of the health workers of the existing system was required. This involvement was also felt necessary as the project was not conceived of as something outside or independent or alternative or parallel to existing health systems. Its main objective was to demonstrate how and in what manner it is feasible to incorporate the philosophy and methodology of community participation working with the existing health system which the country has built over the years. In the community the organizations like Panchayats, Mahila Mandals, cultural and social organisations, songs and drama parties etc., are in existence. All may not be available in one single community but are rather likely to be dispersed in different communities. However, in order to but are give some uniformity to the project strategy it was decided that during the first few months of the project it may be ensured that each village has the groups/institutions like village health clubs, youth clubs etc. Wherever, one or more do not exist, the project workers were asked (as well as trained also) to promote these.

These local groups provided some easily identifiable platform for the communication dialogue to which the group could lend concrete form or identify, necessary continuity and appreciation as well as approach. These groups also gain visibility to local health concerns of the community. Women and School health and youth groups acted in coordination with the health committees as their supportive extension arms. The village health guide and trained birth attendants as community members were closely linked with these groups.

Community Health Action

Actual learning and health education takes place when the

dialogue stage gets transformed into concrete action-related projects which the villagers implement to the advantage of the community. It is here at this stage that the widely accepted principle of 'learning by doing' becomes operative. It is this creative activity which pervades the community experiences in cooperation, conflict management, mobilizing community and outside resources and undertaking responsibilities and discharging them. The ultimate aim of all these is to instil confidence for the generations to come and competence in successfully participating for meeting their health needs.

Therefore, the strategy can best be summarised as 'one of stimulation of local initiative, through open dialogue, towards agreed health or health-related activities'. Stimulation as well as communication education-dialogue were woven around identification, implementation, monitoring and evaluation of need based health activities.

Staff recruitment

Having decided about the strategies and methodologies in the project, recruitment of staff was made. On the whole four Action Research Officers (AROs) and one supervisory staff, i.e., Research Officer were recruited and placed in the field situation. On an average each of the action research officer was responsible for 10-12 villages of a primary health centre. Research Officer, being the supervisory staff was also given responsibility of implementation of the theme of community participation in 5 villages. This approach enabled him to understand the process of community participation in a better way and thereby he was in a position to supervise the AROs in a meaningful manner. All staff recruited were experienced in research in the areas of health and family welfare programmes.

Orientation Training of the Field Staff

Although the staff recruited were experienced in the health field yet orientation training for them was organised considering the importance of the central theme of the project on concepts and processes of community participation and extension approach. Staff were also given exposure during the training regarding importance of understanding the health perceptions and values among the people while organising and working with various 'interest groups, such as, village health committees, mother's health clubs, children's health clubs, etc. They were specially given orientation to respect the health culture of the people and perform the role of a catalytic agent for initiating changes in the areas related to health. Their role as a 'doer' or 'provider' of services which they have been playing in the government service earlier, was de-emphasised and their new role of 'enabler' helping the communities to get involved in health activities was greatly emphasised in the training.

The formal training programme organised was of only one week's duration. While in the project, continuing training of workers based upon regular monitoring of feed back information was inbuilt in the project. The experience gained by us during the orientation training convinced us of the enormous difficulties and problems in changing the role of health workers from 'doer' to 'enabler'. Being the government workers they used to implement the governments' orders with authority as happens in bureaucratic situations, rather than as partner as is expected in the participatory approach in the project. However, in the one week's orientation training, the Principal Investigators of the project devoted most of the time on helping workers in unlearning the established perceptions and procedures, what they acquired during long years of government job, and make them prepared to make entry in the rural communities with an appropriate open and receptive frame of mind and thinking.

Selection of the Villages

According to the operational plan of the project, each ARO was supposed to work within a group of 10-12 contiguous villages. Accessibility of the villages, mixed composition of village population representing different caste and class groups, some homogenous and cohesive composition of the communities were some of the guiding principles kept in mind while selecting the villages. Attempts were made also to consult existing community organizations, district health system organisations as well as district organizations while selecting the villages in order to be sure that in these villages there is a high need for increasing attendance to health services and possess adequate service units and communication-education opportunities. On the whole 42 villages were selected for the project distributed in three districts of Gwalior, Datia and Sagar of Madhya Pradesh.

Health Need Survey

On selecting the villages, a survey was conducted in these selected villages in order to know more intimately and intensively the image and status of the ongoing health programmes, the health problems perceived by the community, the knowledge, attitude and concern of the community on these health problems, the leadership community groups, and the communication pattern existing in the community for making and implementing important decisions, past history of the community in participatory community programme, information on locally available technical financial and human resources, the gathering of information about working of Panchayats, Cooperatives and other Voluntary groups. Special emphasis was given to collect this information with respect to women and children and other very poorer sections of the community. On the whole the survey, in addition to the collection of information, was also instrumental in sensitising and socialising the AROs and RO as well as large number of villagers consisting the group of respondents for the survey. Further this was the stage when the community tried to assess the sincerity as well as credibility of the workers. The staff also used this period in establishing rapport with the communities and its various formal and informal groups including opinion leaders. Wherever required, the workers during this period, took special steps in organising women's health groups, children's health groups and in forming village health committees to make them fully representatives of the village communities. In brief, these activities formed the first stage of the project. This stage is therefore, marked with the socialising, rapport establishing and initiating the formation of interest groups. This stage also provided enough opportunities to both the project workers and the people to know each other better.

Four Principles of the Project

The next activity consisted of introducing the project objectivities, methodology of work and procedures to be followed during the implementation of the project. Four principles therefore, were repeatedly emphasised by the project staff during this period. These are: (a) the project aims at promoting competence of the rural communities in meeting some of the health and health-related needs of the communities, (b) in doing so the principle of partnership between the rural communities and the outside resources will be observed as far as possible, (c) the health activities generated within the project will be planned, monitored, implemented and evaluated by the local health committees, the panchayats and other interest groups; and lastly (d) it was repeatedly made clear that the project will not assign any activity to villagers, members of the health committee/mothers club etc. It is the members themselves who are to assign responsibilities to them to fulfil the various health needs. If they so desire they could make use of the official as well as voluntary health resources. District authorities and district health systems were also repeatedly told about these principles and genesis of the project.

Second stage of the Project

The second stage of the project involved organising health dialogue systematically (which was initiated at the first stage) with a view to implementing and achieving certain specific objectives. This could be achieved by holding village programmes, planning workshops under the initiative of the village health committees in order to identify local health problems and other related problems, assigning priorities to the identified problems and selecting a few activities for implementation, depending upon its urgency of the need, financial feasibility and practicability; to develop specific time schedule and division of responsibility for specific works, work out financial implication and identification of resources both within and outside the community and establish linkages with other groups and institutions in the village like, mothers' health club, children's health clubs, etc. In the project villages this planning workshops were organised based upon the findings of initial survey.

Third Stage

Following this, implementation/action committees had started initiating the activities on the one hand while on the other they started seeking cooperation, coordination and help at the level of the community, with the project and inter agency levels depending upon the nature of the project. Several ups and downs are faced by the project in its different stages of its progress. The project is on-going and during a short span of about 2 years it has shown far better achievements and results in the field of health and related areas of formal and informal education, electricity, drinking water facilities, and overall personal and environmental sanitation. In the areas of MCH & FP, the achievement of villages is far better as compared to non-project villages where the conventional approach of providing health to the villagers without closely involving them is being followed. There are indications that involvement of communities for health programmes is possible, practical and far more rewarding. This has been realised and accepted very clearly by the villagers themselves and they feel much more confident and competent for fulfilling their health needs in partnership with the health system and other rural development systems of the government. The health workers of the regular system in the project villages feel that they are respected more and their targets are achieved more easily and quickly when the villagers themselves take responsibilities for health tasks, the health workers realise that they are not working alone. They feel that so many other villagers work with them as educators, motivators and implementors of health tasks.

In conclusion the question arises of the willingness of the health system to extend the hand of partnership and cooperation with the people. While there will be little disagreement on this it must be realised that implementation of this will call for a review of existing approaches, methodology and organisation of the system. Is the health system ready for this?

FIVE

ETHNIC IDENTITY AND NATION BUILDING NORTH-EAST INDIA

A.C. Sinha

Among the many attributes of the state, territoriality is one which is in itself a geographical concept indicating a variety of features. Its another significant attribute may be identified in terms of population, which is a multitude of communities coexisting in the given territory, organised itself into the state for political purposes. Ethnicity and nationality are the two spectrums of the 'mix' between territoriality and population. A student of social behaviour may like to examine the equality of ethnic participation at the various levels with reference to the nation-building efforts in the country. Keeping that in view, the present paper, firstly examines the concept of ethnic identity as such and its various attributes. Secondly, various approaches to the nation building and its critique have been analysed. Thirdly, after briefly describing the North Eastern region as a distinct one, we have endeavoured to explicate the concepts of core (centre/mainstream) and frontier (periphery/margin). Fourthly, we propose to examine the evolution of relationship between the Indian core and the North Eastern peripheral region. And lastly, after briefly commenting on the quality of the existing relationship, we suggest what should be the pattern of interaction between the two in future for a meaningful participation in the nation-building effort of the Indian state by the various ethnic groups.

Ethnic Identity

No ethnic studies in the contemporary social sciences will be complete without reference to Barth's study of Pathans. He adopts a subjective criteria, when he opines that a population "identify itself, and is identified by others, as contributing a category distinguishable from other categories" (Barth 1981). It also presumes a set of rules governing situations of inter-ethnic contracts. Furnival and M.G. Smith proposed an alternative approach on the basis of some objective criterion. This approach emphasizes the importance of the values and institutions of the various groups in the society and the value consensus that exists between them. This objective and poly-ethnic approach minimizes conflict (Kuper 1971). Against the above background, ideological or sociology of dependence approach goes closer to the Marxist bi-polar class analysis. It suggests to consider ethnicity as an ideology of and for value dissensus and disengagement from an inclusive socio- political arena.

Aronson views ideology of ethnicity distinct from the class ideology in which the latter presupposes pursuing major values, not shared by others in the arena. "If ethnicity is an ideology for disengagement, then we need to give priority on the study of ethnicity not to boundaries once established or to mechanism of maintenance but instead of independent variables which make or deepen the appeal of such ideologies, and the consequences of such ideologies for the arenas in which they arise. We must look harder than we have at the 'ethnic entrepreneurs' who formulate and manage the ideologies, and now situations are defined or reinforced to their adantage. . ." (Aronson 1975). This approach asks why and when the ethnic groups come to be and not how they, like all types of groups, build institutions, elaborate an internal culture, define 'outsiders' and struggle to maintain themselves. It presumes that in case consciousness of deprivation and concomitant organizations are not sufficient to unit a group, ethnic ideology or pride in one's ethnic identity provides the answer.

Approach to Nation building

Against the above micro-level approach, some individual efforts such as Karl Deutsch (Deutsch 1963) were made to study the routes of assimilation and mobilization in post-World War-I Zechoslavakia and Finland, a non-sovereign state of Scotland, and a new nation-state of the Third-World, India. However, the most significant attempt to conceptualise the phenomenon of state formation and nation-building was the series of studies of political transformation organised by the Almonal-Pye Committee of the American Social Science Research Council (Almond and Coleman 1960; Pye 1963; La-Palombara 1967; Ward and Rustow 1964; Coleman 1965; Pye and Verma 1965; La Palombara and Weiner 1966; Binder and Coleman 1971 and Tilly 1973). These studies were mainly concerned with the newly emerged polities of the 'Third World' such as Ghana, Turkey, Iran, Pakistan,

India, Burma etc. They also attempted to identify crucial variables in a generic process of change from the traditional polity to the modern 'bureaucratic-participant' state, though the idea of such a participant nation-state was European in origin, these studies failed to provide comparable experiences of nation-building in Eurpoe and the Third World.

Then in Nineteen sixties a series of Studies were made in which varied experiences of nation-buidling in Europe and other parts of the world were compared. In this series mention may be made of Benedix's (Benedix 1964) comparison of nation-building experiences of Germany, Russia, Japan and India. Holt and Turner's work on England and Japan, France and China (Halt and Turner 1966) and Barrington Moore's anlaysis of the economic basis of political transformation in England, France, the United States, Germany, Russia, China, India and Japan (Moore 1966).

Karl Deutsch and his colleagues at Yale and Harvard took up another dimension and build up computer archive of data on the new as well as the old politics. By the early 1970's a relatively vast literature was piled up and it was thought desirable to assess the conceptual contribution to the understanding of genesis and growth of the polities. In such an effort Rokkan (Rokkan 1971) identified the imbalances in the ranges of cases and variables in the studies of the politics in the form of the large-nation bias, the 'whole nation' bias, and the 'economic-growth' bias. He emphasized the need for comparability of the nation-building experiences across the continents. He also identified six 'crisis of development' such as penetration, integration, participation, identity, legitimacy and distribution as challenges, issues and policy options in courses of nation-building. Similarly Kothari (Kothari 1971) reviews the literature on the nation-building under three heads; social mobilisation theory, centre and periphery and modernisation as the favourite themes of the Western academicians. These Western biases were subjected to criticism by the academicians specially from the third world. All these resulted in the publication of a significant work by Eisenstadt and Rokkan on state formation and nation building. (Eisenstadt and Rokkan 1973). This provides, by now, the most authentic source, organised into five major themes; theories of political development, variations in the state formation and nation-building experiences in Europe, variations within the continents settled from Europe, variations within Asia and Africa and data sources for comparative research on nation building.

Mention must be made of two other significant efforts at

inter-disciplinary levels to unravel the internal dynamics of state formation organised at Leiden on 1975. Henry Claessen and Peter Skalnik organised a seminar on the early state in which about two dozen historians, political scientists and anthropologists presented their studies varied in time and space. They examined a number of significant questions on the theory of state formation: Is it possible to describe the characteristics of the Asiatic mode of production to all or only some, of the early states? What was the role of the conquest in the rise and further development of the early state? What was the influence of population growth and/or pressure on the development of the early state? What kind of correlation existed between the development of trade and markets and emergence of early state? What were the methods of resolving internal conflicts in the early state? And what kind of a correlation existed between the development of the early state and the rise of cities and urban life?

The proceedings were presented in a volume, divided into three parts: Thesis, Anti-thesis and Synthesis. Thesis presents the theoretical aspects and working hypothesis. Anti-thesis describes 20 case-studies arranged alphabetically from all over the world. Synthesis at the end, encapsulates a comparable conceptual analysis. The problem of state formation continues to engage Claessen's concern, which is evident by his efforts to organize a session on the Early State and After at the XIth International Ethnological and Anthropological Congress in 1983, in which more than a dozen substantive papers were presented (Claessen 1978, 1984).

The second effort was made in India at the instance of Prof. Surajit Sinha in 1981 in which historians, political scientists and anthropologists examined the issues around polity formation in eastern and north east India. In this workshop papers were presented on Meitei, Mizo, Dimasa, Khasi and Jaintia from the north-east besides the Bhotia state formation in Sikkim. The process of state formation at the regional level in this region was found to be frozen in the 19th century because of the British domination. This line of thinking was clearly marked by the contribution of Goswami on the Mizo state formation, which provided a negative case (Sinha 1981). This line of thinking is being fruitfully examined by the indigenous scholarship in the north east region of India (Bhattacharjee 1984). The small ethnic groups in the region with their various stages of technological and economic development are being effectively brought within the orbit of the Indian state system. In effect an evolved and complex economic and political system is being super-imposed on otherwise simpler ethnic base of the region.

North-East India as a region

The northern highlands of Arunachal Pradesh is, in fact, the eastern extension of the great Himalayan arc. The eastern limit of the Indian Union with Burma is formed by the Purbanchal extending from Naccha Barwa (on the north eastern extremity of Arunachal) to Arakan Yoma on the border of Burma and Bangladesh. The north western end of the region is secured by the Gangetic Delta, which separates the Mikir- Meghalayan plateau from that of the Rajmahal hills in Bihar. The central part of the region is the low-lying plains of the Brahmaputra and the Barek. The communities have moved in and out of the region since time immemorial. The migration of the communities across the international borders from the North and North-East to the region has been significant. To the extent that anthropologists such as Hutton (1968, 1969) and Burling (1965) have shown the cultural and linguistic links between this region and south Asian peoples.

Because of the geopolitical disadvantages, the region has achieved and integrated insularity. Its overall under-development is an aspect of the larger scenario of unequal and uneven development in the various parts of the Indian Union. In 1960's Sen Gupta and Adasyuk (1968) termed this as an economic region of incomplete formation within a meso-agricultural zone of rice-maize-market-gardening and horticultural products. Chaube and his associates also examined 14 indicators of such an incomplete economic formation (Chaube, Munshi and Guha). Undulating topography and tribal concentraion appear to have gone together in the region. Arunachal, Meghalaya, Mizoram and Nagaland out of the seven units of the region have about 80 per cent scheduled tribal population (Ahmed 1982). This concentration of the tribes in the hill states is significant because only 3.57 per cent of the total Indian and 11.43 per cent of the scheduled tribes were found in the region in 1971. Their distribution is also differential in the sense that only 6 persons per sqr. km were found in Arunachal, while 186 persons per. Sqr. km. in Assam against the regional figure of 77 and the national figure of 177 in 1971.

North-East as the perepheral region of India

A casual vistor to North-East Region from the other parts of India is baffled by the remarks: When did you come from India? This may be heard in Mizoram, Nagaland, Manipur, Meghalaya and lately in Assam. The other side of the coin is the reception method to the vistors of those frontier state to the Indian metropolitan cities, where they are asked to produce their foreign passports to establish their identities. Ignoring the mischief mongers it is worthwhile to consider the confusion created by the genuine mistaken identities. While the former set of Indians after postponing their cultural, religous, caste and linguistic 'superiority' for the time being find the 'backward' tribals ungratefully not identifying themselves as Indians, the latter find themselves lost in the crowded mainstream because of unfamiliar language, food and complexity of communication. And invariably when not properly recognized, they tend to conclude that the statements made in favour of national unity, secularism, non-discrimination etc., are just oral platitudes. One may cancel these stray experiences as exceptions in a huge country like ours. However, such incidences may also be taken as symptomatic expressions of the complex relationship between the Indian core and the north eastern frontier region. Not only from academic but even from practical point of view, certain questions in this context demand our attention: Where is the Indian core or mainstream and what should the frontiermen do with it? In other words, what does it symbolise for a how should the frontliermen identify themselves with it? What is India after all? Is it just a 'state' or is there an Indian society? In that context, what does it mean to be an Indian? How does one normally behave as an Indian?

When the British empire was being built, their entire attention was diverted to acquistition of territories, which were to be governed and ruled from the coastal fortresses of Calcutta, Madras and Bombay. And that's why, three presidencies of Bengal, Madras and Bombay were not only initially extensive but were ethnically, linguistically and otherwise diverse. The National Congress was committed to their break up and establishment of the linguisitc states. However, demands on the ethnic grounds were initially ignored but States of Nagaland (1963), Meghalaya (1972) and Mizoram (1986) were conceded in the case of north east India. However, similar demands from elsewhere were not entertained. In fact, "the Congress party never accepted ethnicity - except in the case of creation of the north eastern states - as the basis for the formation of states; it favoured language as the factor determining the recognition of states". (Singh 1985).

It needs no efforts to identify the Indian Union as a state consisting of 31 administrative units of states and territories. By its own admission, it is a plural society, where multiplicity of race, caste, religion, language etc., are logically recognised. One may also recognise India like any other 'state' as a complex interaction between the spatial (concrete, communicational and other locational objects) and analytical aspects (such as social and behavioural). From purely a legal point of view, the Indian society should coincide with the human multitude within the political boundaries of state. Naturally, this Indian society in typical Durkheimian approach to social structures may consist of material referents such as human resources, transmitted commands, coersion etc., and symbolic and mental referents like consent, fear, persecution, resistance etc. In such a situation, it is but natural to express distinct peculiarities of the national phenomena in terms of bi-polarities like rich and poor, urban and rural, dominant and subordinate, bourgeois and proletariat, developed and underdeveloped and main-stream and periphery. With a view to uncovering the locational and behavioural aspects of the above phenomena, the issues around the concept of core (centre/mainstream) and periphery (frontier) in Indian national context may profitably be examined.

Some scholars presume 'state' to be unicellular organism with a nuclei (centre, core, capital), bodies (territorial expanse), outer membranes (the boudaries) and the stomi (ports, border posts etc.). It is also considered as a system in which a continuous surveillance by the dominant of the subordinates' behaviour and deployment of threats and punishments are normal ingredients (Stressolodo 1980). All those are performed in terms of power, which is defined as control over communication flaws, located in the state at the points where selection is possible, decisions are made and information is transmitted. Through this politico- cybernatic model of state the extensive territorial entity of India is nothing but a heirarchy of power centres branching out to a seat of ultimate decision making power. Naturally, commands follow down fron the centre to the periphery and information travels in the reverse direction.

In the normative model as opposed to the politico-cybernatic model of state 'power' is replaced by the concept of collective consensus on shared norms and values. Emphasis is placed on society, considered to be commonality of immaterial elements such as images and moral codes. Status and prestige are peacefully and unanimously accorded to those who fill the most strategic roles in society. It is presumed that there exists a central zone as realm of values, beliefs and emotions in structure of society. This central zone also provides a set of activities, roles and personnels within the network of institutions. In this way, the central zone is intimately connected with what society considers to be sacred and ideal aspoused by the ruling authority (Shils 1961). From this point of view, the large territorial societies such as India have a number of sub-systems such as polity and economy, and status system such as ecclesiastical and kinship are organized through common and overlapping set of values and personnel. Needless to add that the above sub-systems characterize the pattern of authority symbolized by the individual behaviour.

In case, one examines the expanse of the Indian Union closely from its capital to the frontier regions, some interesting features may be noted. Firstly, the core of the Indian Union may be identified with Delhi, Uttar Pradesh, Bihar, Madhya Pradesh, Rajasthan, Haryana and Himachal Pradesh. This is predominantly a Hindi speaking, Hindu, area which had traditionally been a strong-hold of the Indian National Congress. Needless to add that 40 percent seats in the Indian Parliament belong to this zone. Secondly, an associate to the core may be identified with the States such as Gujarat, Maharashtra, Karnatak, Kerala, Tamilnadu, Andhra Pradesh, Orissa, West Bengal, Tripura and Assam. These states are non-Hindi speaking but predominantly Hindu areas either under the Indian National Congress or other National Political Parties. Incidentally, about 52% seats in the Indian Parliament are controlled by them. Thirdly, at the outer fringe of those two zones, we find Jammu and Kashimir, Punjab, Goa, Lakshadweep, Andaman Inslands, Mizoram, Manipur, Nagaland, Meghalaya, Arunachal Pradesh and Sikkim. These are the frontier states mainly inhabited by non-Hindu and Non-Hindi speaking communities, and have a strong tradition of regional political parties. (Chaube 1984). They elect only about 8 per cent of the members of the Indian Parliament. It may not be out of place to put onrecord that Jammu and Kashmir and Lakshadweep are the only Muslim majority states; Punjab is the only Sikh dominant state; Sikkim is the only Buddhist dominant state and Nagaland, Meghalaya, Mizoram and Arunachal Pradesh are the tribal states within the Indian Union which are all located on the periphery. For the purpose of broad generalization, the first two categories may be identified with the mainstream, while the third zone may profitably be termed as peripheral to the core in various ways.

We feel this is an opportune time to focus on the national exercise in identifying, analysing and evaluating the exigencies of social change, economic growth and political implications of small (frontier) states in India. The Indian Union consists of 31 political-administrative units (22 states and 9 Union Territories). In our present discussion all the 31 units will be referred to as the 'state' irrespetive of their being 'state' or Union Territories). Among these states, the first six large-size states contribute to more than fifty per cent of the total area as well as the total population of the Indian Union. On the other hand, fifteen small units (states) together make up only 8.9 per cent of the area and about 5.5 per cent of the Indian population. In case, we consider the size of the population along with smallness in territory, we get a list of 17 states which are small. Goa, Pondicherry, Chandigarh, Dadra and Nagar Haveli and Delhi are, in fact, structurally and behaviourally parts of their neighbouring larger states. Thus, they are to be excluded from the list. In case we examine the cultural distinctiveness of the states, (i.e., presence of at least one-third population belonging to the scheduled tribes/castes) we come across only some states which are small in territory, population resources, and have particularistic demographic characteristics. Incidentally, these are the states which are geographically inaccessible because of their location on the Indian frontiers. They may be identified as Andaman and Nicobar islands, Arunachal Pradesh, Lakshdweep-Minicoy and Admindivi islands, Mizoram, Nagaland, Meghalaya, Manipur, Tripura and Sikkim (Table 5.1). Those states may be classified into two sets: One,the six states from among the members of the North-East Council and their neighbour, Sikkim, all located on the distant North- Eastern international frontiers and geographically inaccessible mountainous region; Two, the two island states scattered on the expanse of the Bay of Bengal and the Arabian Sea, posing strategic challenge of their own. It may be noted that they are located on the geographically inaccessible regions. The second feature that emerges is that the most of these states are of crucial strategic significance because of their location on the international frontiers with China, Bhutan, Burma and Bangladesh. Thirdly, five of the states e.g. Arunachal Pradesh, Lakshadweep, Meghalaya, Nagaland and Mizoram are predominantly tribal states, while nearly one-third population of Manipur, Tripura and Sikkim belongs to the scheduled tribes and there are the scheduled castes inhabiting these states (Sinha 1984).

Rationale for a defiant North-East Frontier

These frontier states are tenuously linked to the centre (or the capital), where the strategic elites are located, significant decision are taken, commands are transmitted to the peripheries and informations are demanded from them. The key terms, which qualify the relationship between the two are 'power' legitimacy, authority, rules, compliance etc. Such relations are formal, mechanical and legal, which sprang up because of some historical accidents, but they are sought to be of paramount significance. The pattern of this relationship smacks of colonial attitude of the past, to which a paternalistic vaneer of development and planning for the backward regions has been added by the new rulers. Possibly, it would have been ideal to look for a 'moral' consensus of shared norms and values', commonality of ideal images and moral codes, a realm of beliefs and actions and an over all set of sacred national objectives as the common heritage of the core and the periphery. Perhaps only such a common commitment will inspire confidence in the future and only then the real and imagined injustices supposed to be inflicted on the frontiers would set right.

TABLE 5.1
Table showing population, area and ethnicity in the small states

Unit State	Area in sq.kms.	Total Population	Population Density	Percentage of Scheduled Tribes.
1. Andaman and Nicobar Islands	8,293	1,15,133	14	15.72
2. Arunachal Pradesh	85,573	46,75,117	6	79.02
3. Lakshadwip	32	31,810	994	92.86
4. Manipur	22,356	10,72,753	48	31.18
5. Meghalaya	22,489	10,11,199	45	80.48
6. Mizoram	21,087	3,32,390	16	94.26
7. Nagaland	16,527	5,26,449	31	88.61
8. Sikkim	7,299	2,08,843	29	38.00
9. Tripura	10,477	15,56,342	149	28.95

The north-east frontier is vague, distant and amorphous to the mainstream. It is said to be the land of the naked, head-hunting and exotic peoples. Even the famous Kamakhya temple is mythologically associated with marginal power to convert the humans into birds and beasts. The bulk of the mainstreamers are oblivious of the frontier states. In case they could locate them on the map, all they know is the territories and not the communities. Physical distance from the core is coupled with the insufficiency of the communication networks. There is no quick, effective and convenient (the least comfortable) means of communication between the core and the region. In such a situation, those who go to the region, consider themselves something of pioneers, explorers and adventures. The white collar functionaries come to the region on punishment, occassional promotions and out of routine postings. Very rarely a functionary opts for posting in this region. And why should he do so? After all no significant decision, even the one, affecting the distant local situations, is taken in the region. Consequently, a frontier functionary, who lives relatively deprived and inconvenient life, plays no role in the process of decision making; rather he is supposed to obey the orders from the 'above' and on filling the informations. All such functionaries who come to the region on brief sojourn have their powerful patrons, links and well wishers in the core. That is one reason why they do not behave normally. Either they mark their time in nothingness or indulge in acts beyond their normal behaviours.

The frontiermen equally feel the core to be complex, manipulative, mysterious, devoid of sensibility, a jungle of rules and a convenient contrivance of some crafty authority. The moment they get out of their native environs, they confront language, food, transport and communication, etc. as uncomfortable and unfamiliar. "There are historical reasons for that. What is called "Indian Great tradition" by some sociologists hardly penetrated into these difficult border terrains during pre-British Indian empire. Later, these were conquered by the British, but were excluded from regular administration and opportunities of free contact with plains. Neither the Indian Railways nor the Indian national democrartic movement reached out to these areas" (Guha 1982). It is a fact that the better part of the north-east frontier become parts of India effectively only during the last 150 years or so. Even the Ahom land, better part of the Brahmaputra valley east of Kamrup, came into effective Hindu fold (and thus to mainstream) as late as the 17th century. That is one of the reasons that social structure, commensality, marital pattern and festivals and feasting are unique to Assam. In such a situation, the various frontier states adjoining the Brahmaputra valley, are not in a position to identify a collective code of conduct, a shared belief and historically transmitted traditions along with their western neighbours. On the contrary, they are afraid of an unequal social system of the mainstream. Many of them believe that if absorbed in the mainstream, they may be mistreated as the untouchables and reduced to a beast of burden.

By tradition the hunting and pastoral frontier communities consider the settled plains agriculturalists as inferior breeds. They do not accept the natural barriers by temperament, and the political boundaries are least acceptable arrangement of relationship for them. Individual attainments such as physical prowess, swordsmanship, archery, hunting, riding etc., coupled with an element of defiance are the prized ingredients of their behaviour. (Lattimore 1962). Such communities are not only located on the geographically inaccessible tracts, but are also part of 'societies' in the sense that a section of their kith and kin are located on the 'other' side of the legal boundaries. Linguistically, culturally, socially and even economically they are separated by an artificially 'divide' which they have never really recognised as such. In fact, the above over-lapping sets of loyalities naturally provide an alternative mode of behaviour in their hours of distress. Explorers, adventurers fortune-seekers, fugitives fron the law and other types of men fired with an imaginative scheme rush to the 'frontiers' from the core to make quick monetary gains. Thus, a number of bonanza shanty towns emerge where, infact, nobody rules and the 'business' as usual is secured through an unwritten code of violent conduct, through which a tenuous working equilibrium is attained.

Against this backgound, the various types of the Bengali ethnocentricism (and thus Hindu, which represents the mainstream) and actual historical claims relating to script, language, cultural attainments, political awareness, contributions to the economic development, etc., in terms of the region, are seen as efforts of the mainstream to dominate the peripheries. And naturally a situation emerges between them, which can be understood only in terms of dominance subordination syndrome. Here one would like to share the apprehension of a distinguished scholar: "In their eagerness to project themselves as 'nationalistic' 'progressive' and 'secular' many social scientists have been vocal in condemning the loyalties to such entities as religon, caste,language and religion somewhat indiscriminately. But it will be useful to keep in mind two points here: First, the human need is not only for impersonal ties with entities such as political parties and bureauratic state on the one hand and for privatized ties provided by primary groups such as family and kin-group on the other but also for immediate struture and processess which blend and balance the two. In a country like India such ties are often provided by caste, religion, language and region, which are often labelled as communal, parochial, and anti-national. But these loyalties and ties need not be so dismissed. Second, there is a qualitative difference in their loyalties and ties between different levels and contexts. These can co-exist and one need not displace the other." (Oommen 1984).

Commonality of Ethnic and National Identities

It may not be out of place to mention concept of metropolitan and peripheral economies in terms of the marginalized so-called primitive communities. Similarly, proposition of unequal regional development and consequent exploitation of the peripheries by the urban industrial metropolitan mainstream may be relevant (Amins 1980). The mainstream with its superior techno-economic organisation and decisive control on the resources tends to logically extend its economic infra-structure to exploit the peripheries.The emergent peripheral petty middle class tries to collaborate with the domominant metorpolitan elements with a view to sharing the "benefits of development", but they come to realise within no time that the collaboration is to their disadvantage. Thus,the more aware are of the exploitative nature of the metropolitan control,the more defiant they become in their dealings with it. Morevoer there are discrepencies in the ethnic political and state boundaries, which is played upon by the vested interests, against the common interests of the masses.

In this complex spectrum of relationship between the centres' dominance and frontiers' defiance can there be certain shared values, ideas, ideologies and objectives for a corporate living? India is a plural society and a participative democratic state. We claim to have a tradition of unity within diversity. The Indian Union is a confederation of sub-nationalities, with regional (ethnic?) centres for certain decisions and their implementation. However, it is also a fact that the political centre and regional sub-centres have not been able to develop a system of shared functions to best satisfaction of everybody. No sensible Indian would like to weaken the strength and effectiveness of the centre in terms of undertaking and implementing strategic decisions. At the same time, it will be desirable and healthy tradition to increase a sense of partiçipation, belonging and unity of purpose with regards to the national ideals, values, and objectives among the regional sub-centres. This can only be done by encouraging them to take their own decisions keeping in view the national ideals desired from the nation-building efforts. Only then a chain of politico-cultural sub-centres will emerge in the frontier regions which may project virile traditions and absorb the local shock-waves. It is high time to realize that the Indian Union does not belong only and even mainly to the mainstream and the frontiers are to be ruled and subjugated and treated as supplicants. It must also be borne in mind that frontiers do not need paternalistic proppings, but a recognition that they are trusted to take signficant decisions affecting national life, and that they are able and capable to contribute to the national commonwealth and nation-building efforts as equal and proud partners.

NOTE

* The work 'Hindu' denotes a joint family of different faiths,different peoples....It is evolved out of the heterogeneous ways of life of hundreds of tribes and communities that lived in India for ages. This form of Hinduism is a multi-centred decentralized, structure formation of the

ways of life of all those people. Of course the central norms of the Hinduism is represented by the beliefs and thoughts of the Indo-Aryan groups because of dominating role of those people in making of the Indian History. But influences of non-Aryan communities should not be minimized. Thus, peripheral beliefs will have no place in the religious books of the Hindus, some of these beliefs will certainly be part of Hindu practice." (Barlinge, S.S. 1986-1-2).

Reference List

Ahmad A (1982) The linguistic pattern of north eastern region. First national symposium of language and social and regional identities in India. New Delhi

Almond GA, Coleman JS (1960) Politics of developing areas. Princeton University Press

Amins S (1980) Class and nation historically and in the current crisis. Monthly Review Press. London

Aronson DR (1975) Ethnicity as a cultural system. In Henry F (ED) Ethnicity in America. Mouton Publishers. Paris

Barlinge SS (1986) Four phases of Hinduism. In the seminar on historical and contemporary character of Hinduism. New Delhi

Barth F (1981) Process and form in social life. Routledge & Kegan Paul. London

Bhattacharjee JB (1984) Editorial note. J Soc Sci Hum 2 Burling R (1965) Hill farms and paddy fields. Prentice Hall NJ

Benedix R (1964) Nation-building and citizenship. Wiley. New York

Binder L, Coleman JS (1971) Crisis and sequences in political development. Princeton University Press

Chaube SK, Munshi S, Guha A Regional development and the national question in the northeast India. Soc Scient 37

Chaube SK (1984)Cultural frame and the dynamics of federalism in India. Soc Sci Prob 1

Claessen HJM (eds) (1978) The early state. Mouton Publishers. Paris

Claessen HJM (1984) The internal dynamics of the early states. Cur Anthrop 25

Coleman JS (1965) Education and political development. Princeton University Press

Deutsch K (1963) Nationalism and social communication.MIT Press

Eisenstadt SN , Rokkan S (1973) Building states ar d na ions. Saga Publications. London

Guha A (1982) National development and India's northeast region some conceptual aspects in a historical perspective.

Seminar on regionalism and nationalism. Dibrugarh
Hutton JH (1968) The sema nagas. OUP. Bombay
Hutton JH (1969) The angami nagas. OUP. Bombay
Holt RT, Turner E (1966) Politial basis of economic development. Princeton university press
Kuper L, Smith MG (eds) (1971)Pluralism in Africa. Calorrnia University Press. Berkley
Kothari R (1971) Variations and uniformities in nation- building. Intern Soc Sci J 23
La Palombara J (1967)Beaurocracy and political development, Princeton University Press
La Palombara J, Weiner M (1966) Political parties and politcal development. Princeton University Press
Lattimora O (1962) Studies in forntier history collected papers 1929-1958. Oxforx University Press. London
Moore B Jr (1966) Social origins of dictatiorship and democracy. Beacon Press. Boston
Oommen TK (1984) Insiders and outsiders in India promoridial collectivism and cultural pluralism in nation-building. XVIII All India sociological conference. Surat
Pye LW (1963) Communication and political development. Princeton University Press
Pye LW, Verma S (1965) Political culture and politcal development-Princeton University Press
Rokken S (1971) Nation-Building. Cur Social 19
Sen Gupta P, Adasyuk G (eds) (1960) Economic regionalization of India
Shils E (1961) Centre and periphery in the logic of personal knowledge. Essays presented to Michael Polanyi on his birthday. London
Sinha AC (1981) Managing the social consequences of smallness in north eastern region.In : Abbi BL (ed) CRRED. Chandigarh
Sinha AC (1984) Studies in the Himalayan communities.Books Today. New Delhi
Sinha SC (1981) Tribal polity and state systems in precolonial eastern and north eastern India. Centre for studies in social sciences. Calcutta
Singh KS (1985) Tribal society in India. Manohar. New Delhi
Stressolodo R (1980) Centre periphery and system boundary a culturalogical perspective. In:Goattmann J (ed) Centre and periphery spacial variation in politics. Saga Publications. Beverly Hills. London
Tilly C (1973) Formation of national states in western Europe. Princeton University Press
Ward RE, Rustow DD(1964) Political modernization in Japan and Turkey. Princeton University Press

SIX

SURVIVAL AND REVIVAL OF ETHNIC IDENTITIES OF THE CHAKMAS AND MIZOS OF MIZORAM

B. B. Goswami

I

Issues concerning the socio-cultural aspirations of the people are often discussed in International bodies to attain regional peace through cooperation. Such an important announcement was made by two members of South Asian Association for Regional Cooperation (SAARC) held at Dacca in 1986. Mr. Rajiv Gandhi, Prime Minister of India and Lt. Gen. H.M. Ershad, President of Bangladesh made a joint commitment to sort out the problem of tribal unrest in the Indo-Bangladesh border area. The Mizo underground of India occasionally took shelter in Bangladesh and many Chakmas of Bangladesh infilterated into the Indian territory. The village Parva situated at the trijunction of India, Burma and Bangladesh, a hideout centre for the MNF insurgents, was largely inhabited by the Chakma Shanti Bahini followers. Yet in Mizoram the Chakma did not render much help to the Mizo underground. This is because the ethnic identity and aspiration widely differ between the Mizo and the Chakma. In view of the above, survival and revival of such identities are brought into relief through brief ethnography in this paper so as to show that integrational issue is not only a national problem but a local problem too.

II

The Scheduled tribe Chakma of Mizoram India constitutes 7 percent of the total population. Bulk of the Chakma live in the Chittagong Hill Tracts (CHT) of Bangladesh, Bordering Mizoram. In Mizoram as well as in Bangladesh, the Chakma live in plural ethnic state. Their neighbouring ethnic groups in Mizoram are the Mizos, the Pawi, the Lakher, the Riang and other Tripura tribes. In the Chittagong Hill Tracts the Moghs, the Kuki, the Riang, the Marma, the Banjogi and other tribes are their neighbouring ethnic groups.

According to the Chakma one of their beliefs is that they are of Kshatriya origin and have been living at one time somewhere near Nepal foot hills. Sometimes, in the 14th Century they invaded Arakan Hills and settled there after marrying the women of that area. This is, however, not supported by evidence (Loffler 1964). Even early writers such as Hutchinson (1906) holds that Kshatriya origin myth was popularised when the Chakma came in contact with the British during Kalindi Rani's time (19th Century). Kalindi Rani was a devout Hindu ruler who worshiped Durga, Kali and other Hindu God and Goddesses. She might have been provided with the Kshatriya myth by her Brahmin priests at Rangamati, the capital from where she ruled. It appears that Kshatriya myth pervaded among the other ethnic groups also living in the foot hills viz. the Mogh. The Mogh holds that they were at one time rulers of Maghadha in Bihar (Rizvi 1970).

Serajuddin (1984) does not give any credence to the theory of Muslim origin of the Mongoloid Chakmas as enunciated by the early British writers, [(Hutchinson : 1906) wrote, "The origin of the tribe is doubtless due to unions between the soldier of Nawab Shaista Khan, the Governor of lower Bengal, under the Emperor Aurangzeb about 1670 AD and the hill women.")] or the belief by the Mogh that the Chakma are the progeny of Mughal soldiers married to Arakanese women. Serajuddin argues that a few captive Mughal soldiers by the Arakanese king cannot give rise to such a large population. According to Serajuddin "The North India Kshatriya origin of the tribe is not acceptable, nor is its alleged Muslim origin" (1906 : 91). In the 18th Century names of the Chakma Chiefs, one comes across Muslim names but Serajuddin argues that it does not mean that the Chakma adopted Muslim religion. For example, during 19th and 20th Century Hindu names predominate but the Chakma are not Hindus. Serajuddin writes, "Muslim names were confined to the ruling Chakma Chiefs, and they adopted these names in deference to the ruling power of their time. The explanation given by the Chakmas for the Muslim names of their Chiefs is simple enough. Chaman Khan, a Chakma Chief, married into the family of the Wazir of Chittagong and received the Muslim title." (ibid : 90).

The Chakma are a Mongoloid people who entered CHT from Burma. They have definite association with the tribes, migrated from erstwhile Shan area. Grierson (1968) holds that the Chakma alphabets are, "almost identical with the Khmer character which was formerly in use in Cambodia, Laos, Annaur, Siam and at least the southern parts of Burma." The migration from Arakan (Burma) started in the 15th Century and by 18th Century they settled themselves in the hills and foot hills of CHT along the course of Krnafuli river which enters Mizoram.

The Chakma developed statehood from chiefship even in the early 18th Century. In the 18th Century under the control of Arakanese King their territorial jurisdiction included all the hills from the Pheni river to the Saugan and from Nizampur road to the Hills of the Kuki Raja (Serajuddin ibid). They subsequently came in contact with the Mughal for trade. When they stopped payment of tax to the Mughals, the latter attacked them in 1724. Though temporary peace prevailed they had to surrender to the East India Company's Government in 1787 (ibid). "The Mughals did not claim territorial jurisidication over the hills" (Serajuddin : 94), the British did. Nowadays, the Chakma population are distributed in the area around trijunction of India, Burma and Bangladesh.

The Chakma are Hinayana Buddhists. The men's dress consists of dhoti and Panjabi (kurta). It is the women in the hills who maintained cling to their traditional dress. The Chakmas of Mizoram consider themselves as more backward than their counterpart living around Rangamati in Bangladesh. Yet all of them are proud of their old script, history, mythology, folklore and literature. Their religion relates them through Hinayana Buddhism with not only the ethnic groups of their region but with civilizations of Burma, India and Sri Lanka. Most of the chakma houses follow the religious calendar published in Rangoon. The Chakmas have resisted themselves from adopting Christianity. They proudly boast that when other neighbouring tribes such as the Pawi and the 'Lushai' were primitive and fearful savages, they had attained statehood.

Though Chakma speak their own dialect, educated Chakmas can speak Bengali but do not know Mizo. They get their education largely through Bengali medium and read Bengali literature. Their social organisation has been described by Loffler (1964). They are a patrilineal people. Barash (1967) writes, "The concept of 'tribe' has at best only minimal significance when applied to the Chakma who in specific economic and technological respects, are proto-peasant and in other cultural characteristics, notably in ideology and religion are tribal in terms of a Burmese model".

The Chakma practice jhum cultivation, along with permanent wet rice cultivation wherever possible. In this matter they do not require any help from other communities. They rear cattle.

The Chakma migration from Arakan to CHT has been referred to earlier. After the British control of CHT the Chakma moved along the Karnafuli river upto the origin of its source. The Kalindi Rani's territory in 18th Century went upto the border of the present day Mizoram, where Col. Lewin's bust was placed. The British in 20th Century wanted to put a halt to the Chakma migration in Mizoram. E.S.Hyde issued (on 22.3.44) the following order to stop and control Chakma migration in Mizoram (Goswami 1979 : 54-55).

(i) Owing to the large number of Chakmas now settled in the South Lushai Hills, most of whom have considerable families, no further applications for settlement will be considered but for the most exceptional reasons.

(ii) No passes for new separate houses will be considered except where the applicant is

(a) The grown-up married son of a Chakma who has been settled for at least 10 years in the Lushai Hills.

(b) The grown-up married grandson of such a settler.

In both these cases the applicant himself must also be a permanent resident of the Lushai Hills. Passes for daughters will not be considered. Those who marry outside Chakmas, must go to their husband's villages. If they marry Lushai-Chakmas the husband will be covered by the rules above.

(iii) The site of each Chakma basti will be decided by the chief in consultation with the Karbari and will be reported to the Circle Inspector. This site will not be changed without permission from the Sub-Divisional Officer or Superintendent. The name of Karbari with the location of the basti will be reported for record in this office.

(iv) The bastes shall consist of not less than 15 houses which are to be concentrated in a village site, or along a lane which shall not be more than 1/2 mile long. No dwelling houses shall be build outside this site other than jhum houses, granaries etc.

(v) The Chakmas will make and maintain throughout the year a footpath from their bastis to the chief's village.

(vi) The rules about outing Jhums on the river banks will be strictly observed and orders from their office will be obtained before any departure is made from these rules.

(vii) Chiefs will be responsible for the general control of Chakmas in their ram. They will normally work through the Karbari, who will be removed on the recommendation of the chief if he is found to be either ineffective or of bad character.

(viii) Mass movement of a whole or the large part of a basti from one chief's ram to another will require the sanction of the Sub-Divisional Officer or Superintendent. Individual priming (migrating) of houses and families will be allowed as in Lushai villages."

After the Independence of India, the Chakma reacted to maintain their ethnic identity in two ways. In Bangladesh they reacted towards ethno-historic and developmental programmes. When S. Mujibur Rahman, on a trip to Rangamati declared "Now we are all Bengalis" the Chakma reacted sharply saying that their culture, tradition and language are different from the Bengalis. On this ethnicity issue only, Manabendra Naryan Larma, a Chakma, was elected to the Bangladesh Parliament defeating an Awami League candidate.

The Karnafuli Multipurpose Project was conceived by the erstwhile East Pakistan as a developmental project. Indian Government also submitted its protest towards the Project. The Dam created by this Project submerged an area of 400 sq. miles which included 54,000 acres of settled and cultivable land. It also submerged land in India. This Project created a disruption in the Chakma socio-economic life. The Karnafuli Project and Bengali nationalism and culture were two forces, to threaten their socio-economic life, the root causes for Shanti Bahini Military action in 1976.

In India, the Chakma were involved in the political activities of Mizoram District Council. Though remaining at the periphery, spatially as well as politically, they played decisive role in putting a party in power in the Mizo Hills District Council (Goswami 1979 : 55). In 1972, when Mizoram became an Union Territory, the Chakma achieved their own District Council with headquarters at Borapansari. This provision was made to protect their ethnic identity as well as to initiate change as per the needs of the community. But they feel that the area where they live has not received the appropriate attention for developmental programmes. Borapansari is not properly connected by good roads and has no good schools and colleges. They complained that the Mizo are taking away the lions share from the central grant for developmental programmes. They allege that they have not been provided with medical facilities, drinking water supply, even corrugated galvanised iron sheet roofing for Chakma villages.

The Mizo raise the issue of the Chakma infiltration in their area in recent .times. On 14 June, 1982 Ex-Chief Minister of Mizoram released a Memorandum submitted to the Prime Minister alleging alarming increase in the Chakma population. On the other hand, the Chakma allege that some of the areas where the they are living in Mizoram since long, have not been included in their District Council. The Central Government, however, has taken up the issue of the Chakma infiltration in Mizoram and Tripura with Bangladesh Government.

The ethnic tension between the Mizo and the Chakma, thus, is accumulating over time on the matters of ethno-history and development. The same has been observed in Bangladesh as stated above.

III

The Scheduled tribe called Mizo are largely confined to Mizoram. They have their own traditional dress which is worn by men and women. Men in service has, however, wear western garments. Same is more or less true for women working outside North-East India. They belong to Kuki-chin group and speak Dulien dialect. The world Mizo has been popularised since Independence of India (Rao 1978 : 232). In earlier British documents most of the present day Mizo were called Lushai. In 1873 Campbell (1873 : 59) distinguished the Mizos (Lushai of the hills) and the Chakmas (another tribe of the lower hills) in this way "They form one of the numerous tribes generically known as the "Toungtha" as children of the hills and thus distinguished from numerous other tribes in the same direction, generically known as the 'Khyoungtha' or children of the river. The latter in their purity belong to Aracan, speak its ancient dialect and are Buddhists; the former are mixed race, speaking various dialects and do not profess the Buddhist or Hindu religion." The present day Mizo not only disown the word Lusnai but also they have changed the name of the district Lushai Hills to Mizoram through an Act of Parliament called the Lushai Hills District (change of Name) Act 1954, which has now been declared as a State. Ethnic plurality of the state can be observed by the fact that in Mizoram there are three District Councils called the Chakma District Council with headquarters at Borapansari, the Pawi District Council witn headquarters at Lawngtlai and the Lakher District Council at Saiha. As early as 1912 Shakespear wrote that "the term Lushai (nowadays Mizo)as we now understand it, covers a great may clans (XIII) ... In most cases the dialects of the minor clan have been entirely forgotten (41) ... During the census of 1901 an unsuccessful attempt was made to get a complete list of the clan families and branches. The causes of failure were the ignorance of the people themselves as to what clan or family they belonged to and the tendency to claim to be true Lushais" (42).

The Mizo believe that they came out of a cave (Chhinlung). This is a common belief which they share with many other ethnic groups. The details regarding who came out of the cave first or last and how they came out of the cave are the treasured oral traditions of the Kuki-chin ethnic group (Shakespeare 1912 : 94).

It appears that due to historical and other reasons, views of the Mizo and the Chakma towards other are based on the notion of negatively stereotyped outgroup. Prejudices are getting stereotyped. It has been observed that the Chakma and the Mizo both are Mongoloid and trace their mythical origin from Shan state, practised swidden cultivation and had centralised political organisations. They live in contiguous areas. The Chakma, however, had civilizational contact with the outside world much earlier than the Mizos and had also attained cultural, political and economic sophistication. Yet they feel that being a minority in Mizoram their identity as well as development may not be safe in the hands of the Mizo. They now and then want Central Government's intervention. The Chakmas are Buddhist and the Mizo are Christians. Their world view differ. The Chakma are minority having different script and language. The Chakma are called by the Mizo as Takam, unwanted dirty people. The Chakma traditionally consider the Mizo as ruthless people. There are lyllabys in which the children are asked to go to sleep by repeating the refrain that Kukis are coming to loot their village. (Goswami 1975).

The Mizo (Sailo) Chief entered their present day habitat in hordes through Burma about 300 years ago. One of the Mizo tradition speak that they once lived in Shan states. They were constantly in move from one place to the other in search of food and shelter. After entering Mizoram they dislodged many of the earlier inhabitants towards west. The tribes akin to them living in the South Manipur area (popularly known as Kuki) and Jampui area of Tripura are culturally nearer to them. Though historical experiences of the people living outside Mizoram are slightly different, yet the people of these areas express oneness because of common cultural and societal factors and similarity of the hazy mythical past.

Before their conversion to Christianity, the Mizo believed in their own traditional religion. Nowadays all the Mizos of Mizoram are the followers of Christianity. The Roman script and alphabets have been provided to them by the Missionaries. When the British came into contact with them, the Mizos Chiefs were in a habit of attacking the British territory in CHT and Cachar tea plantation. As a matter of fact the Mizo Chiefs upto 1871-72, resisted any idea of British expansion to their territory. The British were always in the alert. They, however, succumbed to the British armoury might, and the area was annexed in 1872.

The Mizo practise swidden (jhum) cultivation. They rear pig. The areas where wet cultivation is practised are limited to a few acres. Their patrilineal social organisation has been summarised by Goswami (1979). He notes that nowadays the features of the 'complex structures' are replacing the fundamental facts of 'generalised exchange'. This is important because this is the third stage in the process of change in the Mizo society. The existence of asymmetric alliance is the first stage and the process of integration through the said system is the second stage (Goswami 1973).

Literacy is Mizoram is quite high. Due to the Missionary efforts most of the Mizo became literate. Many of the literate third generation Mizos have now excelled in many fields of education and development (Thanga 1978 : 172). But all these are post-Independence developments.

The Mizo unrest developed because of politicisation of culture (Goswami 1979). A situation of crisis was blended with culture and tradition to attain political ends. The Mizo insurgents thought it was for their survival. It is, however, a political integrational problem (see for details, Goswami 1979).

The British after annexing the area established Salio Chief

rule in a firm manner, which was earlier loose and incomplete. The process of consolidation gave foothold to the Chiefs as rulers of their reactions. This was the first stage of consolidating 'we' feeling among the Mizo. The second stage of cohesion was at the people's level, so as to build up an acceptable cultural boundary through Christianity. At this stage they discarded the word Lushai, which meant a specific ethnic group, and popularised a more broad based blanket word Mizo. The Mizo ethnic aspiration was thus got consolidated. The third stage gave birth to institutionalised and non-institutionalised politics. The emphasis culminated with a territorial demand for the Mizo in three forms viz. 'Free Independent Mizoram', 'Greater Mizoram' (including areas from Manipur, Assam and Tripura) and the demand for a 'State of Mizoram in India.' The last politicised ideological demand has now been achieved by the MNF by discarding the first one. Initially MNF used the imposition of history and tradition in context to religion. It ignored the constitutional mobilisation for attaining power and used disjunctive activities. When the MNF found that the entrenched political parties and leaders did not lend their full support they expressed faith in constitutional techniques (for details of Mizo Unrest see Goswami 1979), and have now attained a state of Mizoram in India.

The support for attaining the idealised political aim, neither the Chakma nor the Lakher their neighbouring ethnic groups in Mizoram, lend their full support. The Chakma support for the Mizoram underground came through Shanti Bahini of Bagladesh. The Mizo undergrounds fought for safeguarding their own ethnic identity, which they thought may be submerged in the total identity of India. The unedited text of the memorandum of settlement of Mizo issue, signed on June 3, 1986 which is appended herewith mentions that the new state of Mizoram should take necessary action to protect and pressure the rights and privileges of Minorities such as of the Chakma and should take action for socio-economic development. (Point No.9) The Chakma are still dissatisfied and apprehensive. The Mizo now aspire for 'Greater Mizoram.'

NOTES

1. The views expressed in this paper are purely personal.

Reference List

Baresh LM (1967) The concept of a 'Tribe' in East Pakistan The case of the Chakma of the Chittagong Hill Tracts (In)

Abstract, American Anthropological Association, 66th Annual meeting

Campbell (1873) The Looshais, Journal of the Anthropological Institute of Great Britain and Ireland

Goswami BB (1973) Structural Phenomenon of kinship with regard to the Lushai (In) Tribes, Caste and Peasantry, Ethnographic and Folk Culture Society, Lucknow

———(1979) Mizo Unrest : A Study in Politicization of Culture Aalekh Publishers, Jaipur

Grierson GD (1968) (reprinted) Linguistic Survey of India, Vol V, Part. I

Hutchinson RHS (1906) An Account of the Chittagong Hill Tracts, Calcutta

Loffler LG (1964) Chakma and Sak, International Archiv fur Ethnographie

Rao (1978) The Sociology of Mizo Politics, (In) North East India (Ed) by SMDubey, page 232

Rizvi SNH (1970) East Pakistan district gazetteers : Chittagong Dacca

Serajuddin AM (1984) The Chakma Tribe of the Chittagong Hill Tracts in the 18th Century, Journal of the Royal Asiatic Society

Shakespear J (1912) Lusei Kuki Clans, London

Thanga LB (1978) The Mizos, Gauhati

SEVEN

GENETIC, SOCIO-CULTURAL AND HEALTH CARE AMONG TRIBAL GROUPS OF JAGDALPUR AND KONTA TEHSILS OF BASTAR DISTRICT (MADHYA PRADESH)

Salil Basu

Tribal population groups of India provide an unique opportunity for the study of genetic factors in the most natural environmental conditions. Natural environmental conditions, imply the conditions which have not come under the impact of modernisation and acculturation. As we all know, tribal population groups of India are distributed almost all over the country, except in a few states, in defined pockets characterised by their individual socio-economic, cultural and socio-biological set up. They inhabit widely varying geoclimatic conditions and are exposed differently to the various climatic and environmental stresses and strains.

All diseases are genetic in origin to some extent and they manifest themselves in interaction with the enivronment; in a nutshell the disease and process of disease manifestations. have a complex etiopathology. Delineation of the causative factors behind disease requires indepth investigations into the socio-cultural, socio- biological milieu of the population groups. It may include diverse factors such as the sanitation, hygiene, parasitic load, mating-pattern, preferential marital alliances, nutritional pattern, health seeking behaviour, genetic markers etc.

All socio-cultural, socio-biological correlates have to be taken into consideration in drawing at any conclusion from the various factors affecting health and diseases in a particular population group and these may vary from one group to another.

There are about 427 recognised scheduled tribal groups in

India constituting approximately 7.76% of the total population of the country (Census 1981).These tribal groups inhabit widely varying ecological and geo-climatic conditions in different concentration throughout the country and are distinct biological isolates with characteristic cultural and socio-economic background. A brief review of the distribution of the tribals in India - statewise is shown in Table-7.1 (Census 1981). It is clear that the distribution of tribal population is uneven, some of the states (i.e. Nagaland, Meghalaya, Tripura, Manipur, Madhya Pradesh, Orissa, Sikkim) and Union Territories (i.e. Arunachal Pradesh, Dadra & Nagar Haveli, Lakshadweep, Mizoram) exhibit high percentage of tribal population groups.

TABLE 7.1

Distribution of Scheduled Tribal Population Groups of India Statewise (1981) Census

*	States	Percent	States	Percent
	Andhra Pradesh	5.93	Tamilnadu	1.07
**	Assam	10.98	Tripura	28.44
	Bihar	8.31	Uttar Pradesh	0.21
	Gujrat	14.22	West Bengal	5.63
	Himachal Pradesh	4.61		
	Karnataka	4.91	UNION TERRITORIES	
	Kerala	1.03	Andaman & NicobarIsl.	11.85
	Madhya Pradesh	22.97	Arunachal Pradesh	69.82
	Maharasthra	9.19	Chandigarh	Nil
	Manipur	27.30	Dadra & Nagar Haveli	78.82
	Meghalaya	80.58	Delhi	Nil
	Nagaland	83.99	Goa Daman & diu	0.99
	Orissa	22.43	Lakshadweep	93.82
	Rajasthan	12.21	Mizoram	93.55
	Sikkim	23.27	Ponidchery	Nil

* There are no S. Tribes in the States of Punjab, Haryana and Jammu & Kashmir.

** 1971 Census.

Distribution of Tribal Regions in India

The tribal areas can be broadly divided into seven regions (Planning Commission, 1981).

1. Southern Central region comprising of Madhya Pradesh,

Southern Orissa, Eastern belt of Andhra Pradesh. This region is mainly inhabited by Gonds.

2. Central Northern region including Chotanagpur tribal belt of Bihar, Eastern Madhya Pradesh, Northern Orissa, Western Tribal region of West Bengal. This area shows the highest tribal concentration dominated by Santhal, Oraon, Munda etc.
3. Western Tribal region comprises of Southern tribal belt of Rajasthan, Eastern tribal belt of Gujarat, Western belt of Madhya Pradesh, Northern Maharashtra, Dadra and Nagar Haveli. Daman, Bhils, Gamit,Dhodias & Warli are the important tribal groups of this region.
4. North Eastern Tribal region comprises of Hilly areas of Assam, Meghalaya, Arunachal Pradesh, Sikkim, North West Bengal and plain areas of Assam and Tripura. Bhotias, Naga, Khasi, Moro & Miri, Mompas etc. are important tribal groups.
5. North Western Tribal region extends from Hills of Western U.P. and Northern Himachal Pradesh. Lahaulis, Jaunsaris and Kinnarua are the major tribal groups.
6. Southern Tribal region is located at the junction of Tamil Nadu, Karnataka and Kerala. Soliga, Kurumba, Malvali are the important tribal groups of this region.
7. Oceanic group represents the tribal communities in Andaman, Nicobar & Lakshdweep. Jarwas, Onges, Great Andamanese and Sentenelese are the important tribal groups.

Among the scheduled tribes, numerically, the most important are (a)the Gonds of Madhya Pradesh, Maharashtra and Andhra Pradesh, (b) the Bhils of Rajasthan, Gujarat, Maharashtra and Madhya Pradesh, and(c) the Santhals of Bihar, Orissa and West Bengal.The smallest tribal community is the Andamanese (Vidyarthi 1983).

Tribals of Bastar District

Bastar district of Madhya Pradesh is predominantly inhabited by tribal population groups; total percentage of scheduled tribes in Bastar district has been found to be 67.78 (Census 1981).

There are eight tehsils in the district (Jagdalpur, Konta, Kanker, Bhanupratappur, Bijapur, Narayanpur, Kondagaon and Dantewara) with approximately 3900 villages. The major tribal groups of Bastar district are (a) Gonds and their sub-groups i.e., predominantly Muria, Maria, Hill Maria, Abhuj Maria, Dhurwa etc., (b) Halbas, and (c) Bhattras. According to 1971

Census, the numerical strength of these predominant Bastar tribes is as follows:

Gonds	=	8,58,654
Halbas	=	57,052
Bhattras	=	71,095

Keeping in view the high concentration of Muria, Maria (Sub-groups of Gonds), Bhattras and Halbas in Jagdalpur and Konta tehsils, the first phase of research study was initiated among these four tribal groups in two tehsils of Bastar district. In brief, the major objectives of the study were to ascertain socio-economic concomittant, mating- pattern, preferential marriage alliances, food habits, physical growth, health seeking behaviour, fertility, mortality, morbidity trends, sanitation, hygiene, parasitic load, genetico-envirormental disorders and to promulgate the preventive and promotive health care among these Bastar tribal groups.

The detailed sampling design was drawn after an exploratory field survey to understand the distribution of various tribal population groups. In each tehsil (i.e. Jagdalpur/Konta), ten villages were selected on the basis of preponderance of individual tribal groups (Fig.7.1). Randomly selected households from each village formed the core of investigation. With the help of structured questionnaire and extended genealogies, all relevant field data were collected from 949 tribal families i.e., 298 Muria, 179 Maria, 255 Halba and 217 Bhattra. Suitable cross-checks were maintained from elderly members of household, local "DAIS" and PHC records. Some major research findings of study and their implications to health care have been discussed below :

Social organisation

All four tribal groups i.e., Muria, Maria, Halba and Bhattra are strictly endogamous in nature enshrined in their socio-biological dictums. The social organisation is governed by the totemistic exogamous clans, normally animalistic in nature i.e., Nag (Snake), Bagh (Tiger), Kukur (Dog).

Socio-economic status

Income and Occupation - Among all the tribal groups it is very difficult to work out the income pattern, however, it can be fairly assessed from the land holding and the annual crop. 70% of the tribals have land holdings between 0-10 acres with large families, mostly joint families to support. The agricultural produce is insufficient to feed the family. To supplement their

FIG'1 STUDY AREA

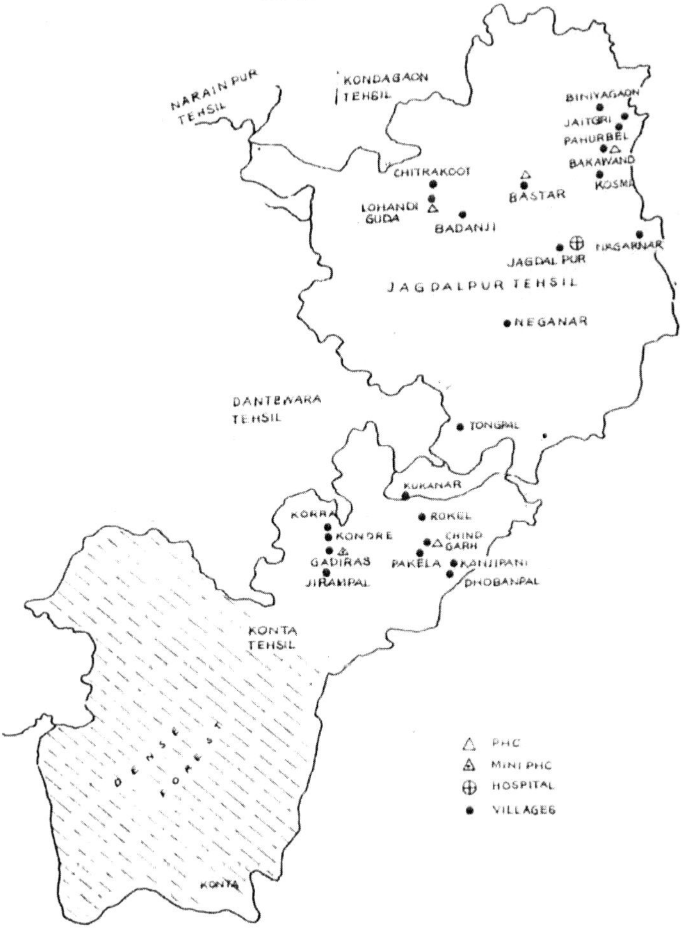

income they resort to occasional agricultural labour, bamboo cutting, fishing and basketary. Besides that, the young in the age group of 16-25 go for contract labour as and when feasible - nevertheless their own agriculture/cultivation should not suffer. The typical scenario of income and occupation in Bastar District among the tribal population groups can be described as agricultue, the source of additional income may be selling vegetables, fish, tendu leaves, sal seeds, etc., which anybody in the household would do, normally it is the women.

Food habits

The staple food among the tribal population groups is rice, millets, wild fruits etc. They prepare a concoction which is known as 'Madia Paje'. It is made from grounded rice and millets which is kept overnight for fermentation after boiling. Vegetable, Dal, fish etc., are also added to develop taste. The non-vegetarian foods such as pigs, mutton, chicken, fish, crabs, field rats are also taken as and when available. Liquor (Mahua) forms one of the most important constituents of their daily consumption which is also consumed by women and children.

The oil of wild seeds 'Tora' is used for cooking, and other purposes including applying on injuries etc.

Mating-pattern

Conceptually, illustration of mating-pattern is considered to be part of socio-cultual practices of a society but its biological impacts are generally ignored. Mating-pattern encompassing the selection of a mate, marital alliances such as religious sanctification of consanguineous marriages etc., contribute significantly to the ultimate mortality and morbidity profile of the population groups.

Consanguinity

Among all the four tribal population groups, consanguinity was practised to a varying degree, subject to the avilability of mates. The highest frequency of consanguineous first cross cousin matrilateral marriages was observed among the Murias and Marias (approx. 18%) and the lowest among Bhattras (5%). Such marriages are considered as a matter of right, signified by offering of gifts etc., at the time of birth of female child in the mama's house to show the claims on the girl. This is normally referred to as 'guda mol' with varying nomenclature for the girl. Bride price, security and assurance that the girl will be looked after better in mama's house are the principle reasons contributing to the perpetuation of consanquinity among all the four tribal groups. Halbas also practice consanguinity though they follow more Hinduised customs and practices.

Fertility and Mortality

Fertility and mortality profile of the four tribal groups have been gathered from the genealogical study of 344 mothers who have completed their reproductive life span. Fertility as such among the tribal groups has been found to be quite high i.e., Muria, Maria, Bhattra and Halba show 5.28, 6.08, 4.88, 6.06 pregnancies per mother respectively. It has been observed that Bhattras exhibit highest rate of infant mortality (148.56/1000 live births) followed by Murias (123.35/1000 live births). Halbas (92.78/1000 live births) and Marias (85.44/1000 live births) display almost equal rates of infant mortality. Moreover, Bhattras show a very high rate of neonatal mortality (101.79/1000 live births) as compared to Muria (57.27/1000 live births), Maria (45.89/1000 live births) and Halba (61.85/1000 live births).

Sanitation and Hygiene

Sanitation among the four tribal groups is very poor. The houses are built of mud walls with thatched roofs devoid of proper ventilation. Within the household compound, an enclosure for the animals is made which leads to poor environmental sanitation. During the rainy season it becomes a breeding ground for mosquitos and leads to spread of malaria.

The source of water and especially drinking water is from the ponds, ditches, wells and rivulets etc. As a taboo, they do not take water from the hand pumps which have been dug by the governmental agencies. In some areas they use these hand pumps for getting drinking water supply.

Personal hygiene is also quite poor among the tribal population groups. Once again this can be relegated to the availability of water and poor awareness about the importance of personal hygiene. The children are the most affected group.

Genetic Structure

Endogamous groups: From the foregoing discussion it is amply clear that the tribal population groups of Jagdalpur and Konta tehsils are distinctly endogamous in nature following the totemistic clan exogamy. This is true for all the four groups i.e., Murias, Marias, Bhattras and Halbas.

The present investigation undertook an indepth study of various genetic traits among the tribal groups of these two tehsils. In total, 1015 blood samples were collected from tribal couples and were subjected to various genetic investigations. As mentioned earlier, a nuclear family formed the basic unit of study. All possible precautions were taken to obtain a randomised sample leaving out relatives. As such attempts were made to collect samples from children also but it was found to be extremely difficult. The blood samples were obtained by finger prick using a disposable lancet. Blood was collected in EDTA and subjected to a battery of genetic tests, which are listed below:

(i) Blood groups - ABO, Rh, MN, Kell, Duffy (Fy^a & Fy^b), JK^a.

(ii) Glucose-6-Phosphate Dehydrogenase.

(iii) Sickling

(iv) Pyruvate Kinase, Hexokinase, Adenylate Kinase.

Standard microtitre plates were used for studying the ABO, MN, Rh blood group systems. Tube technique was followed for the rest of the systems. Non-availability of the sera for MN, Duffy, Kell Jk^a system was responsible for lower number of samples studied for these systems. Glucose-6-Phosphate dehydrogenase enzyme deficiency was studied employing the fluorescent spot test method of Beutler et al. (1979). Sodium metabisulphite/Sodium diothionite was used as a reducing agent to investigate sickling. Cases of sickling were further confirmed by electrophoretic procedure. Where individuals were found to be deficient of G6PD, or were sicklers, attempts were made to screen the whole family, however, such attempts were not always successful.

Fluorescent spot screening methods of (Valentine 1967) were adopted to study Hexokinase, Pyruvate Kinase deficiency, Glutathione Reductase, Adenylate Kinase.

The above investigations were carried out in the field itself. Hemolysates were transported to the base laboratory in Delhi and subjected to advance electrophoretic procedures for studying the haemoglobin variants. IEF, using Ampholine (LKB 3.5-10.5), was employed to study abnormal haemoglobins among the tribal population groups.

Results of these investigation in relation to their significance in health care are discussed below :

Blood Groups

Preliminary analysis reveals that among all the four tribal groups blood group B is predominantly distributed followed by O blood group (Table-7.2). The frequency of Rh negative gene in all the four groups was found to be low i.e., ranging between 3-12% (Table-7.2). This shows a high selection pressure in the tribal groups. Only four cases of 'Duffy Negative' ($Fy^{a-}Fy^{b-}$) were observed in a sample of 540 individuals investigated for the Duffy system (Table- 7.5). Frequencies of other blood group systems like MN, Kell, Jk^a have been shown in Table 7.3 & 7.4.

Sickle Cell Disease

As mentioned earlier, 1015 blood samples from couples were collected. Since the samples from children were not easy to obtain, possibility of tredging on to a homozygote was ruled out especially in case of the sickle cell gene. Our intensive study shows that the frequencies of sickle cell trait among different tribal population groups i.e., Muria, Maria, Bhattra and Halba are 14%, 18%, 12% & 8% respectively. This frequency itself is high and forewarns the alarming impact it may have on the morbidity profile of these population groups who are as such at a primitive stage of development, following traditional medicine and magico-religious practices.

TABLE 7.2

Frequency(percentage) distribtution of ABO and Rh blood group systems among the tribals

Groups	ABO System				Rhesus System	
	A	B	C	AB	Rh^+	Rh^-
Muria n=315	28.25	35.56	25.71	10.48	92.1	7.9
Maria n=199	27.13	37.21	33.15	2.51	93.47	6.53
Halba n=392	21,43	35.72	34.69	8.61	96.23	3.77
Bhattra n=109	22.02	33.03	35.78	9.17	88.07	11.93

TABLE 7.3
Frequency (percentage) distribution of MN blood group system among the tribals

Groups	MN Blood Groups M	N	MN
Muria n=130	16.92	47.69	35.39
Maria n=102	20.59	39.21	40.20
Halba n=106	22.64	43.40	33.96
Bhattra n=104	12.50	47.12	40.38

TABLE 7.4
Frequency (percentage) distribution of Kell and JK^a bloodgroup systems among the tribals

	Kell System			JK^a System	
	-ve	+ve	n	+ve	-ve
Halba n=212	93.39	6.61	106	92.45	7.55
Maria n=198	89.90	10.10	102	93.14	6.86
Muria n=192	89.58	10.42	96	95.83	4.17
Bhattra n=109	85.32	14.62	41	92.68	7.32

TABLE 7.5
Frequency (percentage) distribution of Duffy blood group system among the tribals

	Duffy System			
Groups	FY^{a-b-}	Fy^{a+b+}	Fy^{-ab}	Fy^{a+b-}
Halba n=160	1.25	44.38	24.37	30.00
Maria n140		65.71	28.57	5.72
Muria n=134	1.49	50.57	26.87	20.89
Battra n=106		57.55	29.24	13.21

Thalassaemia

Field conditions did not permit in depth investigation of thalassaemia among these population groups but on subjecting the hemolysates to advanced electrophoretic procedures such as IEF, facilitated identification of cases of thalassaemia which were confirmed during subsequent visits and obtaining repeat samples. From a sample of 958, 18 cases of thalassaemia were detected. Three cases of hereditary persistence of foetal haemoglobin were identified. These findings on one hand signify the presence of the gene in the population groups of Bastar and on the other hand prompt thinking on their health impacts in terms of morbidity and mortality profile. Cases of Hbs thalassaemia were also detected. In these cases, Hbf levels were found to be higher in consonance with latest reports showing that high Hbf levels provide protection against hemolytic episodes. No clinical impairment or perceptible morbidity was noticed in these cases.

Other hemoglobin variants

While investigating the sickling phenomenon, formation of HbC crystals was an indicator of presence of other hemoglobin variants among the tribal population groups of Bastar district. The presence of HbC, HbD and also syndromal conditions with HbS was confirmed by the electrophoretic procedures. However, it may be noted that the frequency of HbC, HbD gene is very low among all the four tribal groups. None of the samples analysed showed homozygous state for HbC or HbD.

G-6-PD Deficiency

All the collected blood samples were subjected to fluorescent spot screening test for G6PD deficiency. In total 958 individuals were subjected to the screening test. Because of elaborate requirements of a spectrophotometer in the field, it was not possible to carry out the quantitative estimation of G6PD which would have further provided information on the homozygotes in the case of females. The results of analysis show that the G6PD deficiency is present in all the four tribal groups ranging between 10-19%; lowest among Murias (10%) & highest among Bhattras (19%), while Marias and Halbas exhibit 17% & 12% respectively.

Pyruvate Kinase

Pyruvate kinase is another important enzyme of the glycolytic pathway - the deficiency, resulting in the shortened red cell life span and subsequent chronic hemolytic anaemia. Screening of the collected blood samples was carried out using fluorescent spot method of Beutler et al. (1977). Six hundred and seventy two blood samples were studied. Nine cases (1.57%) were found to be deficient of the enzyme pyruvate kinase. The findings are significant in view of the fact that this shows the presence of various abnormal alleles among the tribal population groups. Probably this is the first report about the presence of this abnormal allele in the tribal population groups. The deficient individuals of PK deficiency were apparently normal but they complained of weakness and lethargy.

Hexokinase

Hexokinase is another important red cell enzyme which plays a significant role in reducing the red cell life span. Mild to severe cases of hemolytic anaemia in individuals with hexokinase deficiency have been reported. Fluorescent spot screening method (Valentine 1967) was employed for detecting hexokinase deficiency. Only 7 individuals were found to have this enzyme deficiency among the tribal groups of Bastar. All those individuals were suffering from mild anaemia.

Adenylate kinase

Similarly 3 cases of Adenylate kinase deficiency were seen

among the tribals of Bastar District. The incidence of these disorders and its impact on mortality may be more clearly discernible in case a strict surveillance on infant and child deaths is augmented.

Morbidity profile

In the background of extreme poverty, prevalent primitive beliefs and taboos, any investigation on the morbidity profile is bound to lead us to erroneous interpolation. Lay terms such as fever, 'Phula' (Oedema) etc., are the most common terms heard as the cause of death. During the present investigation, information on morbidity was collected, especially for a period of last three months in order to eliminate recall bias and providing an opportunity for cross-checking from the hospital/PHC doctors. This technique provided quite reliable information on morbidity.

Among the children, diarrhoeal diseases, malaria and fevers (unqualified and unknown etiology) & various infections were most common. Unfortunately these take a heavy toll of child mortality in Bastar District. There are hardly any significant difference in child care practices between the four tribal groups. Among adult population, malaria was the most commonly encountered disease, besides the prevalence of tuberculosis, leprosy, skin diseases, venereal diseases, peptic ulcer and nutritional disorders of various kinds.

The distribution pattern of diseases in these population groups does not show significant variations between the four tribal groups.

Health seeking behaviour

The study of the health seeking behaviour of the tribal groups of Bastar district was attempted using a structured questionnaire and by participant observations. It was observed that all the four tribal population groups have an indomitable belief in wrath of gods and goddesses as the cause of illness/disease thereby promoting the perpetuations of magico-religious practices. Intensive investigation did show that the tribal populations seek the relief from disease etc., first of all through 'Sirhas' who are supposed to be in touch with spirits/gods/goddesses and after diagnosing the cause only, they can resurrect them from the wrath. Next, in their preference is use of herbal medicines obtained through the local people or from the jungle. Treatment from PHC or an allopathic medical practioner is the last resort. Surprisingly those individuals who got cured at PHC/or health centre have not been able to perpetuate the benefits of modern medical care. Some of the indigenous herbal medicines used by the tribal groups for the treatment of their diseases include the following:

Name of Jadi/Medicine	**Name of the disease**
Gudmal and Dev Beeja	Diabetes
Scale of Sergi, Menda tree, Seeds of 'Tora'	Wound
Seeds of Dev Beeja and Kosam tree	Fevers
Dhuma Jad, Bela dora Jad	Venereal diseases
Huda Jadi	Weakness, Dehydration

Another important aspect of health seeking be maternal child care. Maternal care during pregnancy is poor among all the four tribal groups. Right from the inception of pregnancy to its termination, no specific diet is consumed by a woman. Inoculation against tetanus; iron, calcium and other vitamins intake is generally, not observed by the expectant mothers.

Most of the deliveries are conducted at home attended by elderly ladies of the household. Services of ANMs, LHVs are utilized only in difficult cases. The placental cord is cut with an arrow head (Tir) in case of a male child and with a knife (kadri) in case of a female child. No specific precautions are followed at the time of conducting delivery which results in increased susceptibility to various infections.

A specially prepared concoction from various herbs, 'Kasa Pani', is provided to the mother on the third day after the delivery. This practice is to be seen among Murias, Halbas and Bhattras. However, among Marias 'Gila Bhat' i.e., soaked rice is given to the mother instead of 'Kasa Pani'. The idea behind giving 'kasa pani' is that it gives soothing effect, helps in recovering the energy lost and also acts as a sort of antibiotic. It has been found in the present study that the maternal mortality directly related to pregnancy and child birth is appreciably high. In addition, a lot of females suffer from ill health due to pregnancy and child birth in the absence of well defined concept of health consciousness.

As far as the child care is concerned, the neonates and the infants are the worst sufferers among these tribal groups. Malaria, unspecified fever, diarrhoea, respiratory diseases, meningitis etc., take a heavy toll. Vaccination, immunization and drug therapies have been found to be poor in these groups. Similarly, the breast feeding infant in the first year does not receive any supplementary nutritious diet. In fact, majority of these tribal people start supplementary diet after the child attains one year of age.

In short, it can be said that the poor health seeking behaviour among these four tribal groups is the result of social and living conditions, malnutrition, illiteracy, ignorance, superstitions, improper and poor sanitation, poor safe drinking water, unawareness of health education, under utilization of health resources, cultural lag, poorly developed mass media, poor medical and health opportunities (variety, quality and quantity of health services) and infrastructure on the administrative side.

Health Care

The results of the foregoing study present a dismal picture about health care among the tribal population groups. The findings are pointers to the multifarious/multiple problems existing among tribal population groups. In the following pages, attempts have been made to analyse the findings of the study with respect to their implications on the health problems.

Socio-economic factors

Tribal population groups of Bastar live in extreme poverty, depending mainly on agriculture and forest produce. The poor food habits contribute to malnutrition especially among children and pregnant mothers ultimately leading to increased susceptibility to morbid conditions. Added to that, extremes of magico-religious misbeliefs and taboos tend to aggravate the problems. Poor sanitation, hygiene including personal hygiene also add to the prevalence of infectious diseases. One of the most important parameter in this connection is lack of safe drinking water. Tribal populations mainly depend for their requirements of water on ponds, rivulets and occasionally wells. At many places it has been seen that they refrain from getting water from the hand pumps etc. Waterborne fungal and bacterial infections are the major morbid conditions seen among the tribal population groups.

As far as programme efforts in this area are concerned

lately the ICDS scheme, immunisation programme, provision of safe drinking water, educational efforts on sanitation and hygiene have been undertaken on priority but with little success. Nonetheless, it may be pointed out that the reasons for the failure or slow progress of these programme areas are primarily because of the fact that these programmes have been pushed without an understanding of the cultural background of the tribals. On the basis of the available information, we are attempting to develop a liaison with the district health authorities for developing an effective strategy for health care delivery among these tribal groups.

It is an established fact that the practice of consangunity has an impact on the fertility, mortality and morbidity profile. In such populations, higher incidence of reproductive wastage i.e., abortions and still births, more frequent neonatal deaths are seen. The observed data from the tribal groups of Bastar point out occurrence of high rates of neonatal mortality with gross under-reporting of abortions and still births.

In view of these findings it may be accepted that it would be impossible to bring about an overnight change in the old age practices. The only recourse is to vigorously promulgate preventive, promotive and educational efforts in the background of existing socio-cultural milieu of tribal life.

Genetic Structure

The study of socio-biological parameter i.e., mating pattern has shown that the tribal population groups of Bastar District are distinct bilogical isolates following totemistic clan oxogamy as a rule. This renders these population groups as distinct biological isolates meaning thereby that they have a characteristic gene pool.

The study of ABO blood group system on one hand has helped to delineate the individual tribal groups, on the other hand has provided knowledge on the possible incompatible matings among these groups. As such, it is well known that incompatibly mated couples (for ABO system) are at a higher risk of undergoing early abortions and neonatal deaths. However, the blood group distribution among these tribals is not significantly different from the other population groups.

Most important finding was on the Rhesus blood group system. The frequency of Rh—ve gene among the tribal groups is much lower than the average frequency in other Indian population groups. Low frequency of this gene is a pointer to the high selection pressure at this locus with a resulting loss of fetuses and newborns at various stages.

Duffy blood group system was studied especially in relation to malaria, since it was reported that Duffy negative individuals have an advantage of being resistent to malaria. The low frequency of Duffy negative individuals in the tribal groups seemingly is not sufficient to comment on this phenomenon.

Hemoglobinopathies and Allied Disorders

Sickle Cell hemoglobin is the most widely studied molecule as far as the tribal population groups of India are concerned. The investigators have mainly emphasised on understanding the generic lineages and disclosing the distribution frequencies of this abnormal gene in various population groups. The frequency of this abnormal gene has been found to vary between 2-40% (Roy et al.1985). Very little efforts have been made to address to health implications of sickle cell disease in the existing highly variable socio-culture milieu in different regions and areas.

The experimental evidence has been brought forth to prove 'malaria - sickle cell' hypothesis. Bastar District is as such a high malarial endemicity zone with predominance of P. falciparum. The high frequency of sickle cell gene as observed among the tribal population groups points out the extent to which this abnormal gene may be adding to the morbid conditions. Sickle cell heterozygotes (HbAS) are prone to frequent hemolytic episodes, are more susceptible to infections, chronic ulcers etc., while the homozygotes (HbSS) conditions are usually fatal in childhood. In the background of poor sanitation and hygiene the morbid conditions are aggravated. Besides that the heterozygous carriers of sickle cell gene during pregnancy are prone to variety of clinical problems especially anaemia which may be fatal. Though, the figures on the occurrence of sickle cell trait in Bastar are from the living couples, it is quite difficult to estimate the deaths which might have taken place because of this factor alone - especially among the children and mothers. The present health care system has to be geared for the diagnosis of sickle cell trait by carrying out a very simple laboratory investigation, which can be established within the present set up. The laboratory technicians already working in the primary health centres may be provided training in this aspect.

Another important parameter is the Glucose-6-Phosphate Dehydrogenase deficiency. The individuals who suffer from this genetic abnormality are prone to hemolytic episodes, upon ingestion of antimalarial drugs, anti-biotics, fava beans etc. It has been reported that Glucose-6-Phosphate Dehydrogenase enzyme deficiency also provides a protection against malaria. In a highly malarial endemic zone i.e., Bastar District, the vigorous efforts are being made to control malaria which includes DDT spraying and extensive and indiscriminate use of anti-malarials such as chloroquine followed by a course of radical treatment i.e., primaquine. The tribal population groups of Bastar District show a high frequency of this deficient gene. Inevitably, it may be perceived that the programme efforts are completely ignoring the consequences of administration of anti-malarial drugs in communities showing high frequency of the susceptible disorders which may normally be fatal.

Detection of the G-6-PD deficiency in such remote areas though may sound to be a difficult procedure but the fluorescent spot screening method is simple to perform and the reaction mixture can be preserved for long durations. Proper training of health manpower within the system can be built in with minimum inputs.

Another group of disorders causing hemolytic anaemia taking a heavy toll of life is thalassaemia - especially among the children. In carrier states, the thalassaemic individuals would be apparently normal but will contribute to the mortality picture among the children. The presence of other enzyme deficiencies particularly which contribute to the occurrence of reduced red cell life span such as Pyruvate kinase, Hexokinase, Adenylate kinase etc., are indicators of the variety of abnormal hereditary traits prevalent among the tribal population groups of Bastar District.

During the recent workshops held at the National Institute of Health & Family Welfare, the participants deliberated at length on the promulgation of health care measures for the genetic and genetico-environmental disorders among the various population groups of India. Nevertheless, the problems of the tribal population groups figured because of specific genetic and genetico-environmental disorders prevalent among the tribal groups having serious health implications. In the Workshop on Genetic Epidemiological Approaches to Health Care (Roy et al. 1986), it was reiterated that within the health care infrastructure certain priority components on health care for genetic and genetico-environmental disorders can be built in.

In conclusion, I may suggest that the MCH programme of the government should involve specific inputs for improving nutritional conditions of the pregnant women, ante-natal and postnatal care, more strenuous efforts of the ICDS programme, detection of the genetic and genetico-environmental disorders such as sickle cell, G-6-PD deficiency, thalassaemia and other abnormal conditions etc. For these specific training courses may be organised especially for the medical and paramedical personnel engaged in delivery of health services among the tribal groups of not only Bastar District but all other tribal areas.

Efforts of all other developmental agencies in a coordinated fashion will surely result in improved socio-economic conditions, sanitation and hygiene, provision of safe drinking water etc. The education and communication methods should be utilised to promulgate not only better utilisation of health care services but also adopting preventive & promotive health care approaches.

Reference List

Basu SK (1978) Hemoglobinopathies in India: A Public Health Problem. Health & Population Perspective & Issues 1: 319-339

Beutler E, Blume KG, Kaplan JC et al. (1979) International Committee for Standardisation in Hematology: Recommended Screening Tests for Glucose-6-Phosphate Dehydrogenase Deficiency. British Journal of Hemetology 43:469.77

Census of India (1971) Office of the Registrar General and Census Commissioner of India, New Delhi

Census of India (1981) Office of the Registrar General and Census Commissioner of India, New Delhi

Planning Commission (1981) Report on development of Tribal Areas. National Committee on the Development of Backward areas, Govt. of India, New Delhi 7-8

Roy SN, Basu SK, Jindal Anil (1985) Population Genetics and Health Care: Issues and Future Strategies. Technical Report Series No 8, NIHFW, New Delhi

Roy SN, Basu SK, Jindal Anil, Kshatriya Gautam K. Genetic Epidemiological Approaches to Health Care. Technical Report Series. NIHFW, New Delhi, 1986 (in press)

Valentine WN, Oski FA, et al. (1967) Hereditary hemolytic anaemia of Hexokinase deficiency. New England J Med. 276:1

Vidyarthi LP (1983) Tribes of India (in) Peoples of India. Some Genetical Aspects. ICMR, New Delhi : 85-103

EIGHT

GENETICS AND HEALTH OF THE WEAKER SECTION: AN ANTHROPOLOGICAL INSIGHT

R.K. Gulati

The Indian sub-continent constitutes a large variety of populations, sub-populations both larger and smaller, dispersed through the length and breadth of the country. These groups though they occupy the same ecological set-up, have their own cultural behaviour, religious practices, occupation and other functional aspects of their life. Living together these groups develop an exchange system to fulfill their economic needs but they may not share the socio-biological way of life. Both their heredity endowment and ecology play an important role in giving shape to their socio-economic position. This is one of the foremost reasons for the formation of many groups with varied socio-economic positions in all regions of India.

One cannot really assess very objectively the socio-economic categories of the populations, as in a region ecology is also different from one place to another. Various economic surveys in India show different pictures and that is why we do not get a clear cut image of the population below poverty line. However, it has been reported that 40 - 70% of the population live below the poverty line. Such a large vulnerable population in our country is of great concern in view of the extraneous social pressures and their impact on the genetics of their health. Our late Prime Minister, Indira Gandhi had told the United Nations first world conference on Human Environment in 1972 that poverty is the greatest pollutant, this stressing that a third of the world's population should not be condemned to live undernourished, existence in slums and without work. It is worth mentioning here that there is no reference to a large number of these groups in our old written records.

There seems to be no need to show any correlation between the social groups and their genetic make-up, but the groups manifest in their genotypic make-up either directly or indirectly their cultural way of life. In the diagrammatic representation certain facts of such manifestation are revealed.

In this paper emphasis has been laid on effect of the various external environmental factors on the health and genetics of the weaker section of the society to show how the well-being of these groups can be maintained in the present day changes due to industrialization, urbanization, migration and modernization. the reason why anthropologists are concerned about this problem is that they contribute to a large extent to national production, economy and an over-all the well-being of the nation.

Malnutrition

Effects of malnutrition on some socio-economic groups in our country which are more vulnerable than the rest of the population on account of a variety of factors are evident from the following account:

Rural areas

Out of 5,76,000 villages in our country, 150,500 have been classified as the difficult scarcity or health problem areas. 43.86 million to 123 million people are estimated to be worst affected. As roughly 38% of the population is of children between 1-14 years of age, 38 million children would thus be in the lowest decennial of poverty and about 3.1 million lactating mothers (infants below one year estimated 3.1%) will be in the extreme state of poverty. Thus the rural populations suffer a high rate of nutritional deficiency. Poor environmental hygienic conditions play a very important role in undermining the nutritional status of the rural populations. A recent study reveals that the simple correction of anaemia in village children did not bring about a decline in the rates of diarrhoea and respiratory infections as the state of environmental hygiene continued to be unsatisfactory and thus negate any advantage due to the improved nutritional status.

Agricultural labourer

In our country this class is the most thoroughly exploited and suppressed one. It is an irony of fate that though primarily they are responsible for producing what others eat, they do not get sufficient food for their sustenance. Their sufferings are more than those of the industrial workers on account of the very nature of their work. Economically too, they remain the sufferers.

Tribals and hill people

Tribal population has been estimated to be about 7% of India's population. They are spread over different parts of the country and inhabit mostly the hilly tracks which isolate them physically, culturally and economically from the non-tribal population. Despite the difficult terrain, A.S.I., and N.I.N., Hyderabad have surveyed many tribal areas.

By and large, the tribals are extremely poor. Their only source of derived income is from selling forest produce like honey. Some of them cannot even afford clothing in winter with night temperatures below 10° C. Their diet consists of forest produce and some locally grown millets and rarely milk or rice included. Children are breast fed for over one year and no special provision of diet for pregnant or lactating mothers is made. One of the study reports reveals that only 23% were found in good health, 33% in poor or very poor state, 17% had dental caries, 11% were anaemic and 5% had vitamines A, D and B deficiencies. 40% of the children were underweight while 51.8% to 72.6% were having nutritional anaemia. Malnutrition and malaria seemed to be their worst enemies affecting 41% of the population. Even some tribal groups face extinction due to these factors. Some of the tribal groups, on the other hand, were found to be astonishingly free from Vitamin A and B deficiency and the dietary studies showed that green leafy vegetables contributed a fair amount of beta carotene and riboflavin.

In the hilly regions a study revealed the high incidence of goitre i.e., 30-90% of the population were found to be affected and more than 10 million people were the sufferers. Though etiology of endemic goitre is multifactorial, yet it attributes to the deficiency of iodine in nutrition.

Besides endemic goitre, a survey in Kumaon hills in U.P., brings to light nutritional disorders like those of lower weight, less head circumference and low height. Even triceps skinfold were below standard. Among the parasitic infestations roundworm was found the commonest was. Haemoglobin values were found to be low at a height of 12,000 ft., in a Himalayan village.

The reasons for the high prevalence of nutritional

deficiency in tribal and hill areas are:

(i) Rugged terrain and inaccessibility leading to isolation on account of difficult movement of men, material and knowledge.
(ii) Overall poverty due mainly to lack of resources, ignorance and awareness.
(iii) Poor expansion of cultivable land. Over the generations the area of land in a family does not incrase in proportion to increase in family size. Number and types of crops are restricted in the hills.
(iv) Availability of less calories as compared to the requirements.

Urban slum areas

Urban slums have been the outcome of the migration from rural areas to urban towns in search of employment in the process of industrialization. At present a quarter to one third of urban population in our country lives in slums in comparison to 5% three decades ago.

Studies in urbanized towns like Jaipur and Calcutta show a higher incidence of morbidity rate in the lower socio-economic groups though protien in takes were not so low.

Malnutrition increases infant mortality. In a Calcutta study, three out of every six babies born in slums were found to die soon. There was a widespread growth retardation and majority of children were found to be suffering from current long duration malnutrition. Nutritional status of urban slum children on the whole, was worse than those of the rural pre- school ones. Low nutritional status of the slum population may be attributed to reduced food availability, the reason being of less purchasing power.

Reduced mental efficiency

Malnutrition affects the development of brain and the studies show that among the children who had a bout of severe Protein Calorie Malnutrition, there incomplete restoration of functional capacity of the brain despite the intensive therapy resulting in apparent clinical cure.

Medico-genetic problems among the tribal groups

Tribal groups in India face differential problems related to their ecology. Ecological conditions and socio- economic factors including a wide gamut of variables viz., mating practices, preferential alliances, age at marriage, income, occupation, nutritional status, education, climatic conditions etc., do affect in one way or the other the medico genetic profile of the groups. However, selection, mutation, migration etc., have their role to play as important in-built components.

Industrial pollution

Vulnerable sections of the society are the affected by the industrial development in India terms of medico-genetics. Lack chemical, brass, limestone, jute, fertiliser and drug industries. The fumes and dust emitted by these industrial units make workes suffer from the disease like bronchitis, silicosis, T.B., etc. In case of the leather industry the workers are the sufferers of bacterial and fungal infections. Due to unplanned water management and added pollutants to water the agricultural labourers are the most affected by the bacterial and fungal diseases. Constructions of dams and reservoirs, without proper scientific screening, made the life of the poor people more susceptible a to new type of crippling disease such as "genu valgum" in certain parts of South India. Thus, unplanned development and improper management of effluent makes the life of industrial workers miserable in terms of health.

Endemic goitre

The most tragic manifestation of this condition in the progeny of victims is by way of Cretinism, deaf mutism and idiocy. In a study, 4% of the population in a Himalayan tract was found to be deaf mutes in an area where the prevalence rate was 40%.

The areas affected are mainly in the sub-Himalayan regions and parts of the adjoining plains. The incidence in the regions of endemicity has been recorded to be as high as 40% in some studies. The highest rate was found in females between 12-18 years and males between 9-13 years of age.

Northern part of India is part of the great goitre belt which extends from Afghanistan through Jammu and Kashmir eastwards for more than 4000 miles over the southern slopes of the Himalayas into Assam and Burma. Viewed more closely, the areas affected are extending from Gilgit to Kashmir along the Karakoram range into Ladakh and then into sub-Himalayan regions of Himachal Pradesh and Punjab, viz., Kangra, Pathankot, Gurdaspur, Hoshiarpur, Hamirpur, Kyelong, Kulu and Spiti, and pervading the Shivalik hills and districts of Tehri, Kasauli,

Ambala, Dehradun, Kumaon (Almora and Nainital).

Haemoglobinopathies and well-being of community

Haemoglobin S(Sickle-cell) is the most commonly found abnormal haemoglobin in India. In a homozygous condition its effects are severe and fatal. Sickling in India has been reported mostly from the tribal groups and lower castes. Its highest frequency is found among the Paniyans of Nilgiri hills, Tamilnadu (34.43%). The lowest frequency has been reported among the Todas of Nilgiri hills (0.05%). In Western India Sorathis show the highest (30.6%) whereas the lowest is among the Parsis of Gujarat (0.02%). In Eastern India Santhals of West Bengal show 1.7% and Griza Oriahas of Assam with 29%. In Central India, the frequency ranges from 1.38% among Mehtar of Malva (M.P.) to 38.21% among Mahar of Bastar (M.P.).

In Orissa the highest frequency is among the Konda paroja (13.3%). The frequency of sickling among aboriginals of Chotanagpur has been found to be 8.3%.

In North India, frequency of sickling is highest among Garasia of Sirohi, Rajasthan (23.64%).

Although a number of haemoglobin variants are obsarved in this country, only a few of them (HbS either in homozygous state or in association with beta thalassaemia, HbE with thalassaemia or thalassaemia homozygous or its variants) are of clinical importance. As HbS frequency is high mostly in the tribes and scheduled castes, constituting approximately one fifth of the total population of this country, attention needs to be paid to identify the different groups in them with high incidence of these deleterious genes. Cases of such genetic disorders have high morbidity rate; intercurrent infections are rather common and most of them terminate fatally in childhood. Those who survive sometimes become crippled as in sickle cell disease, and thus became a burden to the family. Prognosis of the disease depends greatly on the environment of the patient. Those with a better standard of nutrition and living conditions progress well with prompt attention, whenever there is infection and thus avert hazardous crisis.

Haemoglobin E homozygotes enjoy reasonable health unlike sickle-cell homozygotes, while HbE-thalassaemia cases suffer from moderately severe clinical disability.

The prevention of common genetic diseases like sickle cell anaemia, sickle cell thalassaemia and thalassaemia major, can be resorted to by population screening and genetic counselling.

Impact of consanguinity

Consanguineous marriages are prevalent in India and particularly in South India the incidence is quite higher. Geographical locations, availability of mates, various socio-economic factors like dowry, land, poverty, interpersonal relationship between the new bride and her moter-in-law and religious sanctions are the major factors responsible for this practice in South Indian states and in Maharashtra. High frequency of consanguinity has also been reported among the Muslims of Delhi and Lucknow, West Bengal and Rajasthan, and scheduled castes and tribes of Madhya Pradesh.

A survey conducted in Bangalore has shown that 30% of cases of mental retardation occur in the offspring of consanguineously related parents. The chances of mental retardation are more in families which have consanguinity in more than one generation. Also, the number of children affected are more in such families. Earlier studies elsewhere have disclosed that consanguinity definitely increases biochemical defects attributable to recessive genes. Instances are there where no harm has been reported.

In another systematic study conducted by the inventor of telephone, Alexander Graham Bell showed that a large number of blind and deaf people had parents who were cousins. Similar studies in other parts of the world also show that congenital deafness is more frequent among children of parents consanguineously related. It has been noted that when a recessive condition is sporadically seen, it is exclusively due to consanguineously related marriages.

The effect of consanguinity on human reproduction, morbidity and mortality is less certain though studies conducted in USA, France and Japan show that the rates of mortality and morbidity are shown to have increased in the offspring of the consanguineous marriages as compared to those of non-consanguineous marriages (UNSCEAR 1962).

In studying the effect of consanguinity on fertility and reporductive compensation in Hirado Japan, Schull et al.(1970) have observed that the number of living children is less in consanguineous matings than those in non-consanguineous matings. Basu(1975) has also reported similar findings among the North Indian Muslims, whereas Schull and Neel (1972) found it to be equal in consanguineous and non-consanguineous couples in the

Hirado population, Japan. Similar observation has been noted in a hospital survey from Karnataka (Radha Rama Devi et al. 1981). Rao and Mukherjee (1975) on Pattasali population in Andhra Pradesh found higher mean number of pregnancies and live births and lower mean number of living children in consanguineous matings than in non-consanguineous matings.

Several investigators in their studies have expressed divergent views regarding the effect of consanguinity on mortality. Kumar et al. (1967) from five hospitals in Kerala, Murty and Jamil (1972), Basu (1975), Rao and Mukherjee (1975), Sundar Rao (1978) in Tamilnadu, Puri et al. (1978) in Pondicherry, Reddy and Naidu(1978) in Andhra Pradesh have observed higher fetal, neonatal and infant mortality in consanguineous matings as compared to non-consanguineous matings. Some studies do not show appreciable effects of consanguinity on fertility and mortality (Jacob and Jayabal 1971; Schull and Neel 1972, Roberts and Bonne 1973; Freire-Maria and Krieger 1975; Radha Rama Devi et al. 1981).

It is revealed from the above studies that there are instances where no harm has accrved and the effects of consanguinity are not the same in all cases. This is probably due to the fact, as Sanghvi (1974) suggested, that high rate of consanguinity practised by the Dravidian populations of South India through generations gradually eliminates the deleterious genes by segregation. But there is an imminent need to understand the biological significance of cansanguinity.

In a nutshell it is apparent that poverty as a factor affects the weaker section. Different social pressures (see Fig.8.1) in interaction with other environmental forces have a lot of bearing on their genetico-cultural way of life. Thus to have a genetically and physically stronger section of society, it is advisable to keep in mind the anthropoligical perspective. This will help in the implementation of various programmes designed for the well-being of the large part of the population in our country.

Acknowledgement

The author extends his deep gratitude to his colleagues Shri S.S. Bandyopadhyay, Dr. S.N.H. Rizvi, Dr.(Mrs.) G.R. Lakshmi, and Shri Teja Lal, for their academic and other help in preparation of this paper.

EXTRANEOUS SOCIAL PRESSURE AND ITS EFFECT ON GENETICS AND HEALTH

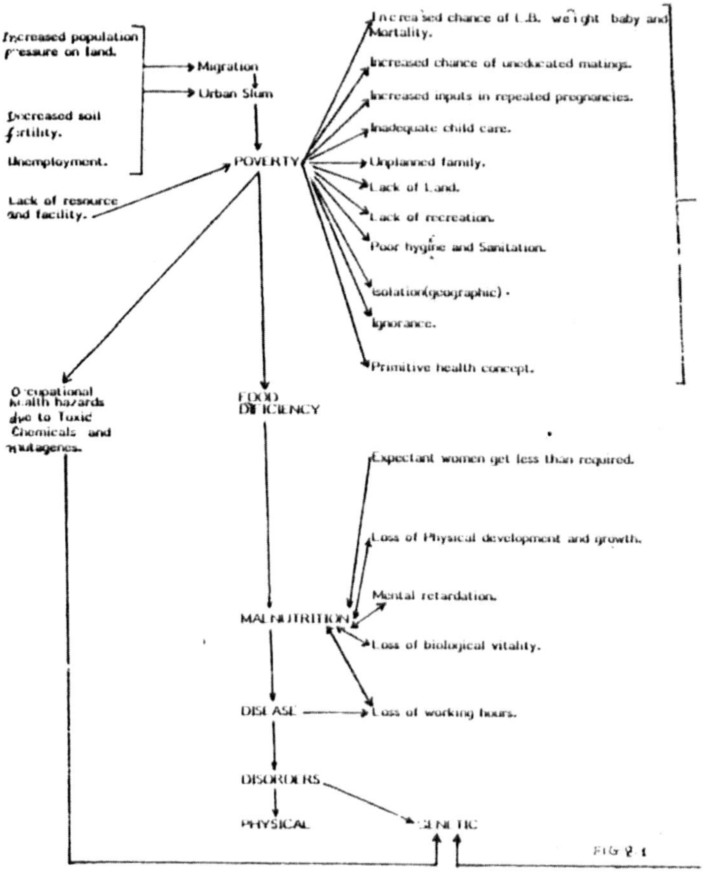

FIG 2.1

Reference List

Bansal IJS, Singhal P (1983) Anthropology in Indian Context. Today and Tomorow's Printers and Publishers, New Delhi

Kawata Kazuyoshi (1963) Environmental sanitation in India. Medical College, Ludiana

Roberts DF, Bonne B (1973) Reproduction and inbreeding among the samaritans Soc Biol 20:64-70

Roy S, Basus, Jindal A (eds) (1985) Population aenetics and Health care Issues and future strategies. HIH&FW, New Delhi

Sanghvi LD (1966) Inbreeding in India. Eugen Quart 134:291-301

Shukla PK (1982) Nutritional Problems of India: Prentice Hall of India Private Limited, New Delhi

Singh IP, Tiwari SC (1980) Man and his Environment. Concept Publishing Company, New Delhi

NINE

GENETIC DIFFERENTIATION AMONG THE TRIBAL POPULATIONS OF ORISSA, INDIA

A.K. Kapoor

The sub-division of Indian population into a large number of endogamous groups, especially, castes, tribes and communities, provides ample scope for understanding the nature and the extent of genetic variation within and between them. With the above stated objectives, the present study aims to investigate, on the basis of six serological and bio-chemical systems, the magnitude of genetic differentiation and the degree of gene diversity among the five tribes of the tribe-dominated eastern province Orissa, India.

Method and Material

The present analysis is based on six serological and bio-chemical systems (A_1A_2BO, MN, Rh, ABH secretion in saliva, phenylthiocarbamide (PTC) taste sensitivity and sickling of RBC) for which data were obtained from the earlier studies (Das et al. 1963 a & b; Das and Mukherjee 1964; Das et al. 1966; Das et al. 1967). They conducted their study in Koraput district of Orissa since it has maximum concentration of tribal populations. The five tribes taken for study are the Bado Gabada (BG), the Bareng Paroja (BP), the Parang Gabada (PG), the Ollaro Gabada (OG), and the Konda Paroja (KP). All these tribes live in close proximity and in large concentrations. Ethnographic account of these tribes are not well documented. Das et al.(1968) pointed out that these tribes are endogamous group maintaining their individual identity. They practise clan exogamy. However, they avoid consanguinity in any form. The Bado Gabada speak Indo-Aryan languages, the Ollaro Gabada and Konda Paroja Dravidian language and the Bareng Paroja and Pareng Gabada Munda language. All the five tribes are speculated to have been originated from common veddoid stock.

Table 9.1 summarizes the populations taken for the present study and the serological and bio-chemical systems tested in them.

The significance of differences in the occurrence of gene frequencies for different loci among the different populations was tested with chi-square.

FST values for each allele of every locus were computed according to the method of Wright (1943, 1951).

Genetic distances among the five tribal populations of Orissa was computed according to Nei's(1972) distance measure. A dendrogram was also constructed from the genetic matrix (Nei 1975). Following Nei (1973) the total gene diversity (H_T) was partitioned into the gene diversity within sub-populations (H_S) and between sub-populations (D_{ST}). The coefficient of gene differentiation, i.e., $G_{ST}=D_{ST}/H_T$ was also calculated.

Results and Discussion

Gene frequencies for A_1A_2BO, MN, Rh blood group systems ABH secretor factor, ability to taste PTC and sickling of the different tribes are presented in Table 9.1.

The inter group differences based on chisquare heterogeneity and contingency chi-square analysis of gene frequency are presented in Table 9.2 and 9.3. It can be infered that inter group differences are statistically significant for Rh blood groups and sickle cell trait. However, PTC is the only marker which does not reveal significant heterogeneity between any of the paired population comparison.

When the chi-square values are pooled for all the loci, all the paired populations under comparison show significant differences (table 9.2). Similarly when all the populations are pooled (table 9.3), the resulting contingency chi-square analysis show statistically significant differences for all the loci.

The F_{ST} values calculated for each allele of the different loci of the five tribes are listed in Table 9.1. For diallelic loci, we are presenting the computation for only one of the two alleles. The average F_{ST} obtained from different F_{ST} values comes out to be only 1.07%. Here too, the F_{ST} values for Rh blood groups and sickle cell trait are the highest and PTC the lowest, corroborating our earlier results based on contingency chi-square analysis.

TABLE 9.1

Distribution of various blood groups, Secretor, Taster and Sickle cell gene frequencies among the tribal populations

System	Allele	TRIBAL GROUPS							
		Bado Gabada (BG)	Bareng Paroja (BP)	Pareng Gabada (PG)	Ollaro Gabada (OG)	Konda Paroja (KP)	Weighted Mean P_1	Variance F_1	Values of FST
A_1A_2BO	O(r)	0.5092	0.5220	0.5109	0.4832	0.5064	0.5046	0.00001	0.00069
	$A_1(P_1)$	0.1887	0.1753	0.1554	0.1935	0.2106	0.1873	0.00034	0.00223
	$A_2(P_2)$	0.0420	0.023	0.0272	0.0097	0.0119	0.0217	0.00013	0.00656
	B(q)	0.2601	0.2754	0.3065	0.3136	0.2711	0.5046	0.00044	0.00217
ABH	Se	0.4255	0.5095	0.4293	0.3606	0.4580	0.4487	0.00291	0.01179
PTC	T	0.2937	0.2683	0.2730	0.2751	0.2691	0.2759	0.00008	0.00043
Rh-Hr	R1(CDe)	0.7130	0.7766	0.7352	0.7819	0.7844	0.7613	0.00077	0.00424
	r (cde)	0.0050	0.0633	0.0045	0.0707	0.0046	0.0337	0.00099	0.03042
	R_2(CDE)	0.0470	0.0427	0.0773	0.0891	0.0839	0.0701	0.00037	0.00573
	Ro(cde)	0.1388	0.0742	0.1506	0.0397	0.1108	0.0966	0.00184	0.02116
	Rz(CDE)	0.0962	0.0432	0.0324	0.0165	0.0165	0.0382	0.02075	0.02057
MN	M	0.7594	0.7097	0.8289	0.7844	0.7711	0.7702	0.00152	0.00860
Sickle cell trait	Hb_A	1.0000	1.0000	0.9357	0.9866	0.9309	0.9622	0.00091	0.02505

Average FST = 0.01074

Variance = 9.54×10^{-5}

TABLE 9.2

Chi-square Heterogeneity between paired populations based on analysis of gene frequencies

Analysis of	Combinations df	A_1A_2BO 3	ABH 1	PTC 1	MN 1	Rh-Hr 4	Sickle Cell 1	Total 11
Gene frequencies	BG x BP	1.8933	5.8326*	1.3509	2.8205	38.4526**	0.0000	50.3493**
	BG x PG	4.5857	3.8030	0.9263	6.4745*	17.1907**	13.4084**	46.3886**
	BG x OG	15.1122**	3.7453	0.7402	0.7758	92.8686**	2.6561	115.8982**
	BG x KP	10.7069*	0.8436	1.3123	0.1664	31.9412**	14.4635**	59.4339**
	BP x PG	1.3406	0.2583	0.0474	18.3640**	40.5513**	13.4084**	73.9700**
	BP x OG	7.4516	19.7162**	0.0982	6.7869**	20.0783**	2.6561	56.7877**
	BP x KP	5.2984	2.1513	0.0014	4.5102*	37.6773**	14.4635**	64.1021**
	PG x OG	7.4556	15.9556**	0.0097	2.8567	68.4489**	15.6111**	110.3376**
	PG x KP	8.9146	0.9827	0.0338	4.6980*	5.8923	0.0632	20.6046*
	OG x KP	2.9775	8.1980*	0.0791	0.2302	46.3039**	17.6507**	75.3944**

* 0.01 P 0.05

** P 0.01

TABLE 9.3
Chi-square values resulting from contingency X^2 Analysis of gene Frequencies

Locus	Orissa Tribes X^2	df
A_1A_2BO	26.8730**	12
ABH	24.9195**	4
PTC	1.8715	4
MN	19.3181**	4
Rh-Hr	179.4628**	16
Sickle Cell trait	43.8386**	4
Total	296.2835**	44

** P 0.01

TABLE 9.4
Values of Genetic Distances

Group	Paired Populations	Genetic Distance Minimum Dm	Genetic Distance Standard D.	Maximum D'
Orissa	BG x BP	0.0029	0.0048	0.0049
	BG x PG	0.0030	0.0050	0.0043
	BG x OG	0.0035	0.0055	0.0059
	BG x KP	0.0023	0.0038	0.0026
	BP x PG	0.0042	0.0069	0.0052
	BP x OG	0.0052	0.0085	0.0097
	BP x KP	0.0026	0.0042	0.0035
	PG x OG	0.0054	0.0087	0.0092
	PG x KP	0.0014	0.0024	0.0023
	OG x KP	0.0031	0.0049	0.0051

Using gene frequency data the genetic distances between the five tribes of Orissa were computed (Table 9.4). The net codon differences (Dm) per gene per locus between two populations does not exceed 0.0054, thereby indicating that the gene differences between any two populations is accounted for by not more than 0.54% of total population. The dendrogram obtained from the distances matrix is presented in figure 9.1. It is evident from dendrogram that Pareng Gabada (PG) and Kond Paroja (KP) form one cluster and are narrowly separated from Bado Gabada (BG) and Bareng Paroja (BP)which tend to form another cluster. Ollaro Gabada, however, are seperated from all the four by fairly good distance. This fact, however, remains unexplained in the absence of well documented history.

TABLE 9.5
Gene Diversity Estimates among the five Tribes of Orissa

Locus	HT	GST
A_1A_2BO	0.6278	0.00176
ABH	0.4948	0.01179
PTC	0.3994	0.00043
MN	0.3540	0.00860
Rh-Hr	0.4036	0.01175
Sickling	0.0627	0.02505
Average	0.3904	0.00989
Variance (S^2F)	0.0074**	0.00016**

** Sampling variance after Nei & Roychoudhury (1974)

The estimates of gene diversity for individual locus all the loci are presented in Table 9.5. Once again the G_{ST} value for sickle cell trait comes out to be the highest and for PTC the lowest, amongst all. The total gene diversity (H_T) among the five tribal populations is 0.3904. Gene diversity within (H_S) and between (D_{ST}) sub-populations is 0.3865 and 0.0039 respectively. The gene differetiation among these five tribal populations is only around 1%. It can, therefore, be inferred that intergroup variations are smaller than intragroup variations and that a small fraction of gene diversity accounts for the differences between populations.

Following Nei's (1972) method, further genetic distances were calculated among two low caste Hindus in West Bengal, six tribes in Bihar and five tribes in Orissa with the help of gene frequency data of five polymorphic loci, namely A_1A_2BO MN, Rh, ABH secretor and Hb (Table 9.6).

The data were collected from published papers (Kumar 1957; Kumar & Mukherjee 1975; Chakraborty and Yee (1973). The dendrogram was constructed from the matrix of genetic distances and form two clusters (Fig.9.2).

In the first cluster two low caste Hindus, namely Duley and Tentulia Bagdi have separated away from six tribes of Bihar and one tribe of Orissa. In most castes the genetic distance between Duley and Tentulia Bagdi is larger than that between any two of six tribes in Bihar. Bareng Paroja, is closer to Desi Bhumij, Ho than to other four tribes, namely, Santhal, Oraon, Dudh-Kharia and Munda. Among remaining four tribes of Orissa

TABLE 9.6

Genetic distances ($D \times 10^2$) among two low caste Hindusof West Bengal, six tribes of Bihar and five tribes of Orissa (based on frequency data for five polymorphic loci A_1A_2BO, MN, Rh, ABH and HbB)

		(1)	(2)	(3)	(4)	(5)	(6)	(7)	(8)	(9)	(10)	(11)	(12)
(1)	T.Bagdi												
(2)	Duley	0.57 +0.42											
(3)	Santal	0.64 +0.34	0.54 +0.37										
(4)	Oraon	0.65 +0.39	0.59 +0.31	0.09 +0.04									
(5)	Dudh Kharia	0.69 +0.30	0.82 +0.52	0.33 +0.22	0.47 +0.27								
(6)	Munda	1.36 +0.74	1.28 +0.71	0.46 +0.24	0.65 +0.37	0.21 +0.16							
(7)	Desi Bhumij	1.51 +0.95	0.96 +0.60	0.56 +0.34	0.63 +0.51	0.95 +0.41	0.60 +0.38						
(8)	Ho	0.73 +0.54	0.54 +0.31	0.55 +0.32	0.67 +0.31	0.71 +0.46	0.72 +0.56	0.28 +0.12					
(9)	B. Paroja	0.97 +0.67	0.73 +0.38	0.48 +0.23	0.54 +0.31	0.58 +0.31	0.45 +0.30	0.20 +0.12	0.23 +0.15				
(10)	P. Gabada	3.14 +2.17	2.05 +1.62	1.78 +1.10	2.12 +1.44	2.04 +0.96	1.31 +0.42	0.63 +0.26	1.13 +0.53	0.84 +0.41			
(11)	K. Gabada	2.17 +1.26	1.23 +0.89	1.22 +0.58	1.37 +0.77	1.42 0.58	1.00 +0.62	0.28 +0.04	0.51 +0.18	0.51 +0.06	0.30 +0.12		
(12)	B.Gabada	2.29 +1.31	1.16 +0.80	1.64 +0.80	1.75 +0.86	1.76 +0.91	1.44 +1.02	0.65 +0.39	0.73 +0.51	0.56 +0.30	0.59 +0.08	0.44 +0.20	
(13)	O. Gabada	2.35 +1.55	1.57 +1.00	2.18 +1.47	2.35 +1.41	2.42 +1.73	2.13 +1.90	0.90 +0.62	0.66 +0.40	1.01 +0.72	1.94 +0.55	0.58 +0.29	0.65 +0.40

(Cited from Roychoudhury, 1981)

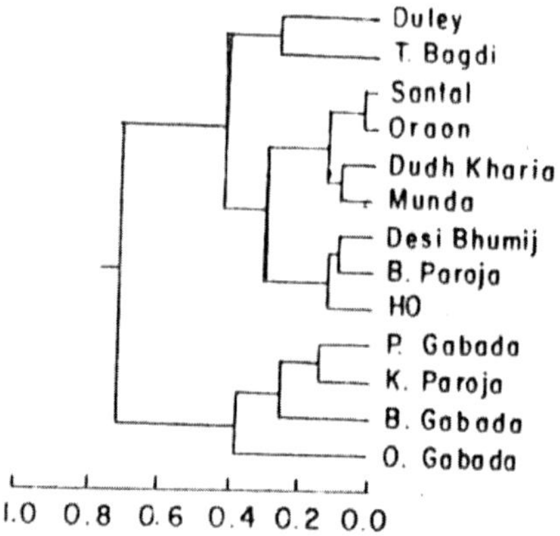

Fig.9.2. The dendrogram for two low caste Hindus of Wes Bengal six tribes of Bihar & five tribes of Orissa (based on gene frequency data for five polymorphic loci.), (Cited from Roychondhury, 1981.)

FIG.9.1 DENDROGRAM OF FIVE TRIBAL GROUP OF ORISSA

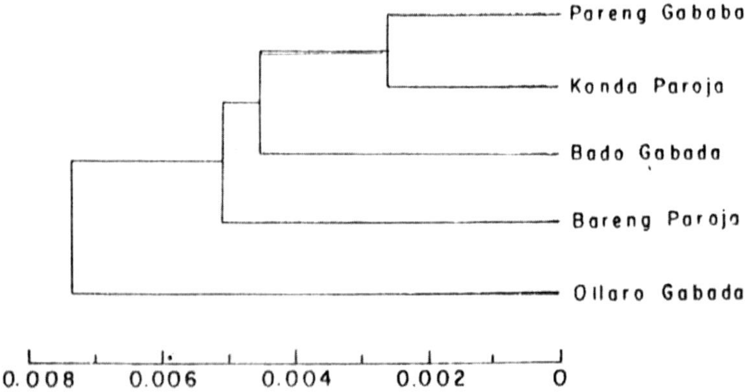

in the second cluster, the genetic distance between Pareng Gabada and Konda Paroja is the least, while that between Bado Gabada and Ollaro Gabada is the largest.

To sum up, therefore, five tribes of Orissa, although living in close proximity and under the same ecological environment, reveal differences between each paried populations when all the loci are pooled and at individual locus, when all the five tribes are taken together. Some interesting observations are obtained for Rh blood group system, sickle cell trait and ability to taste PTC. While the former two, as revealed by F_{ST} and G_{ST} values in the present investigation, can be considered as being under differential selective pressures, the last one, i.e. PTC can be thought to be under some common selective pressure, operating in these five groups.

The gene differentiation in these five tribal populations is very small, thereby indicating that intergroup variations are smaller than intragroup ones. More than 99% of the total gene diversity is accounted for by individual variability. However, it should be noted that the inference made in this paper is based primarily on the type of anlaysis we have presented which is only approximation to reality. Only six polymorphic characters have been used in the present investigation and data on a large number of common genetic loci are required to advance further comments in this direction.

Reference List

Chakraborty R, Yee S (1973) Phenotypic bioassay of five tribes of Orissa India. Hum Hered 23: 270-279

Das SR, Bhattacharjee DN, Sastry, Mukherjee DP (1963a) Blood groups ABH secretion sickle cell trait and colour blindness in the Bado Gabada and Bareng Paroja of Koraput Orissa. Bull Anthrop Survey India 11:145-151

Das SR, Mukherjee DP, Bhattacharjee PN (1963b) PTC taste threshold distribution in the Bado Gabada and Bareng paroja of Koraput Orissa. Acta Genet Basel 13:369-377

Das SR, Mukherjee DP (1964) PTC taste sensitivity survey among the Pareng Gabada the Ollaro Gabada and the Konda Paroja of Koraput Orissa. Acta Genet Basel 14:168-176

Das SR, Sastry DB, Mukherjee DP (1966) Blood groups and ABH secretion in the Pareng Gababa the Ollaro Gabada and the Konda Paroja of Koraput Orissa, Acta Genet Basel 16:169-183

Das SR, Mukherjee DP, Sastry DB (1967) Sickle cell trait in

Koraput District and other parts of India. Acta Genet Basel 17:62-73

Das SR, Mukherjee DP, Sastry DB (1968) A somatological survey of five tribes in the Koraput Orissa. Bull Anthrop Survey India 17: 400-422

Kumar N (1957) A genetic survey among the Tentulia Bagadi and the Duley of Hooghly district in West Bengal. Bull Deptt Anthrop 6:81-88

Kumar N, Mukherjee DP (1975)Genetic distances among the Ho tribe and other groups of central India. Am J Phys Anthrop 42:489-494

Nei M (1972) Genetic distance between populations. Amer Nat 106:283-292

Nei M (1973) Analysis of gene diversity in subdivided populations Proc Natl Acad Sci USA 70:3321-3323

Nei M (1975) Molecular population genetics and evolution. North Holland and Pub. Co. Amsterdam

Nei M, Roychoudhury AK (1974) Sampling variances of heterozygosity and genetic distance. Genetics 76:153-170

Roychoudhury AK (1981) The genetic composition of the people in eastern India. J Indian Anthrop Soc 16: 153-170

Wright S (1943) Isolation by distance. Genetics 28: 114-138

Wright S (1951) The genetical structure of populations. Ann Eugen 15:322-354

TEN

GENETIC STRUCTURE STUDIES AND WELL-BEING OF WEAKER SECTIONS: AN OVERVIEW WITH SOME NEW THOUGHT FOR BIOLOGICAL ANTHROPOLOGISTS

Lalit K. Kashyap

Last year while participating in a national seminar on "Population Structures among Tribes" at Tribal Research Centre, Ooty, I shared some of my views for strengthening bio-anthropological studies for the tribal health and development (Kashyap 1985) and this year while reviewing the contributions of anthropologists towards the studies on Scheduled Communities in the 73rd Annual Conference of the Indian Science Congress at Delhi, I tried to find out how much applied work is being done by both the biological and social anthropologists for the welfare of the Scheduled Communities (Kashyap, 1986). After these two exercises, questions like the utility of genetic structure studies for weaker sections and negligible reviews of bio-anthropolo- gical studies compared to social anthropological research in India, were haunting me. I am thankful to the organisers of this Seminar for asking me to present my views under the theme 'Genetic Structure and Well-Being of Weaker Sections' and thereby providing an opportunity to find out answers to some questions which were bothering me for quite some time.

Reviews of research in anthropology have been attempted from different angles from time to time (Roy 1922; Majumdar 1956; Ghurye 1956; Dube 1962; Bose 1963; Singh 1969; Vidyarthi 1972, 1980; Srinivas & Panini 1973; ICSSR 1974, 1985; Basu & Biswas 1980; Gopala-Sarna 1984; Sinha 1985; Kashyap 1986). Among other things, it has been established in these reviews that the social anthropological researches were patronised by the Britishers to understand the intricate dynamics of the Indian tribes and castes for subserving their colonial interests, whereas bio-anthropological researches of that time were aimed mainly to classify Indians under racial categories, to propogate the myth that Indian masses belong to "inferior" races, fit to be ruled by the racially "superior" whites. After the independence of India in 1947, social anthropologists besides continuing basic research, started studies to meet the new requirements of social planning and development. On the other hand, with racial anthropology falling into disrepute throughout the world after the Nazi episode, the bio-anthropologial researches confined mainly to finding out the finer differences among human populations. With the gradual (i)addition of new genetic markers to the existing arsenal of the bio-anthropologist (anthropometry, somatoscopy, blood groups, dermatoglyphics, PTC tasting and morphological traits) (ii) advance in evolutionary theory and (iii) availability of various statistical tools for finding out genetic distance/affinity and heterozygosity/homozygosity among the human populations, the armoury became fit for finer genetic structure studies.

Before proceeding further, let me clarify the meaning of the three key-words of this paper: Genetic Structure Studies (GGS), Weaker Sections and Well-Being. The type of genetic structure studies started after the independence (as described above), and which were generally conducted at micro-levels (hence the usage of terms like micro-evolution and microdifferentiation became popular) taking into consideration social and demographic variables also at times are taken as GSS for this paper. Such GSS were mainly conducted on the tribal groups initially, because of their well-defined endogamous mating pattern and their availability in large numbers in a particular geographic area and later, to find out some genetic variants or private polymorphisms and associations with certain diseases. The Scheduled Tribes (STs) and Scheduled Castes (SCs) being the main recognised 'Weaker Sections' of India are the main focus of this paper, however, few examples of other backward classes (OBCs), some mionority groups and communities-in- crisis are referred at places, treating them also as a part of such sections. Dictionary meaning of the term 'Well- being' (as per the Oxford Student's Dictionary of Current English) is welfare, health, happiness and prosperity. In the words of the renowned biological anthropologists of Oxford, Geoffery Ainsworth Harrison (1982) 'Well-Being' is a biological state within a condition where no 'disease' is recognised and people are regarded as 'healthy',some of these states are likely to be aspects of adaptations of fitness. The states of 'Well-Being', like morbidity have both physical and mental components and a subtle blend of the two. Keeping these meanings of the key words in mind, a quick overview of the progress of genetic anthropology is attempted as the first part, and its role in the well-being of weaker sections as the central part of this paper. The third part of the communication includes some new areas of applied research for the well-being of both the Weaker-sections and biological anthropologists.

Material & Methods

For the first and second part of the paper secondary sources were utilized, particularly the content analysis of the two journals, The Anthropologist-a foremost journal from India mainly devoted to bio-anthropology and The American Journal of Physical Anthropologists (AJPA)-a leading international journal of biological anthropology. Contents of a volume each, at random, of two other Indian journals exclusively devoted to bio-anthropology, viz., the Acta Anthropogentica (Vol 2) 1978 and the Indian Journal of Physical Anthropology & Human Genetics (Vol 10) 1984 were also utilized. All the publications of all the volumes of AJPA from 1951 to 1975 and of the Anthropologist from 1954 (year of the inception of this journal) to 1973 (with the exception of two volumes: IV and XI due to their non-avail- ability at the time of writing this review) were classified into 15 convenient categories. First 10 categories,(i) blood groups, (ii) dermatoglyphics, (iii) other traits (including morphological traits, skin reflectance studies, PTC tasting, colour blindness and studies on twins), (iv) population genetics, (v) demo-genetics, (vi) behavioural genetics, (vii) bio-chemical genetics, (viii) cyto-genetics, (ix) eco-genetics and (x) clinical/medical genetics were placed under the rubric of genetic structure studies. Rest of the work of non-genetic nature by bio-anthropologists was classified under five other categories, viz., (xi) evolution & race (xii) primatology & paleoanthropology, (xiii) growth & development, (xiv) dental anthropology and miscellaneous. The 20 years review of the Anthropologist (number of papers being 146) was divided into two equal periods, whereas the review of the AJPA (number of papers being 1416) was based on clustering of its contents into five equal, five yearly intervals. A paper covering different aspect of GSS like blood groups, dermatoglyphics and biochemical markers was represented in three different heads. Thus, after giving such weightage the N for AJPA became 1640 from 1416. For the third part of the paper, besides quoting some empirical primary studies various tertiary sources like the publications of the Government of India on the welfare of weaker sections were utilized.

Results and Discussion

(I) Rise of the Genetic Structure Studies in India

In India, the proper bio-anthropological researches started from the beginning of this century only. The 1901 and 1931 Census operations contributed significantly in the field of ethnology and bio-anthropology by providing data on physical and racial types based on anthropometric measurements and somatoscopic observations. Brains behind these bio-anthropological studies were H.H. Risley, E.A. Gait, T.C. Hodson and J.H. Hutton. Risley (1908) published his pioneer work 'The People of India' and gave the racial affiliations of Indians besides providing racial basis of castes. In 1931 Census, B.S. Guha also joined these operations under the Census Commissioner Hutton and provided his own racial classification of Indian populations in 1935 (Guha 1937). Other Indians followed Guha, examining his classification for various unstudied populations or describing the same populations with added morphological/genetic markers. Work of Biswas (1936), Sarkar (1936) and Ghurye (1937) may be mentioned here. During this period, D.N. Majumdar was also actively engaged in racial surveys with the expert guidance on statistical methods of P.C. Mahalanobis and C.R. Rao. It may be mentioned here that Mahalanobis (1925) was quite interested in racial studies, well before the Guha's classification. Due attention in these studies was paid to the tribes of India.

A solid foundation for GSS, was laid by Sanghvi, whose papers (Sanghvi and Khanolkar 1949 and Sanghvi 1953) are still the most widely quoted ones in genetic anthropological studies. During the last forty years, a number of studies on genetic variations of Indian populations have been added. Phenomenal progress made in GSS is due to the rapid advances made in laboratory techniques (revealing new genetic markers), biostatistics (providing new methods for calculating genetic distances/diversity/affinity) and population genetic theory (producing new models for interpreting the genetic data). Vogel and Motulsky (1979) have identified three major landmarks which have revolutionised the genetic anthropology, (i) the advent of molecular biology in late 1940s and 1950s, (ii) foundation of human chromosome research in late 1950s and 1960s and (iii) discovery of the histocompatibility gene complex in late 1960s and 1970s. More recently, new techniques of DNA analysis are coming up to study individual/population/racial differences in man. Notable among these is the genetic variation of mitochondrial DNA (mtDNA) which has a great potential in tracing ancestry, admixture and affinity of different groups of people. The available data on genetic markers on different tribes and castes has been subjected to rigorous statistical analysis and genetic distances have been calculated. Besides the proliferation of studies on genetic microdifferentiation mainly due to the above referred developments, another group of bio-anthropologists working on the evolutionary forces (natural selection, mutation, migration, drift and founder effect) responsible for the observed genetic differences have produced a number of good papers. Foundation of this line of work was laid by the work of JBS Haldane, RB Fisher and Sewall Wright but the impetus to such studies was given by the landmark paper of Washburn (1953) in which he coined the word 'New Physical Anthropology' and appealed to bio-anthropologists to look at the forces behind the observed genetic variation. Indian anthropologists were quick to respond to these developments. In India, BM Das (1964) may be regarded as the pioneer in micro-evolutionary studies. Demogenetic and population structure studies are the later off-shoots of this line of development. Amit Basu may be taken as the first to fruitfully utilize these developments in his GSS on Pahira tribe.

The hypothesis that some polymorphisms may be genetic substrate against which the environment acts to determine susceptibility and resistance to common diseases led to the development of the field of eco-genetics. Association of genetic markers with diseases, explanation of G6PD-deficiency, thalasaemia, certain hemoglobinopathies in endemic malarial areas, generally among the tribal populations, are the concern for this group of bio-anthropologists.

There may be many studies, in which bio-anthropologists have worked on all these lines of work in a single project. Neel (1978) has produced such a holistic work after his studies on Amerindian Tribes, particularly the Yanomama. In India K C Malhotra's work on the tribes of Maharashtra may be considered in this category of holistic GSS.

It may be surmised from the publications in the Anthropologist (Table 10.1), that 3/4th of the efforts of Indian bio-anthropologists were devoted to GSS between 1954 to 1973. It may be seen that there is a decline in simple descriptive studies based on only blood groups or dermatoglyphics from the first decade (1954-63) to the second decade (1964-73). In the same period, studies in eco-genetics, clinical genetics and cytogenetics have increased. Trend discerned from the content analysis of the AJPA (Table 10.2) reveals that gradually the number of papers in biochemical genetics, eco-genetics, clinical genetics, behavioural genetics have increased and simple blood group reports have declined from 1951 to 1975. However, only

TABLE 10.1
Relative position and trend of genetic structure studies as reflected from papers published in the Anthropologist. (1954-1973)*

S.No.	Topics	Period 1954-1963	1964-1973	Total
1.	Genetic Structure Studies, based on :			
	a Blood Groups	6 (10.71)	6 (6.67)	12 (8.22)
	b Dermatoglyphics	27 (48.21)	28 (31.11)	55 (37.67)
	c Other Traits **	7 (12.50)	19 (21.11)	26 (17.81)
	d Population Genetics	0 (0.00)	1 (1.11)	1 (0.68)
	e Demogentics	1 (1.78)	1 (1.11)	2 (1.37)
	f Behavioral Genetics	0 (0.00)	0 (0.00)	0 (0.00)
	g Biochemical Genetics	2 (3.57)	2 (2.22)	4 (2.74)
	h Cyto-Genetics	0 (0.00)	3 (3.33)	3 (2.05)
	i Eco-Genetics	1 (1.78)	3 (3.33)	4 (2.74)
	j Clinical/Medical Genetics	1 (1.78)	3 (3.33)	4 (2.74)
	Total	45 (80.35)	66 (73.33)	111 (76.03)
2.	Evolution and Race	0 (0.00)	6 (6.67)	6 (4.11)
3.	Primatology and Paleoanthropology	2 (3.57)	4 (4.44)	6 (4.11)
4.	Growth and Development	8 (14.28)	11 (12.22)	19 (13.01)
5.	Dental Anthropology	0 (0.00)	2 (2.22)	2 (1.37)
6.	Miscellaneous	1 (1.78)	1 (1.11)	2 (1.37)
	Grand Total of Total Pubisihed Papers	56	90	146

* Volumes IV (1957) & XV (1968) of the Anthropologist were not available for this analysis, hence the actual analysis is without these two volumes. However, a special volume published in 1969 has been included.

** Include Morphological traits, skin reifectance studies, PTC tasting ability, colour blindness andstudies on twins.

TABLE 10.2

Relative position and trend of genetic structure studies as reflected from papers published in the American Journal of Physical Anthropology (1951–1975)

S.No.	Topics	Period					
		1951-1955	1956-1960	1961-1965	1966-1970	1971-1975	Total
1.	Genetic Structure Studies, Based on:						
	a Blood Groups	27 (12.86)	37 (19.27)	38 (14.18)	36 (7.79)	23 (4.53)	161 (9.82)
	b Dermatoglyphics	4 (1.90)	2 (1.04)	9 (3.36)	20 (4.33)	29 (5.71)	64 (3.91)
	c Other Traits*	11 (5.23)	14 (7.29)	28 (10.45)	30 (6.49)	33 (6.45)	116 (7.07)
	d Population Genetics	8 (3.81)	5 (2.60)	10 (3.73)	26 (5.63)	35 (6.89)	84 (5.12)
	e Demo Genetics	0 (0.00)	0 (0.00)	5 (1.87)	7 (1.52)	17 (3.35)	29 (1.77)
	f Behavioral Genetics	0 (0.00)	0 (0.00)	1 (0.37)	2 (0.43)	8 (1.57)	11 (0.67)
	g Biochemical Genetics	3 (1.43)	4 (2.08)	21 (7.84)	24 (5.19)	31 (6.10)	83 (5.06)
	h Cyto-Genetics	0 (0.00)	0 (0.00)	0 (0.00)	5 (1.08)	2 (0.39)	7 (0.43)
	i Eco-Genetics	2 (0.95)	2 (1.04)	1 (0.37)	17 (3.68)	7 (1.38)	29 (1.77)
	j Clinical /Medical Genetics	1 (0.48)	2 (1.04)	0 (0.00)	3 (0.64)	16 (3.15)	22 (1.34)
	Total	56 (26.67)	66 (34.38)	113 (42.16)	170 (36.80)	201 (39.57)	606 (36.95)
2.	Evolution and Race	10 (4.76)	2 (1.04)	6 (2.24)	13 (2.81)	10 (1.97)	41 (2.50)
3.	Primatology and Paleoanthropology	82 (39.05)	55 (28.64)	68 (25.37)	129 (27.92)	130 (25.59)	464 (28.29)
4.	Growth and Development	37 (17.62)	43 (22.40)	59 (22.02)	150 (21.64)	102 (20.08)	341 (20.79)
5.	Dental Anthropology	7 (3.33)	12 (6.25)	11 (4.10)	29 (6.28)	38 (7.48)	97 (5.91)
6.	Miscellaneous	18 (8.57)	14 (7.29)	11 (4.10)	21 (4.54)	27 (5.31)	91 (5.55)
	Grand Total	210	192	268	462	508	1640
	Total Papers Published	190	176	219	394	437	1416

* Includes Morphological traits, skin reflectance studies, PTC testing ability, colour blindness and studies on twins.

about 37% of bio-anthropological work was devoted to the GSS upto 1975. In India, if we look at another journal (Indian Journal of Physical Anthropology & Human Genetics, Vol X), we may find GSS still in its infancy, as studies on a single population that too based on a single trait/marker like blood groups, PTC tasting ability or finger/palmar dermatoglyphics are still produced. On the other hand, there are journals in India, like Acta Anthropogenetica (Vol. 2) where about 90% papers are devoted to GSS based on biochemical markers. Thus, it may be said that the GSS are actively pursued by the Indian anthropologists.

From a review of papers presented in Anthropology Sections of ISCA, it was deduced (Kashyap 1986) that about 21.68% papers by bio-anthropologists were devoted to studies on Scheduled Communities (20.48% on STs and 1.20% on SCs). Thus, it may be said that a sufficiently large number of bio-anthropologists are engaged in GSS and the weaker sections are getting reasonably due attention in these studies. Achievements of such studies in the well-being of weaker sections is summarised in the following part of this paper.

(II) Genetic Anthropological Studies vis-a-vis Well-Being of Weaker Sections

Main contribution of GSS so far is the proper ethnic placement of various tribes/castes and their genetic relationships with other Indian populations on the basis of ABO/Rh/MN and other blood groups, ABH Secretor, PTC Tasting ability, protein polymorphisms, abnormal haemoglobins, etc. All these exercises were conducted in the backdrop of the racial classification of Indian tribes (like the Negrito, the Proto-Australoid and the Mongoloid) and the Indian languages having ethnic affiliations (like Indo-Aryan, Dravidian, Austro-Asiatic and Tibeto-Burman). Other contributions are in identification of the high risk groups in respect of hemoglobinopathies, other diseases specific to tribal areas, inbreeding levels, etc. Through microevolutionary/demogenetic/population structure studies, in a number of cases evolutionary course of a tribe/caste has been predicted, genetic load calculated, morbidity pattern pointed out and sub-divisions within a group identified.

1. Ethnic Placement of tribes/castes and their genetic relationship with other groups

Position of tribes/castes in respect of selected serological/biochemical markers is given below. Information is heavily drawn from a review article of Roychoudhury (1983).

(a) Blood Groups

Out of the 21 blood group loci found to be polymorphic in human populations the ABO system has been studied in largest number of Indian populations. Tribal populations living on Indo-Tibetan borders generally show higher frequency of A over B, contrary to the 'B more than A' characteristic of the populations of Indian subcontinent. Higher frequency of A over B in these border tribals shows their affinity with Mongoloid populations. In the Gangetic plains and most of the tribes in Bihar, Orissa, MP and Gujarat 'B more than A' pattern has been observed. Same is the case in Andhra tribes where the Raj Gond, Lambadi, Naikpod, Pardhan and Yonadi show a preponderance of B over A, with the exception of Koya Dora and Yerukala tribes. In deep south Paniyan, Kurumba and Adiyan and also the STs of Lakshadweep show higher frequency of A over B. Extremely low frequency of A (1%) among the Kotas of Nilgiris has been reported. With the picture of ABO system being almost complete on Indian populations, Bhalla (1984) has prepared illustrative maps showing the gene diversity in tribal populations of India on the basis of ABO, MNS and Rh polymorphisms. Pingle (1985) tried to find out the genetic relationship of 38 tribal populations of the Peninsular India. There are many other similar attempts to show the ABO diversities in the tribal groups in different regions of India.

In the case of MN system of blood groups most of the Indian populations have a higher frequency of M (60-75%). In general, the tribes have gene frequencies lower than 65% in Gujarat, 65 to 75% in Andhra Pradesh and Madhya Pradesh and higher than 75% in North East India, Orissa, Tamil Nadu and Kerala.

The frequency of Rh negative or Rh(d) gene varies from 15 to 30% in majority of Indian populations. This gene is practically absent among the tribals of North East Himalayas and in some tribes of Bihar, Orissa and South India. Kotas are distinguished from other tribes of Nilgiri Hills by the absence of cde gene.

Other blood groups like Diego, Kell, Duffy, P, Kidd, Lewis and Lutheran have been studied in a few populations of India. The Diego blood group factor is essentially a Mongoloid characteristic, for it is absent in Caucosoids and Negroids. The diego gene has a frequency of 2 to 4% among the Khasis, Bhutanese and Nepalese. The presence of this gene in Rajbanshi caste in Cooch Behar and Jalpaiguri District of West Bengal indicate Mongoloid influence. This gene is totally absent in

Kurumba and Irula tribes of South India.

(b) Gm and Inv Polymorphisms

The antigens of the Gm system have been tested in a number of tribes in India. The $Gm^{1,5}$ haplotype known to be a marker for Mongoloids is found with high frequency in Oraons (Bihar), Tharus (UP) and Koya Dora, Konda Kamara and Lambadis (AP). This haplotype is completely absent in the Toda, Irula and Kurumba of South India. THE Inv^1 allele of the Inv system varies among non-tribes indicating not much difference between tribes and non-tribes, in respect of this marker.

(c) ABH Secretor

Frequency of secretor gene (Se) varies from 65 to 70% among Nocte, Galong Abor and Angami (Nagas) of North East India; from 50 to 60% among the tribes of Bihar; from 35 to 50% among the tribes of Orissa. A decreasing trend in the frequency of Se gene is observed as one moves from North East to Bihar, Orissa, and Kerala.

(d) PTC Taste Sensitivity

The Panyan and Kadar tribes have higher incidence of tasters (46-73%) and the same is the case with tribes of Orissa (46 to 50%) and Gujarat (52%).

(e) Defective Colour Vision

The incidence of sex-linked defective red-green colour blindness is reported to be highest in culturally advanced groups and lowest in the tribes, supporting Post's hypothesis of relaxation of selection. The tribes of Gujarat (2.6%), Orissa (0.9%), AP (1%) and Maharashtra (1 to 2.4%) show a smaller incidence of colour blindness. In contrast Santals of West Bengal have a high incidence of colour blindness (5%). Recently the Post's hypothesis has been questioned by some workers in GSS.

(f) Protein Polymorphisms

Tribes are characterised by low frequency (2 to 3%) of the third complement system (C_3) as against 2-14% among non-tribes. The frequency of Bf^F gene of properdin factor is lower in the tribes of Himachal Pradesh than the neighbouring non-tribals. For the acid phosphatase, the frequency of P^a allele ranges from 11% in the Kadar tribe of Kerala to 40% in the Parsis of Bombay.

The G6PD deficiency of type B is prevalent in many parts of India. A high incidence has been reported among Koya Doras (13%) and Santals (14%).

(g) Rare Variants of Proteins & Enzymes

Rare variants are considered to be useful genetic markers for characterising populations. The absence of Dchi-a variant of serum transferrin distinguishes Lambadi-tribe (who are believed to have migrated from North) from the other tribes of Andhra Pradesh. This variant is absent among the tribes of Nilgiri Hills. Some other variants reported among Indian tribes are : the Pgm^{6K} allele of phosphoglucomutase locus-I and Peh^{BK} allele of peptidase-B in Kadars, one slow moving variant of albumin in Lambadis and of transferrin in Gonds.

(h) Abnormal Haemoglobins

The incidence of Hbs, related to sickle cell trait, has been reported to vary from 5 to 30% among the tribals in Nilgiri-Wynad-Mysore area, South Gujarat and Bastar. HbS is conspicuously absent among the Kota, Kadar and Kurichia of Nilgiri Hills and Ho, Munda, Oraon, Kharia and Santals of Bihar. Another abnormal haemoglobin E has been detected among the Kacharis, Totos, Khasis and Manipuris.

(1) Genetic relationships of tribes within themselves & with other Indian populations

Generally on the basis of genetic distance analysis (based on gene frequency data of a number of loci), tribes in a region have been found to be genetically different from the neighbouring non-tribes. Tharus of Kumaon were found to be different from the three non-tribes living in the tribe's neighbourhood. Tribal Kanets were found to be different from the Koli caste in HP. In Andhra Pradesh the Koya Dora and Konda Kamara tribals were found to have a marked genetic distance with Malas and Modigas (SCs) of the same area. In Nilgiris, Kota and Toda showed genetic affinity with non-tribals whereas rest of them formed a cluster together. Three tribes of Maharashtra, viz., Bhil, Pawara and Katkeri showed great genetic distances from the caste Hindus of the same area. All these results show that by and large, tribes have remained isolated in most of the regions. Genetic distances between tribes have also been calculated and a lot of variation amongst the tribal groups have been recorded. Tribes of North east India are different from those in Bihar and Orissa. Similarly, the tribes of Andhra and Nilgiris differ genetically. In a genetic distance study in Gujarat among seven tribes, except for the Koli, other tribes (Bhil, Dubla, Naika, Dhanka, Dhodia and Gamit) were found to be genetically closer to each other. In another genetic distance study of 11 tribes in Central India (Bihar, MP and Orissa), results did not correlate much with the linguistic differences, for example, the genetic distance of Santal was smaller from Oraon than from the Munda, although the language of the Santal and Munda is Mundari and that of Oraon is Dravidian. It is probable that in this case geographic proximation seems to be more important than the linguistic affinity for genetic exchange. On the other hand, in a GSS of five tribes of Orissa, the tribes were found to have a low genetic affinity in spite of geographic proximity. Thus, the efforts of bio-anthropologists are continuing to understand the genetic distance/affinity of the weaker sections of the society.

2. Haemoglobinopathies

In early 1950s Lehman and Cutbush found Sickle Cell trait in southern India, since then a large number of studies on haemoglobinopathies have been carried out on a number of Indian tribes. The Sickle Cell trait among tribals varies widely, ranging from more than 20% among the Pardhan, Gamit, Paniyan, Kurumba, Irulas, Raj Gonds, to less than 5% among Lambadi, Dhurwa, Santhals and Todas. Sukumaran (1978) has reviewed the incidence of haemoglobinopothies among the SCs and STs. Selective advantage hypothesis relating to endemicity of malaria and incidence of sickling in populations is yet to be confirmed and tribals and other weaker sections provide an opportunity for such studies. Other Hb abnormalities like Hb D,E,Q,J,K,L are yet to be explored fully in tribal areas of the country.

3. Other Genetical Diseases

The red Cell enzyme, Glucose-6-Phosphate Dehydrogenase (G6PD) deficiency is of considerable importance and has been studied in a number of weaker sections. Percentage of G6PD deficiency has been reported in tribals like Gonds (11%), Angami Nagas (0.27%) and minority groups like Parsi (12-15%), Lohana (3.2%) and Khoja (2%). Hyperendemicity of malaria in the country, particularly in the tribal areas, imposes stress on the public health and the treatment with anti-malarials in G6PD deficient individuals creates further problems with the development of hemolytic complications. Thus, mass-screening of G6PD deficiency is desirable to detect such sensitive groups/individuals, so that alternative methodology of treatment and preventive/promotive health care measures be adopted. There are a number of studies on association of blood groups,

HLA-antigens, chromosomal aberrations and diseases but the coverage of weaker sections is negligible. However, it has been reported by Verma (1978) that many diseases of present civilization like Cardiovascular, Cerebrovascular, diabetes mellitus, cancer, hypertension are rare among the tribals.

4. Inbreeding Studies

Due to societal sanctions or demo-geographical compulsions close breeding has been observed in various weaker sections. In Andhra tribals a high frequency of consanguinity (above 50%) has been reported among Koya Dora, Konda Reddy, Pardhans. Among Kotas 12.69% frequency of consanguinous marriages has been reported. Gonds (59.4%) and Bhils (59.20%) have also been reported to be highly consanguinous groups. Effects of inbreeding on reproductive wastage, mortality, fertility and congenital malformations have been studied by a number of workers. It has been reported (Verma 1985) that there is 1 1/2 times increase in the rate of malformations among the offsprings of consanguinous marriages.

5. Microevolutionary/Demo-genetic Studies

B M Das has recently shown a unification process among the Nagas (fusion) whereas Malhotra has shown the creation of new endogamous groups in some populations of Maharashtra due to social ostracism (fission). Amongst the Ahmadiyyas, the microevolutionary advance has been shown through the simultaneous fission-fusion process (Kashyap & Tiwari 1980). In a number of tribal communities index of opportunity of selection has been calculated, while others have identified a number of sub-groups/divisions in a tribe which was earlier known to be a single entity.

All these studies are likely to be utilized in the future for proper planning for the development of the weaker sections. As most of these studies have a promise to be beneficial in the long run, some bio-anthropologists have become restless and are clamouring for applied research of immediate use to the masses. It is true that bio-anthropologists have yet to reduce the distance between their findings and masses (mainly weaker sections) on the one hand and the bosses (policy planners), on the other. Bio-anthropological research after crossing the stage of a colonial science is still in the phase of imitative research where we are testing the models or applying methods/theories developed in the West, with a few exceptions. Various development stages of the subject as proposed by L P Vidyarthi: (i) Formative (1774-1919), (ii) Constructive (1920-1949) and (iii)

Analytical (after 1950) or as proposed by I P Singh: (i) Formative (upto 1935), (ii) Descriptive (upto 1952) and (iii) Converging (after 1952) remind me of the four-fold classification of Penniman given long ago about the development stages of Anthropology. At times we even borrow the titles for our papers/research projects directly from the West. In a recent debate entitled "Is Indian Anthropology dead/dying?" the word British has been simply replaced by the word Indian. Possibilities of GSS by bio-anthropologists on some live problems faced by the weaker sections of the country are explored below.

(III) Some New Lines of Action for Biological Anthropologists

1. Propagation of the concept of equality through the GSS: deliberate attempt should be made to show that genetically speaking there is no hierarchy among the human populations.
2. Study on the effects of inter-caste marriages: various State Governments are encouraging inter-caste marriages by giving different incentives. Through GSS, impact of such marriages are to be analysed and the results utilised for the eradication of untouchability.
3. Orientation of the research findings of GSS for the success of various National programmes for the welfare of the weaker sections like IRDP/TSP/SCP/ICDS.
4. Rationalization of the list of SC/ST Communities: through GSS administrators may be helped to assign the proper place to controversial communities and in the identification of false certificate holders. Impact of lifting of area restriction in some states and of continuation of the restriction in certain areas on the mating pattern of the concerned communities may be studied.
5. GSS of formation of new Mendelian groups within a SC or ST community: may be due to the conversions, practise of untouchability or economic gains due to the development policies of the government for the weaker sections.
6. GSS of bonded labourers; the Union Government is paying a lot of attention on the identification, release and rehabilitation of the bonded labourers who are in bondage from generations in certain areas. It would not be difficult to find a large number of such groups for bio-anthropological studies.
7. Atrocities on STs & SCs: genetic/biological basis of agression/violence may be studied.
8. GSS of weaker sections residing in the core or periphery of national parks or wild life sancturies: ef-

fects of the symbiotic life of hunter gatherers on their genetic structure or even of the tribals at other stages may yield useful results.

9. GSS of groups displaced by the major industrial or other projects: results of the change in the habitat, intermixture with new populations need to be studied.

10. Counselling to the threatened, declining groups: seventy two primitive tribal groups (Table 10.3) identified so far should form the priority group for the future bio-anthropological research. Possibility for action/intervention biological anthropology in such situations should be explored to help the threatened group or a community in crisis.

TABLE 10.3

Identified primitive tribal groups

S.No.	State/UT		Primitive Tribal groups	No. of Households
1.	Andhra Pradesh	1.	Bodo-Gadaba	400
		2.	Bondo Poroja	400
		3.	Gutob Gadaba	400
		4.	Khond Poroja	400
		5.	Parengi Poroja	500
		6.	Thoti	226
		7.	Dongaria Khonda	900
		8.	Konda Sabaras	600
		9.	Kutia Khond	900
		10.	Chenchu	2860
		11.	Kolam	5255
		12.	Konda Reddi	8722
2.	Bihar	1.	Asur	1404
		2.	Birhor	693
		3.	Birjia	726
		4.	Savar	708
		5.	Hill Kharia	2048
		6.	Korwa	3743
		7.	Malpaharia	9727
		8.	Parhaiyas	2930
		9.	Sauria Paharia	11809
3.	Gujarat	1.	Kathodi	588
		2.	Siddis	896
		3.	Kolgha	6000
		4.	Kotwalia	2580
		5.	Padhar	2037
4.	Madhya Pradesh	1.	Abujhmarias	2446
		2.	Baigas	35387
		3.	Bharias	23559
		4.	Hill Korbas	13461

State	No.	Tribal group	Population
	5.	Saharias	23559
	6.	Kamar	3950
5. Maharashtra	1.	Maria Gond	1189
	2.	Katkaria	28255
	3.	Kolam	11178
6. Orissa	1.	Birhor	20
	2.	Didayi	433
	3.	Mankidias	175
	4.	Lodha	788
	5.	Bondo	774
	6.	Dongaria Kondh	535
	7.	Kutia Kondh	1348
	8.	Lanjia Souras	1636
	9.	Paudi Bhuyan	727
	10.	Soura	1743
	11.	Kharias	23089
	12.	Juangs	4876
7. Rajasthan	1.	Seharia	7000
8. Tripura	1.	Reangs	12935
9. West Bengal	1.	Birhor	120
	2.	Toto	135
	3.	Lodha	9123
10. Uttar Pradesh	1.	Rajis	74
	2.	Buxa	2000
11. Karnataka	1.	Jenu Kuruba	1367
	2.	Koraga	1285
12. Kerala	1.	Cholanaickans	70
	2.	Kadar	66
	3.	Kurumbas	180
	4.	Kattunaickans	1057
13. Manipur	1.	Marram Nagas	908
14. Tamil Nadu	1.	Kattunaickans	260
	2.	Kotas	260
	3.	Todas	240
	4.	Irulas	1160
	5.	Kurumbas	940
	6.	Paniyans	1140
15. A & N Islands	1.	Great Andamanese	5
	2.	Jarawas (Estimated)	50
	3.	Onges	19
	4.	Senteneless (do)	10
	5.	Shompens	18
			287002

Number of Prinitive Tribal groups - 72

Source: Tribal Development A Statistical Profile - Background Paper on Tribal Development No. 12, Govt. of India, Ministry of Home Affairs, New Delhi 1985.

Reference List

Basu A, Biswas S K (1980) Is Indian Anthropology dead/dying ? J Indian Anthrop Soc 15 : 1-14

Bhalla V (1984) Gene diversity in tribal population of India: illustrative maps showing the distribution of ABO, MNS and Rh polymorphisms.In: Malhotra K C, Basu A (eds) Human Genetics (volume I). Indian Statistical Institute, Calcutta pp 420-448

Biswas P C (1936) Uber Hand-und Fingerlcisten von Indern. Z Morph Anthropol 35

Bose N K (1963) Fifty years of science in India, Progress of anthropology and archaeology, Indian Science Congress Association, Calcutta

Das B M (1964) Genetic Variability among some populations of South Goalpera, Assam, Proc Nat Instt Sci (India) 30:315-338

Dube S C (1962) Anthropology in India, In: Madan T N and Gopala-Sarna (eds) Indian Anthropology. Asia Publishing House, Bombay

Ghurye G S (1937) Physical data from Kathiawar. J Anthrop Soc Bombay, Jubilee Volume

Ghurye G S (1956) The teaching of sociology Social psychology and social anthropology. In: The Teaching of Social Sciences in India UNESCO Publications, pp 148-153

Guha B S (1937) An outline of racial anthropology in India, Indian Science Congress Association, Calcutta

Gopala-Sarna (1984) Indian anthropology retrospect and prospect In: Bansal I J S, Singhal P (eds) Anthropology in Indian context. Today and Tomorrow Publishers, New Delhi

Harrison G A (1982) Life Styles well-being and stress. Human Biol 54: 193-202

ICSSR (1974) A Survey of researches in Sociology and social Anthropology (vol I to III), Popular Prakashan, Bombay

ICSSR (1985) Survey of research in sociology and social anthropology (vol I) Satvahan Publications,New Deihi

Kashyap L K (1985) Population structure of an inbred small group of the Bhotia tribe in Kumaon Himalayas - some suggestions to strengthen such studies for tackling problems of tribal health and development In: Reddy K N (ed) Proceedings of the National Seminar on Population structures among Tribes, Ooty. Publication Division, Tamil University, Thanjavur (In Press)

Kashyap L K (1986) Trends in studies of scheduled communities as reflected through content analysis of papers in anthropology sections of Indian Science Congress Association In: Tiwari S C (ed) Proceedings of the 73rd Indian Science

Congress Association, Anthropology Section, Delhi. Today and Tomorrow Publishers, New Delhi (In Press)

Kashyap L K, Tiwari S C (1980) Kinetics of genetic kinship as inferred by isonymy among the Ahmediyyas of Kashmir Valley. Human Biol 52: 311-324

Mahalanobis P C (1925) Race mixture in Bengal. Presidential Address at the Authropology Section in the XII Annual conference of Indian Science Congress Association

Majumdar D N (1956) Anthropology under glass. In: The Teaching of Social Sciences in India UNESCO Publications, pp 161-173

Neel J V (1978) The population structure of Amerindian tribe, the Yanomama. Ann Rev Genet 12 : 365-413

Pingle U (1985) ABO gene diversity and genetic distance between three geographical regions of Peninsular India In: Ahuja Y R, Neal J V (eds) Genetic Micro differntiation in Human and other Animal populations. Indian Anthro- pologist Occasional paper I, New Delhi

Risley H H (1908) The peoples of India. Calcutta Thackerspink

Roy S C (1922) Research in anthropology in India. Man in India II

Roychoudhury A K (1983) Genetic polymorphisms in human populations in India In: Satyavati G V (ed) Peoples of India, Indian Council of Medical research, New Delhi, pp 1-30

Sanghvi L D (1953) Comparison of genetical and morphological methods for a study of biological differences. A J Phys Anthro 11: 385-404

Sanghvi L D, Khanolkar V R (1949) Data relating to seven genetical characters in six endogamous groups in Bombay. Acta Genet (Basel) 6 : 41-49

Sarkar S S (1936) Racial affinities of the inhabitants of Rajmahal Hills. Trans Bose Res Instt 2

Singh I P (1969) Physical anthropology in India: Retrospect and prospects. The Anthropologist 16: 69-83

Sinha A C (1985) Anthropological lacunae in anthropological research paper presented at a UGC seminar on "Perspective in Anthropological Research in India: Planning for the future researches and methodologies" held at the Department of Anthropology, Delhi University, Delhi from September 27-October 1, 1985 (Mimeographed)

Srinivas M N, Panini M N (1973) Development of Sociology and social anthropology in India. Sociological Bulletin 22

Sukumaran P K (1978) Haemoglobinopathies in scheduled castes and scheduled tribes In: Verma I C (ed) Medical Genetics in India, Auroma Publishers, Pondicherry

Verma I C (1978) Medico-genetic problems of primitive tribal communities. In: Verma I C (ed) Medical Genetics in India, Auroma Publishers, Pondicherry

Vidyarthi L P (1972) Social anthropology in India since independence. In : Mathur K S, Verma S C (eds) Man and Society, Ethnographic and Folk culture Society, Lucknow, pp 55-78

Vidyarthi L P (1980) Two-hundred years of social anthropology in India since independence. In : MathurK S, Verma S C (eds) Man and Society, Ethnographic and Folk culture Society, Lucknow, pp 55-78

Vidyarthi L P (1980) Two hundred years of social anthropology in India (1774-1971). Vidyarthi LP, Sahay BN, Dutta PK (eds) ClassicalPublishers, New Delhi

Vogel F, Motulsky A G (1979) Human Genetics. Springer-verlag, Berlin

Washburn S L (1953) The strategy of physical anthropology. In: Kroeber A L (ed) Anthropology Today. Chicago Press, pp 714-727

ELEVEN

PROMOTING OCCUPATIONAL MOBILITY AMONG SCHEDULED CASTES: PROBLEMS AND PROSPECTS

R.R. Prasad

In the traditional Indian social system many of the occupational roles have an ascriptive content. Many castes were correlated with particular occupations. However, not all castes were occupational groups and certain occupations like agriculture, the army, and the teaching professions were open to all castes irrespective of whether they belonged to the higher castes or the polluting castes. But the norms governing occupations were particularly rigid in the case of polluting or untouchable castes. Ascription was the norm for the occupational roles for members who belonged to untouchable groups and such occupations were considered impure. An untouchable could not change his occupation within rural setting.

Although the norms governing occupational mobility among polluting castes were very rigid in the traditional Indian social system, change from one occupation to another within the occupation specific caste or group among the untouchable castes has been taking place as a continuous process in the different parts of the country. Srinivas (1966) has described one such process as Sanskritization by which a low Hindu Caste or tribal or other group, changes its customs, ritual or ideology and way of life in the direction of a high and frequently, "twice-born caste". This has brought individual as well as collective mobility to all occupational castes including the untouchable castes.

While the sources of occupational mobility lay in the political and economic systems, Sanskritization provided a traditional idiom for the expression of such moability. The need for promoting occupational mobility amongst scheduled castes by way of creating political will and strengthening their economic base has, however, also got expression in the strategy of the development of scheduled castes during the sixth Five Year Plan. The Government of India's Report (1985) by the Working Group on the Development of Scheduled Castes (1980-85) listed the promotion of occupational mobility amongst scheduled castes as one of the general objectives of the scheduled castes development because of its importance in the context of the social discrimination suffered by them.

Certain occupations followed by the scheduled castes are somehow, irrationally though, psychologically associated with social stigma. For example, the occupation of scavenging, carcass recovery and flaying, and hide tanning which are carried out by the scheduled castes, are associated with social stigma. But there are some occupations like weaving, basket making, fishing, etc., which the scheduled castes follow, do not carry any social stigma as such. However, their position in these occupations does represent their economic weakness.

As the occupations followed by the scheduled castes fall under the two broad categories (1) clean and, (2) unclean, the efforts aimed at promoting occupational mobility amongst them have to take into consideration the various socio-economic and technological factors. The unclean occupations in which scheduled castes are traditionally engaged have to be converted into clean, sophisticated and hygienic occupations by way of technological interventions. The technological interventions in the unclean occupations should be made with a view either to reduce the physical involvement of the scheduled castes in such occupations to the minimum or to improve the working conditions so as the occupation is not plagued with bad odour, handling and removing of filth physically, and unhygienic surroundings. And for those scheduled castes who are not engaged in unclean occupations, the occupational mobility amongst them should be promoted by strengthening their economic base and releasing them from the grip of the exploitative layers and structures. This would help them in attaining horizontal and vertical mobility.

The present paper attempts to examine critically the problems and prospects of promoting occupational mobility amongst those Scheduled Castes who are traditionally engaged in the unclean occupation of (i) scavenging, and (ii) carcass recovery, flaying, and hide tanning.

The Scavengers

The inhuman practice of removing night soil and filth physically by scavengers is greatly responsible for perpetuating untouchability in our society. So long as the old type of dry latrines remain, the evil practice of scavenging would continue and the scavengers cannot be totally liberated. The members of scheduled castes engaged in this occupation have customarily been assigned the 'lowest' position in the caste hierarchy in our country. A time-bound programme for the conversion of dry latrines into water-borne ones should be launched so that the scavengers can be rescued from the jaws of social cruelty within the shortest possible time.

The programme of conversion of dry latrines into water-borne ones is being implemented in various parts of the country for quite some time. It is estimated that there are about 3245 urban agglomerations in the country out of which only 217 have sewerage covering?, only 20% of the population serviced by the system. It is also estimated that there are about 6.5 lakh scavengers in India catering to the needs of 4.6 crores population using dry latrines in India. Further, according to the data available, there are about 41 lakh dry latrines in the country which ought to be converted into water-brone latrines with a view to liberating the scavengers from the inhuman practice of removing night-soil and filth physically. The requirement of funds for low-cost sanitation as it stands today has ben estimated to be at Rs.900 crores including Rs.400 crores for rehabilitation of displaced scavengers on completion of this programme. Average unit cost at current prices is Rs. 1200 approximately plus price escalation for converting one dry-latrine into water-borne one.

Looking at the magnitude of the problem, very little has been done in this field so far. The Scheduled Castes and Backward Castes Development Division (SCBCD) of the Welfare Ministry, earlier under Home Ministry, is implementing a programme of the liberation and rehabilitation of scavengers under the centrally sponsored schemes of "Implementation of Protection of Civil Rights Act" 1955. The intention of this Ministry is to assist the efforts of the willing States and provide initial support. The programme is being assisted for a few selected towns on certain conditions like 'whole town approach', 'non-recurrence of dry latrines', 'creation of revolving fund' and 'total rehabilitation of liberated scavengers' (both private and municipal). This programme is being implemented by the 15 State Governments with the help of matching assistance from Central Government. So far 51 towns have been selected in these States. 8 towns in Bihar have been made scavenging free and the liberated scavengers have been provided alternative employment. The Central Government has also requested the

State Government(s) to accord highest possible priority to the scheme for conversion of dry-latrines into sanitary ones, thereby eliminating scavenging in urban areas, and (b) to amend the Municipal Acts so as to prohibit construction of new latrines requiring carriage of night-soil manually.

It is no doubt true that efforts aimed at eliminating the inhuman practice of scavenging are highly commendable, but its success will largely be determined by the forces which prohibit construction of new dry latrines, and reversion of the liberated scavengers in the same dirty occupation from new alternative occupations. Although the problem of scavenging is largely confined to the municipal towns it is feared that due to growing rural modernization, the rural elites shall initially replace the open-air latrines with dry latrines and thus the practice of carrying night-soil and filth physically by scavengers may also take roots in the rural areas. Therefore, it has to be ensured that along with the Municipalities, the Gram Panchayats also prohibit construction of dry-latrines in the rural areas so as to destroy the evil of scavenging before it takes obnoxious form. Further, it may not be possible to convert all the dry latrines into water-borne ones with government assistance only. The individuals willing to convert their dry latrines into water-borne ones should also be assisted by making them available the necessary materials at subsidised rates in addition to providing short-term bank loans. Such measures would help in quickening the process of conversion of dry latrines into water-borne ones as the persons still using dry latrines shall feel morally encouraged and financially supported for undertaking the conversion work. However, the most important aspect of this process would be to ensure that the liberated scavengers are simultaneously rehabilitated in alternative occupations which are not attached with social stigma. The occupations thus selected should also be of a nature which generate more income than the liberated scavengers' erstwhile occupation. All this naturally calls for regular and close monitoring and evaluation of the rehabilitation projects.

The Caarcass Flayers

Carcass recovery and flaying forms the basis of the village, cottage, small and large organised leather industry. In every village or in a group of villages there are certain caste groups amongst scheduled castes who traditionally attend to the recovery and flaying of carcasses for obtaining hides to be used for tanning and manufacture of leather footwears, etc. Since time immemorial, there are well-defined groups scattered all over India that carry on these occupation with such scanty means, resources, implements and technical knowledge as have been handed to them from sire to son. For nearly three hundred years at least neither the Indian society even during the old panchayat system nor any of the Indian governments, indigenous or foreign, seem to have taken any substantive interest either in advancing their technical knowledge, improving their socio-economic conditions, or providing them with facilities and means to improve their working conditions. They have survived till now on sheer unexhausted past momentum.

The Chamars have had a customary obligation and right to render carcass recovery and flaying to the village society. Despite the prevailing social attitude of contempt for all those who followed the work of carcass recovery and flaying, the Chamars have continued doing this demeaning occupation. But in the last three decades there has been a movement amongst Chamars to give up their traditional occupation of carcass recovery and flaying and adopt some clean occupations with a view to attaining upward mobility in the caste hierarchy.

The Commissioner for Scheduled Castes and Scheduled Tribe in its annual report for the year 1958-59 observed, " at a number of places, members of scheduled caste communities traditionally engaged in this work (skinning of dead cattle, etc.) had given it up or were being forced by their community panchayats to give it up". The Census Organization undertook a project in 1966 to trace the contours of the social mobility movements among the scheduled caste in different parts of the country. The report revealed that the leather workers' castes like Bairwa, Balai, Bhambi, Chamar, Jatav, Regar and others of Kota, Sikar, Bhilwada, Udaipur and Chittorgarh districts of Rajasthan had left handling the carcasses of cattle under the influence of social reformistic movements initiated by their caste panchayats.

Due to the growing awareness among the carcass flayers about the low status attached to their occupation, majority of them are bent upon giving up their age old occupation and joining the army of landless labourers. This trend got further fillip when the carcass flayers' caste panchayats as a part of their efforts to achieve social regeneration, started forcing the carcass flayers to give up their dirty and obnoxious occupation or face social excommunication. Many of the carcass flayers who have not been able to immediately give up their age old occupation, have been socially excommunicated and are now leading a socially ostracised and isolated life.

Although the carcass flayers' caste panchayats are greatly

responsible for motivating and persuading the carcass flayers to give up their age old occupation, other factors, which are mainly economic are also instrumental in alienating the carcass flayers from their traditional occupation. At many places in Uttar Pradesh, Rajasthan, Haryana, Orissa, etc., a system of awarding contract at the block/panchayat samiti level for the collection of dead animal has been introduced, thus, replacing the old jajmani system whereby the scheduled castes traditionally engaged in carcass collection, hide tanning and footwear manufacturing enjoyed certain rights and privileges of collecting the dead animals of their patrons. With the introduction of a system of awarding contracts at the open auctions to the highest bidder, the scheduled castes traditionally engaged in carcass recovery and flaying, have taken a back seat because their weak financial conditions do not allow them to stand in the open auction before the dominant Hindu castes and Muslim hide traders. But the tragedy is this that interest of the dominant caste/traders is limited only to securing of contracts and making huge profits either by sub-contracting the contract to the smaller contractor/trader or by establishing hide godowns and running it profitably with the help of the poor scheduled castes who work as wage earners. But even the number of such scheduled castes who are working as carcass flayers on daily payment is very insignificant because of the improved means of communication and transport which the hide contractors use. Earlier there were 3-4 carcass flayers in almost each village, now the contractors employ only 3-4 flayers as wage earners at block level and manage to recover almost all the dead animals with the help of tractors and jeep trailors, etc. Thus, the introduction of contract awarding system for collection of dead animals in rural areas has led many traditional carcass flayers belonging to scheduled castes to give up their avocation and migrate to urban areas for seeking wage employment.

While the pressures accruing from the caste panchayat of the scheduled caste leather workers and the introduction of contract system have in a way enabled the traditional carcass flayers to liberate themselves from the polluting occupation of carcass recovery and flaying, and, thus, achieve occupational mobility by adopting the so called clean occupations such as landless agricultural labourers, construction workers, rickshaw pullers, etc., a deeper analysis shows that such pressures have helped attaining occupational mobility only to select caste groups from among the leather workers caste belonging to the scheduled caste. This is so because the occupation of carcass recovery and flaying did not cease to exist merely because the Chamars or other similar caste among scheduled castes have stopped handling carcasses. In fact, the trade of recovering hide from the carcasses and selling them to the organised tanneries continues to be a major occupation for many scheduled caste families. But there has certainly been a change in the nomenclature of the caste groups among scheduled caste attending to the work of carcass collection and flaying. When the Chamars left the occupation of carcass collection, the Bhangis (scavengers) have adopted it in a big way. Initially, these people were offered good wages by the contractors to attract them in this occupation. Gradually, the entire work of carcass collection and flaying has been adopted by the Bhangis in those areas where the Chamars have given it up. Although the Chamars have managed to attain upward mobility by giving up unclean occupation and adopting the so called clean occupations in the form of wage employment, the Bhangis have further submerged themselves downward in the social and caste hierarchy by adopting another unclean occupation of removing carcasses alongwith handling night-soil and filth physically. Earlier, the Bhangis carried out the work of removing carcasses and night-soil only in the urban areas, but when the Chamars started dis-associating themselves with their traditional occupation of carcass recovery and flaying, the Bhangis living in rural and semi-urban areas readily adopted it along with their other main and subsidiary occupations.

The evil persists

From the above discussions, one important question arises. Whether promotion of occupation mobility amongst scheduled castes envisages occupational mobility amongst only a few castes or for all the members of the scheduled castes? If the idea is to promote horizontal and vertical mobility only amongst a few castes among the scheduled castes, then the above case study does not purport to say anything significantly because the Chamars have already attained occupational mobility by giving up the work of carcass recovery and flaying. But, if the objective is to promote occupational mobility among all the scheduled castes, then the above case-study suggests that there is a need to reconsider our policy in this regard. Because even though the Chamars have left the unclean occupation of carcass recovery and flaying, the occupation continues to be followed by another scheduled caste community, the Bhangis. And this does not mean occupational mobility. Because the ultimate aim is to see that the scheduled castes get rid of the social stigma attached to their occupations which give birth to many obnoxious social disabilities including untouchability and commission of atrocity against them.

What is to be done

Naturally, the solution cannot be found merely in persuading the scheduled castes to give up their unclean occupations, but in cleaning the uncleanliness of the occupations like carcass collection and flaying, hide tanning, etc. in which they are traditionally engaged. We have already made considerable headway in liberating the scavengers by converting the dry latrines into water-borne ones and also by rehabilitating the liberated scavengers in alternative occupations which do not carry the stigma of untouchability. But no serious thought has been given to modernize the rural leather industry by devising scientific and hygienic process of deskinning the dead animals, tanning of raw hides and manufacture of footwear with a view to liberating the scheduled castes leather workers from the social stigma attached to their unclean and unhygienic occupation. Since the carcass flayers mostly use their own body as the tools of production, untouchability in the case is embodied on their person. Unless there body is liberated from use as tools of production, untouchability cannot be expelled from their life.

There is considerable scope however for the primary operations of collection of dead animal bodies, flaying and curing operations to be improved with a high dose of modernisation including mechanisation. This will be of enormous social and economic advantage to the country.

At the economic plane, official study teams have reported that only about 15 per cent of the potential hides and skins are being recovered presently for economic gain. Given our vast livestock population, such high non-recovery (as much as 85 per cent) constitute an unimaginable economic loss to the rural households. Any improvement in the proportion of recovery of hides and skins over the pitiable 15 per cent, would constitute an enormous economic gain for the individual household as well as the economy.

Planned development efforts over the last 30 years, however, do not show any serious or significant organisational and technological attempt to improve these primary occupations. The Central Leather Research Institute (CLRI) has made a notable contribution to upgrading of leather industry technology but its work has not extended to the primary level of leather activity. Village leather industry is also supposed to be covered by the Khadi & Village Industries Commission (KVIC), but its contribution too has been marginal. The Industrial Development Bank of India (IDBI) has recently awakened to the industrial and social potential of this industry but is still at the stage of examining various options for intervention.

Should it be any wonder that economic deprivation and neglect continues to compound the social disability of lakhs of scheduled caste primary leather workers, particularly the carcass flayers and hide tanners. There is, therefore, an urgent need to work out a comprehensive attack on the many-sided complex economic and social problems which have long kept the scheduled caste leather workers in the leather industry to subhuman conditions.

The first step in the direction of improving the socio-economic conditions of the scheduled caste leather workers for enabling them to attain horizontal and vertical mobility is to devise an organisational and technical substitute for the carriage of the dead animals to release the shoulders of the carcass collectors from carrying that load. The second step should be to ensure a total replacement of the abominable physical and insanitary conditions in which flaying and curing of carcasses and hides activity is carried out. Technology should be summoned to minimise to the utmost the use of hands and feet of the workers from the carcass flaying and hide tanning activities. It should also be commissioned to minimise pollution of the environment. The third step should be to make availability of proper bathing, washing and laundry facilities for the workers engaged in these primary operations. These facilities must be not only modern to wash out what Gandhiji called "the blot of untouchability"' and to ensure for them a clean healthy physical and social life.

It is often argued that mechanical devices for collecting dead animal bodies, or provision of modern sanitary flaying centres are not economically viable. But it has to be remembered that untouchability is not an economic phenomenon. The extra cost, if any, of modern organisation, technology and mechanical inputs required to banish untouchability from the human race should be debited to the social column in the national ledger (Jain, 1985). If, social subsidy is justified in any sphere of our activity, improvement of working and living conditions of primary workers in the leather industry would be the most deserving case as it would promote occupational mobility amongst scheduled castes.

Reference List

Government of India Ministry of Home Affairs (1985) Report of the working group on the development of scheduled castes

1980-85
Jain LC (1985) Key note address in the workshop on socioeconomic problems of rural leather workers held at NIRD. Hyderabad
Srinivas MN (1966) Social change in modern India. Allied Publishers, New Delhi

TWELVE

DEVELOPMENT AND ANTHROPOLOGY: REBUILDING RURAL AND TRIBAL INDIA

P. K. Bhowmick

'Development' refers to the process of 'gradual unfolding', 'growth' or 'stage of advancement. None of the societies is static, all of them have related movements through adjustments and interactions, either with nature or with the different groups of people in and around. In the true sense of the term, it sums up and designates the most important aspects of change concerning the 'well-being' or 'uplift' of the people, in general, and it ensures stability and comfort in living processes. Broadly speaking, as Mair (1984) says:

> In contemporary contexts, the process is a movement towards a condition that some of the world's nations are supposed to have attained. Those which have not reached it, used to be called 'underdeveloped'.

Generally, these countries are considered 'less developed countries, i.e., LDC'. Development does not necesarily mean inculcation of values vaguely associated with Western Civilization. It is something more : it is utilization of the resources of the region and, at the same time, removes the distressing condition or poverty of the people. Sometimes, it refers primarily to economic backwardness causing malnutrition, ill-health, little awareness of the cause of disease, high mortality rate and high birth-rate. Besides these, there are many contributory factors causing more problems like housing, education, unemployment or under-employment etc. In societies, there are diversities and hierarchy among the groups of people (Castes & Communities) and in many cases these bring in their wake social or economic deprivations through exploitation. All these constellate together and reflect the acute problem related to backwardness and under-developed conditions. These conditions are interlaced with regional disparities.

It is true that due to geographical positions, certain regions are more fertile, than others, some areas are favoured with regular monsoon rain, whereas others are arid uplands or drought prone areas. Naturally, regional imbalances are all the time noticeable and along with these, people's reactions or adjustments vary from place to place. Ultimately, a prevailing disparity continues even in spite of man's utmost endeavour to overcome it.

History tells us about sporadic migrations, attacks and invasions which culminated in some proceses of exploitation and, as such, many countries in the global context came under the colonial power, exposed to the exploitation by their rulers. These resulted in the adverse effects on the underdeveloped countries, their total stagnation and misunderstanding among the people.

II

Anthropology, the science of man, endeavours to study man in his totality. It has a colonial heritage, as the colonial administration in various countries tried to know the manners and customs of the people whom they wanted to subjugate and rule. It tried to peep into the aspects of etisnography, specially of the so-called primitive people as part of evolutionary history of civilisation of mankind. Gradually, many more points were added up to have a comprehensive picture of men, their gradual adaptation procedures, from time to time, encompassing their culture and society. Study of anthropology helps understand people and society and various social relationships and aspects of international situations due to contacts which have been occuring in a society. Such anthropological concepts and methods became structured , and in the course of time, anthropology became a separate discipline altogether, incorporating many procedures. Thus, this subject helped the colonial administrators better management of men and affairs.

In India, we have various phases of systematic development of anthropology. Prof. Vidyarthi (1977) had divided anthropological studies and researches into the following:

(i) Formative period (1774-1919)
(ii) Constructive period (1920-1947)
(iii) Analytical period (1948-till date)

In the formative period, etinography culture-studies were emphasised. As a result, some groups of people were studied and analysed in depth with their cultural specialization, and this type of study specially by the British Anthropologists belonging to the administrative stratum ultimately showed the differences of cultures. Such one-sided studies and their results very clearly divided the society vertically and consequently the people began to identify themselves in terms of cultural differentiations and distinctions. Publicity and propaganda format created this schism among the groups. Such constant efforts of the so-called anthropologists/administrators very adversely affected the minds and action-patterns of the people whose world-view changed accordingly. Gradually, during the constructive period, new dimensions were added when the subject received support through field and case studies. Facts cleared the clouds and understanding grew in a better way and radiated into their minds. Slowly but surely, during the analytical period, new types of researches were undertaken, situations interpreted, interactions and contacts examined with historical authenticity and more problems of integration were diagnosed. The World War II brought most of the countries of the world, freedom and independence. This enabled many rich countries to come forward due to their closeness, for the general betterment of the countries under the colonial rule, in various ways. Anthropological researches and studies started to change the situations more quickly. 'Science of man' became the 'Service of man'. Welfare and developmental activities were suggested, even initiated by the anthropologists; many of the anthropologists were included in the administration work itself. Thus, practical or applied anthropology and, later, Action Anthropology became the watchword of the day when involvement of the anthropologists as social engineers or architects was considered a must for the administration. This type of involvement, speacially in the L.D.Cs got priority and suggestions were made accordingly.

III

India became independent and constitutionally it became a welfare state with republican principles. The problems of the countries were reconsidered by the political leaders as well as indian administrators. The weaker sections of the population as well as the backward zones were demarcated and, through planning and projects, all these problems were sorted out and reconsidered for solution and improvement. Those people who were lagging behind or were deprived of social justice were unmistakably identified, special powers were endowed to the Governors and more constitutional facilities were extended to all these sections of the people of our country. Government took the responsibility for their upliftment and a number of departments were established, advisory committees or evaluation committees constituted; institutes were organised for research work and action was taken up relating to the problems, constraints and compatabilities. Before independence, we had sporadic examples of involvements of the anthropologists to steer clear the difficulties faced by the then administrators. For example, J.K. Bose of the Calcutta University helped the then British administration, specially when F.O. Bell found problems in land settlement operations among the matrilineal Garos of erstwhile Bengal; Dr. Haimendorf involved himself in the welfare of some South Indian tribes at the request of His Excellency, the Nizam of Hyderabad. This type of involvement of the anthropologists at the advisory level of the administration was needed to have a smooth functioning of the administration. But, in the changed circumstances, the role of anthropologists began to change, through action and development of anthropology by regular problem-diagnosing and doing a series of welfare experiments in a few specific situations. A few of the anthropologists were posted at the advisory level. In the Anthropological Survey of India, the Planning Commission wing of the Ministry of Home Affairs (TD), various cultural institutes and many other Departments of Anthropology at the university and college level, anthropologists got themselves acquainted with the problems, associated themselves. They became an integral part of the administration and thus their role changed to action level. Many evaluations were made to note the aspects of change as well as constraints of development.

In India, we had Community Development (1952), National Extension Service (1953) and many other projects relating to overall development. The Tribal concentrated areas were marked (scheduled areas) and special Multipurpose Tribal Blocks were created for the quick development of the people and the region.

Thus, we find that the problems of the region as well as the problems of the people were effectively handled by the expert anthropologists who became involved in the nation-building processes. Again, out of the 427 Scheduled Tribes of our country, 72 groups were identified as Primitive Tribal Groups (PTG) owing to their special socio-cultural articulation and primitiveness, and resistance against their own development, in particular, and the country's development, in general. Thus, we find that the actual work of the anthropologists - their activities and research - as found in their papers, books and reports are helping the administration in various ways. Therefore, anthropology is nowadays not merely a 'curio-study' or a 'traveller's account', but it is a meaningful corollary or adjunct to the development programme initiated in the country. They are, to all intents and purposes, helpful to the development programmes in pinpointing the problem-ridden zones, examining the constraints and the types of resistance and they are working as social doctors or social engineers for solving specific problems of the country.

IV

Problems were many and varied at the time of Independence. Details of India's available resources were not assessed, though the Indian National Congress made an attempt to do so sometime in 1934. More than 82% of the total population live in villages, which were at that time not properly linked with communication facilities. The maximum cultivable land was in the possession of a few persons; the agriculture and the agricultural implements were old and outdated. Thus, poverty stared the poor villagers in the face. Neither sanitation, nor medical facilities, not even supply of drinking water was easily available. Illiteracy, superstition, prejudice and narrow world view retarded the pace of rationalisation and all these enveloped the minds of the majority people. Misunderstanding among the castes and communities was manifested through sporadic outbursts of riots and massacres and this was the go of the day. Over-population and pressure on land created acute unemployment problems and as a result people became restive and tense. For such unskilled people, no remunerative work could be procured immediately. Usurers and money-lenders started bleeding them white through exploitation. Famine, pestilence and epidemics were a hardy annual. There were no industries to offer minimum facilities to these hapless to meet their inescapable needs. In such critical juncture, India won Independence, i.e., removal of the foreign rule with all the concomitant curses of partition of the country. There were a good number of princely states which had friendly alliance with the then British administration, which supported the promoters of exploitation for their personal gain. Nothing of consequence was to be had at that time. New planning was needed to bring about certain factors into play to put an end to in the unfortunate conditions that pervaded our country and to combat all these problems mentioned above. Non-availability of food, clothing and shelter constituted the major part of the problem of the time, and these were to be tackled first. Thus, it became necessary:

> .... to plan, to direct to organise and to coordinate, but it is even more necessary to create conditions in which a spontaneous growth from below is possible.... Community

> Development Scheme is something which is likely to bring about a union between the top and others. (Nehru 1952)

The Government of India had set up the Planning Commission (1950). In this way, there was implementation through the Community Development and Panchyati Raj. Human resources had to be mobilised to utilise the maximum physical resources, technical know-how had to be disseminated, the problems of the people had to be properly resolved. Thus, human contacts, in a specific way, became unavoidable. Training and orientations were needed to reshape the mentality of the people and also the implements. We find in the writings of Professor Dube that the

> Officials who were called upon to implement the development plans on behalf of the State, had to assume an active role of leadership and had to function as innovators and agents of change in the communities under their charge.

Naturally, through various plan periods, envisaged in the Tribal Development Projects, more provisions were made, roads and other means of communication were extended, industries were set up, schools, colleges and universities were opened, orientation and training became a must, as the world was getting smaller and smaller and people were coming closer to each other by sharing their weal and woe, happiness and smile together.

V

The involvement of the anthropologists in the matter of development of India has now become significant. Anthropology is being taught in as many as 28 Universities and in some of the colleges affiliated to them. Both social and physical anthropologists have distinct roles to play, not only to impart education and training, but also in other spheres of researches and evaluations. Anthropologists have been inset in the Planning Cell as experts, in Tribal Cultural Research and Training Institutes, Tribal Welfare Departments in different States, Ministry of Welfare (TD), Census Department, Offices of the Commissioner for the Scheduled Castes and Scheduled Tribes, National Council for Education Research and Training and many other Organisations relating to health, hygiene, family planning and nutrition. There is the Anthropological Survey of India, the biggest in the global context and the Indian Statistical Institute and there are also a good number of local and national organisations and associations where quite a few anthropologists are working in various capacities, either for research or for action projects.

In the course of general development activities the introducing projects and plans, we find induction or replacement of ideas of the anthropologists related to developmental programmes.

India is a country of villages. Naturally much emphasis has been put on agriculture to improve the levels of the standard of living by introducing new techniques and other technical know-how; shifting cultivation problems and disadvantages have been studied by the anthropologists and remedial measures suggested. This has been done in the Naxal belt of Srikakulam; new plants are being replaced for plantation to avoid indiscriminate cutting and felling of trees by the Saoria Paharia; irrigation system is being changed for perennial water sources. To motivate the people for a better life-style at the grass roots, socio-psychological barriers are being removed and the proposals for change are being implemented through human resource development.

Setting up of industries, construction of dams etc., require vast areas and thus shifting of the people becomes necessary. Again, in course of time, new ethnic groups began to migrate. As a result, a healthy planning both for migration and rehabilitation is needed. Special care is being given at the industrial complexes where a good number of people are displaced; for such reasons many suggestions have been made for implementation, i.e., for better living and stability by anthropologists.

The rehabilitation of the Primitive Tribal groups of people and also of the de-notified (ex-criminal) tribes at various places of our country, has been taken up. Many other researches are being taken up with proper and appropriate suggestions in this regard. In most of the cases, these are being implemented by the authorities concerned.

Economic aspects of exploitation and indebtedness, bonded labour and other types of exploitative systems and relationships have been identified by the researches of the anthropologists all over India. Land Tenure systems have been changed in our country through legislation. How far the land reforms are implemented or whether the poorest people are deriving advantages out of them are also some significant aspects for study.

Issues in respect of migration due to breakdown of the rural economy and the march of the village poor towards towns and cities have also been receiving due attention from the anthropologists. Thus, in the entext of a total restructuring of rural economy by utilising waste-lands, surplus man-power, through extension of technical know-how and by harnessing the available human resource, the anthropologists have a role in rebuilding the national economy and reinforcing the variegated groups with more stability.

Economic planning remains also abstract and incomplete, unless it becomes consistent with the totality of goals and values of social progress that must be, besides democratic and universal enough to arouse the social and political idealism of the people. It is the social science that broaden and democratise the strategy of true man-power planning or human resource development in the widest context, and makes the people more responsive to modernisation as their own contributions to it are simultaneously enlarged.

THIRTEEN

HUNTERS-GATHERERS OF THE BAY ISLANDS: PROBLEMS AND NATURE OF CULTURE CONTACT

T. N. Pandit

The Andaman and Nicobar Islands (numbering aboout 300; area 8293 sq. kms.) have been historically one of the most isolated areas in the world prior to the British occupation of the Andaman Islands in 1789. The first British settlement in the Andaman Islands lasted only a few years and was abandoned in 1796. The British came here again sixty two years later (1858) in a more decisive way and established the second and the permanent settlement at Port Blair. The Nicobar Islands had in the meantime been under the nominal control of the Danish East India company but the territory came under British control, through a treaty with Denmark, 1869. Today, the islands, also called the Bay Islands, are an integral part of the Indian Union with the status of a Union territory. The Islands are situated in the Bay of Bengal (the straight distance between Port Blair and Calcutta/Madras is about 1200 kms.). The climate is tropical with heavy rainfall and the land is covered with lush green vegetation. The sea around is rich in food and mineral resources.

The oldest human population in the Islands have been the Andamanese in the Andaman group and the Nicobarese in the Nicobar group. The Andamanese hail from the negrito stock and are probably the oldest inhabitants in this area. They could have come here from the mainland south-east Asia thousands of years when the Negritos were possibly the dominant people in this wide region stretching from the coastal South India to the New Guinea islands and beyond. The Andaman Negritos have been hunter-gatherers all through. The Nicobarese, on the other hand, are of mongoloid stock and have been herders and horticulturists keeping large herds of pigs and cultivating coconut plantations. However, during the last century and a quarter the islands have been politically, economically and socially part of India, there have been large scale migrations from various parts of India either under government sponsored schemes such as the resettlement of prisoners brought to Port Blair jail, the Bhatu (from U.P.), the Mappila (from Kerala) and the Burmese settlers, the Bengali refuges and the ex-servicemen settlers etc., or the voluntary migrants from West Bengal, northern Indian states, such as U.P., Bihar, Punjan and from the southern states of kerala, Andhra, Tamil Nadu and Karnatake etc. As a consequence over the last century and more total population of the islands has risen sharply and as per projections for 1986 exceeds 200,000 (against an estimate of about 8000 in 1901). The population of the municipal area of Port Blair alone is more than 50,000 today. It is noteworthy that the competent of the original tribal populations is barely 12% whereas they were the sole masters and inhabitants of the area prior to its occupation by the European powers in 18th and 19th centuries. In fact the negritc Andamanese population has been reduced to a paltry 500 against the British Administration estimate of about 5000 in 1858. Thedemographic decline has been sudden and sharp. But this is in keeping with the world-wide pattern of destruction of isolated native populations on the entry of the outside people especially the Europeans. However, the Nicobarese have not suffered to this extreme extent as a result of contact with the new migrants whether of European of Indian origin for various reasons. However, it may be emphasised here that the impact and nature of initial and continuing intimate contact with the migrant populations mainly of Indian origin and the consequences of the policies of the British and Indian administration have not only affected the demography and population distribution but the entire gamut of social, economic, and political life of the Andamanese and the Nicorbarese.

The vast majority of the migrant Indian population especially in the villages lives on agriculture; the rest follow the urban trades. So we, have in the Andaman and Nicobar Islands three distinct catagories of communities in terms of their culture and economic activities:

(A) The Andamanese, the traditional hunter-gatherers;
(B) The Nicobar/ese, the herders and horticulturists;
(C) The mainland Indian migrants who are mainly agriculturists but also follow non-agricultural and urban occupations (see-Pandit 1969 and 1985).

If does not need great wisdom to imagine that there are

broadly three major perspectives to the major historical and cultural changes that have been taking place in these islands as a result of their colonisation by the British East India Company first tentatively towards the end of the 18th century, and later more effectively in the mid 19th century. But what is even more interesting, is that the perception of the changes that have occurred have also varied within each category and some times within each community at different levels.

Changes in culture, says Murdock (1960:248-249) "normally have their origin in some significant alteration in the life condition of society.......Among the classes of events that are known to be especially influential in porducing cultural change are increases or decreases in population, changes in the geographical environment, migration into new environments, contacts with peoples of differing culture, natural and social catastrophes such as floods, crop failures, epidemics, wars and economic depressions, accidental discoveries and even such biographical events as the death or rise to power of a strong political leader". It is a fairly comprehensive statement but we shall presently see that most of these factors have been operative in the Bay Islands in their recent history. But we shall restrict our discussion to the situation with reference to the hunters-gatherers.

Hunters-gatherers

The Andaman group of Islands have over the millenia been the exclusive habitat of the negrito hunter-gatherers. The negritos, it has been surmised, probably migrated to the Bay Islands, several thousand years back from the mainland south-east Asia. Here they seemed to have flourished as hunter-gatherers having had plenty to eat from their forest and see resources. Contrary to popular belief - as pointed out by Sahlin (1972:1-40) among others - that considers hunter-gatherers as doomed and starved people who may barely manage to survive, the latter, could be conceptualised as being 'original affulent' societies in terms of the high degree of satisfaction of their felt needs. All evidence points to such a state of affairs prevailing among the Anadaman hunter-gatherers.

The area of the Andaman group of islands is about 6200 kms. Most of the inhabited islands were peopled by the Andamanese. In the 19th century there were at least 12 different tribal communities spread out between the islands in the Great Andaman (ten) and Little Andaman (two) regions. Except for immediate neighbours they were not even aware of each other's existence except perhaps in a very vague manner. Each tribe and each local group or band had its owr local territory (Radcliffe-Brown 1948) to move around in search of wild boar and fruits, roots, tubers and honey, turtles and turtle eggs etc. The seasonal and daily movements meant a life of seminomadism, building of permanent and temporary shelters, a clear cut sexual division of labour. Men being the hunters alone weilded the bow and arrow and spears (fitted with iron or stone points). The canoes and rafts too were rowed by men and they went up the tall trees to bring Women collected fruits, tubers and roots and did minor fishing with baskets around the creeks. They also helped in the construction of the shelters and tending the babies and cooking food etc. The boys and girls grew up to follow their parent's footsteps. Life was peaceful and smooth; some excitement was provided by the occasional appearance of a distant ship (scrupulously avoiding the islands) or the appearance of a ship wrecked crew near the shores. These were promptly dealt with by the Andamanese warriors using their bows and arrows. However occasionally the Malaysian pirate ships succeeded in capturing alive a few people who were taken away to be sold as slaves. But such events were few and far between to disturb the idyllic peace of the islanders. However, the situation changed drastically and for good in 1858 when the British ships laid anchor off the South Andaman coast with their naval personnel and the first batch of Indian prisoners to lay the foundations of a penal settlement at Port Blair and to safeguard the islands for the British political and trade interests. The Andamanese watched first with curiosity and fascination and then with awe and anxiety when the ships kept coming and going, when the forests were cut down and the land cleared and new kind of shelters began to be built to house the new people with their new ways of life. The danger was realised at once and resistance offered in the most forceful manner possible. They resisted the occupation and exploitation of their lands at every step in an unorganised or organised manner. They fought valiantly and gallantly with their bows and spears (see Mouat 1863 and Census 1931). However, the guns had to prevail ultimately over bows and arrows. The story of this resistance is glaring instance in contradiction of the view point offered by Devore (quoted in Eibl-Eibesfeldt 1973:129) that hunter-gatherers do not defend their territory against aggression. Eible-Eibesfeldt (ibid 129-187) has rightly rejected the Devore's above observation with very convincing evidence. The battles in South, Middle and North Andaman was followed by peace and close contact and cultural interaction with the outsiders both Britishers and Indians. This led to disease and epidemics in the second half of the 19th century. The Andamanese died like flies, the causalties in battles fought earlier were nothing compared to the devastation that overtook them now. The Andamanese left the settlement in fear and spread the contagious diseases inside the forests. This happened in the Great Andamans and the story was later repeated in Little Andaman in all its gory detail. But two tribes namely the Jarawa (in Great Andaman) and the Sentinalese (in North Sentinal Island) resisted the proffered hand of friendship and were saved from a similar fate with such lightening speed.

However, the four surviving Andamanese tribal communities today number less than 500. They are the Great Andamanese (28) living in Strait Island, the Onge (101) of Little Andaman, the Jarawa (250, estimated) of Great Andaman and the Sentinalese (100, estimated) of North Sentinel Island.

The Great Andamanese are the surviving members of the ten original tribes of Great Andaman. The survivors were living a scattered life, sometime, as serfs or in govt. service as bush police-men. In 1970 they were brought together for resettlement in Strait island as a single community. In otherwords this has been an attempt to create a community out of disparate uprooted individuals whose sense of belonging together could be traced only to their common tragedy and the dark skin colour and a language evolved out of a mix of original ten tribal languages/dialects interspersed with some Hindi and English words and expressions. A community has sought to be created out of the survivors of the demographically and socially disorganised original communities. Their sembalance of unity is also derived from a negative but an important factor that of a common distance from the dominant settlers. In the changed circumstance this factor assumes considerable significance as their very survival is dependent on the recognition as a group by the former. The settlement at Strait Island has been built and is maintained and sustained by the government agencies. Apart from the material needs supplied periodically, the families are also paid cash allowences. From the "original affluent" state they have come a long way to state of complete dependence. However, their "standard of living" could be said to be higher as their wants have increase multifold and they consume a lot many more items than the Jarawa and the Sentinalese or even the Onge do. Also the marriage rules have been greatly diluted because of the acute problem of finding mates. Some women also have got married to outsiders at timesand lots of them have been having sexual liasons with outsiders. The biological fatherhood has lost its significance. Much of the old culture has vanished though some important old customs survive such as the death rites, the name giving custom and initiation ceremony etc. and, of course, the language in its modified form. Hindi has been fully adopted as a language of interaction with outsiders and partly among themselves. The settler's dress habits have been copied by the Great Andamanese almost fully.

How do they look upon themselves as a group vis-a-vis their past and the other people. The more perspective of their members talk of the old glory that was theirs, the lands that have been lost, the people who are no more, the grim reality confronts them with foreboding. And yet there is a keen desire to survive as individuals, to maximise their advantages by manipulating the concerned individuals, by stead-fastly ignoring the "degradation" that has entered their lives, by seeking little pleasures like having a drink a smoke or a little bit of opium. They think of themselves as 'civilised' in their life-style and consider the other three Andamanese groups as "wild and primitive" types. Their self-image, as manifest in their own behaviour, is not at all bad. But on the other hand most of the settlers regard them as "a degenerate and perasitic community which lacks the desire and the will to help itself". Many regard the government's concern and commitment for their welfare as misplaced and misconceived. There is little appreciation in the public mind for the recent historical experience of these people (not of their own making) that has led to such tragic consequences in their 128 years contact with the outsiders (since 1858).

The Nicobarese and the other three Andaman tribes have no contact with this community and hence they have no opinions about them. However, the author has observed meetings between the Great Andamanese groups and small groups of the Onge and the Jarawa. The former's appearance made the latterfeel that they were nearer to them but they could not converse with each other as their languages could not be mutually understood.

After the Great Andamanese the community in the longest contact with the outsiders is that of the Onge. The first friendly contact was made with them in 1885. Till 1967 the island of Little Andaman was the exclusive habitat of the Onge (Pandit & Bose 1977 :132 - 140). However since then several thousand settlers have come here for permanant settlement. These includes the mainland Indians and also the Nicobarese. The latter have established a village near one of the major Onge settlements at South Bay. For the first time in their thousands of years of stay in the Islands the Onge are living face to face with other propulations which have occupied their hunting grounds and disturbed their migratory pattern. Not only that, they feel outnumbered, outmanouvered and dominated in their own home territory. The Onge resentment over this has been subdued in terms of their overt behaviour but patient observation shows the hurt it has caused their psyche as also their whole way of life. There have been organised attempts of changing their life styles sometimes with or without consent. They have also felt impressed by the new consumer items which they could use. Their huts have been rebuilt with new designs but quite often the onge built the old type huts alongwide the new ones. They do not maintain the new huts themselves but wait for the government engineers to do the job. Due to demographic decline (since 1961 population has come down to 101 from 129, in 1858 the estimate of this population was about 1000) arranging marriages presents a problem. Some eligible males do not have any girls to marry and some men and women have got married in spite the considerable disparity in age. But no social rules have been violated yet. With more intense contact with the outsiders knowledge of Hindi is an asset that conditions the recognition of an individual as an Onge leader by outside agencies irrespective of his traditional position within the community. This has sometime caused resentment and factionalism. The efforts of the official agencies to teach the Onge horticulture and pig-rearing have not met with any great success. But their food habits have changed in as much as they have taken to tea, tobacco, rice, wheat flour, condiments salt, sugar etc. They have also started wearing clothes like pants & shirts and saris and blouses. The concept of personnel belongings has been extended with new consumer items being added. They have also become wage earners on the officially organised plantations and can buy new consumer items at their own cooperative store.

However with all the changes-both material and at the level of ideas - the Onge society is making an effort to adjust to these as best as possible. They continue to be a viable community with social and cultural fibre intact. But the demographic factor is of overriding importance. With a population of 101 it is very vulnerable in terms of its capacity to survive.

The Jarawa, occupying the western coastal and forest regions of South and Middle Andaman remained aloof for 116 years after the establishment of the settlement at Port Blair in Sourth Andaman. In fact, they occasionally suffered casualties during punitive expeditions sent against them during the British regime and in return attacked the settlers whenever they got an opportunity. Obviously having observed the sad fate of the other Great Andaman tribes they decided to remain aloof from the settlement. Their decision to positively respond to our friendly gestures in 1974 must have been a conscious decision taken after considerable thought. It is interesting to observe that the Jarawa, in spite of all the aggression mounted against them in the past and their aloofness that kept them away fromm all kinds of "welfare measures" seem to have survived better. Their state of health is better, their fertility intact and their society following its traditional hunting-gathering pattern of existence, is not suffering from any feelings of trauma or crisis as seen among the Onge and the Great Andamanese. They still kill any intruders that may venture into their forest reserves but also meet the official parties on their occasional visits in a most friendly manner. They do show curiosity for but do not yet feel over-awed by our technology or life-style. They very gladly accept our gifts of coconuts, bananas, iron pieces etc. and sometimes give us small gifts of their neclaces, armbands etc., and sometimes give us small gifts of accounts, bananas, iron pieces etc. and sometimes give us small gifts of their necklaces, armbands etc in return.

The Sentinelese of North Sentinel island continueto remain aloof as they are yet suspicious about our friendly overtures. However, they do not mind accepting gits of coconuts, bananas, iron pieces etc., if deposited on the beach at a safe distance from where they are standing. So they remain a community which has the least contact with the outside world. The Jarawa and the Sentinelese remain two of the well known hunting-gathering communities in the world.

The settlers' attitude towards the Jarawa and the Sentinalese is governed by their perception of their own self interest. We may briefly discuss some of the important points:

The Jarawa, as they live adjacent to the settler's settlements, are often looked upon as a serious hinderence to the exploitation of the forest and sea-resources in that area. It has even been suggested that the area be dereserved and free access allowed to all. They further make a great noise about the "hositlity" of the Jarawa and demand posting of strong police forces for their own protection. Sometimes there are requests for issue of arms to the settlers themselves to deal with the Jarawa.

The timber lobby has an eye on the unexploited timber resources of the Jarawa reserve and keep instigating the settlers etc for opening up the area. Some settlers also greedily eye the land area of 640 sq. kms. that the Jarawa occupy for expansion purposes of the settlement or for rice cultivation. But the Government is firm on keeping the Jarawa forest reserve very much intact and to ensure the latters' protection.

However the long standing demand of the settlers for the completion of the Andaman trunk road (north to South Andaman) running through the Jarawa territory has since been conceded. But number of safeguards to minimise any inconvenience to the Jarawa are to be implemented. The completion of the trunk road will take several years yet.

The situation with regard to the Sentinelese is not the same as they live on a separate island altogether. North Sentinel Island is the exclusive home of the Sentinelese. Except for some poachers with their boats and official parties nobody visits this area. However, who can tell about the future?. Demands for usable land can lead to the kind of developments that have occurred with the Onge in Little Andaman and the kind of demands being voiced by the vocal sections of the settlers in the Andaman Islands.

Reference List

Census of India (1931) Andaman and Nicobar Islands, vol. II Calcutta.

Devore I (1971) The Evolution of Human Society. In Man and Beast Comparative Social Behavious. I. Eibl-Eibesfeldt in The Biology of Peace and War, 1979, London, 129

Eibl-Eibesfeldt I (1979) The Biology of Peace and War, London, 129-187

Mouat FJ (1863) Adventures and Researches among the Andaman Islanders, London

Murdoch GP (1960) "How culture changes" in Man Culture and Society ed. H.L. Shafiro, New York, 247-260

Pandit TN (1972) "Tribes of Andaman and Nicobar Islands. In Tribal situation in India ed. K.S.Singh, Simla, 239-259

———(1985) The tribals and the non tribals in the Andaman Islands: a historical perspective. J Ind Anthrop Soc 20: 111-131

FOURTEEN

ROLE OF NUTRITION IN PHYSICAL GROWTH AND DEVELOPMENT

J.C. Sharma

Nutrition is of prime concern to all living organisms. The quality and quantity of food available play an important role in determining the health and well-being of individuals and populations. Its application involve physical, social, biological and medical sciences. In the field of anthropology it occupies an important place not only because of its relevance to human survival, but also because of its very wide connotation and great many applications. These encompass from food production, procurement and consumption, socio-economic institutions, cultural practices and beliefs associated with food to biological needs of food, nutritional deficiencies affecting growth and development, fertility, mortality, morbidity, health and disease, nutritional variations as a means as well as consequence of adaptation, natural selection and in short the whole process of biological evolution. Such a wide scope of nutrition can justifiably call for designing a full course on nutritional anthropology and a much wider discussion on the topic which however, is beyond the scope of the present paper. In Indian context such an exercise is more relevant and more challenging in view of its great ethnic and geographic diversity coupled with poverty, ingnorance, superstition, where food habits are governed by religious and other ideological considerations more than mere availability of food. It is, therefore, necessary to evolve a multidisciplinary approach to the study of nutritional anthropology.

One of the major areas of nutrition, with which we are presently concerned, is intimately connected with health and well being of the people. It goes without saying that healthy people are a nation's most valuable asset on whom rests the nation's future. Children of today are the citizens of tomorrow who will man different walks of national life. The calibre of each of them will depend on their state of physical and mental growth. It is now well established that the course that a body and mind take to grow is determined by heredity but to a large extent influenced by environmental factors particularly nutrition.

It is also well known, or perhaps not so well known, that for proper physical and mental growth, appropriate and adequate nutrition is necessary besides particular genetic make up which will ensure proper metabolization of nutrients. Individuals differ in their morphology because of their different genetic make up and therefore different metabolic activity. Similarly some individuals may need more nutrition while others need less to achieve a similar morphology. Nutritional needs for energy expenditure vary with age, sex, weight, body proportions, hormonal and physical activity. Table 14.1 shows the energy expenditure per hour of a 70 kilogram man doing different types of activity.

TABLE 14.1

Activity	K Calories/hour
Sleeping	65
Awake lying still	77
Sitting at rest	100
Standing relaxed	105
Dressing & undressing	118
Tailoring	135
Type writing rapidly	140
Light excercise	170
Walking slowly (4.2 Km per hour)	200
Carpentry, metal working, industrial painting	240
Active exercise	290
Severe exercise	450
Sawing wood	480
Swimming	500
Running (8.5 Km/hour)	570
Very severe exercise	600
Walking very fast (8.5 km/hour)	650
Walking up stairs	1100

From Guyton, A.C. Text book of medical physiology 5th Ed. Philadelphia W.B. Saunders Co. 1976. Data compiled by Prof. M.S.Rose.

According to Villee (1977), if a person remains in bed for 24 hours and receives nourishment he will expend about 1800 kilo-calories and additional 200 kilo-calories for the movement of muscles of digestive tract, the synthesis and secretion of the digestive juices and the active up take of the products of digestion. A person living a sedentary life uses about 2500 kilo-calories per day and one doing heavy physical work may expend 6000 or more kilo-calories per day. Most adults achieve a balance between the intake and utilization of calories and their weight remains remarkably constant for years. There is a tendency for middle-aged people to gain weight because physical activity but not appetite decreases with age. An excess of only 10 kilo-calories per day over the energy requirement would lead to an increase in weight of about one kilogram in the course of a year. When the calorie intake is less than the daily energy requirement, the body must draw upon its stored materials. The first to be used are the carbohydrates, stored as glycogen in the liver and muscles. Next fat is withdrawn from strorage in fat deposits of the body and metabolized to supply energy. An average adult male has about 9 kilogram and average adult female about 11 kilograms of stored fat (about 15 per cent & 21 per cent respectively of the total body weight). The calories from the stored fat can supply energy for five to seven weeks of life. During prolonged starvation the cells metabolize their own enzymes and structural proteins, first from the skeletal muscles and then from the heart, internal organs and brain untill death occurs (Villae 1977).

Understanding of nutritional needs of adults is important not only because healthy people are more efficient and more productive in the national economic growth but also they are capable of producing healthy progeny who in turn will growup to become healthy adults. Also, the nutritional status of adults is an index of nutritional status of a community and by comparison with normal or standards can bring out nutritional deficiencies in the population due either to inadequate or inappropriate diet or due to ecological, ideological, socio-economic or epidemiological factors.

Assessment of Nutritional Status

Nutritional status of an individual or a community can be assessed in a variety of ways depending upon the resources and circumstances, which include dietary and deficiency sign surveys, biochemical tests and application of anthropometry. Acute nutritional deficiency particularly protein deficiency can be revealed by the incidence of Kwashiorkor, nutritional marasmus, stigmata healed rickets in the form of bossing of the forehead, pigeon shaped chest, Harrison's sulcus and bowing of legs, bulging bellyes etc. Incidence of Vitamin deficiency such as Vitamin A deficiency manifests in the forms of Xeroses, Bitot's spot, phrynoderma, dry pigmented conjunctiva etc. Vitamin B complex deficiency, manifests signs in the form of angular stomatitis cheilosis, stomatitis, glossitis, swollen & bleeding gums etc. Nutritional deficiency signs should be used alongwith other criteria for these in themselves may at times be misleading because while most of the deficiency signs, particularly due to acute nutritional disorders may manifest clear identifiable symptoms such as those mentioned above but some of these may also be caused by non-nutritional factors. Less acute protein-calorie malnutrition of early childhood which do not manifest any of the easily identifiable symptoms, however, present difficulty in the diagnosis but its prolonged effects can be as disastrous if not more.

Biochemical estimation of nutritional status can be carried out on various body tissues and body fluids but under field conditions, blood and urine which are easily obtainable are most suitable. Haemoglobin estimation can be done with the help of haematocrit and serum, proteins, albumine, Vitamine A, carotene, ascorbic acid and alkaline phosphatase can be estimated from blood plasma. Similarly urine samples can be analysed for urea, thiamine, riboflavin N-methylenicotinamide, iodine etc. These tests can be carried out by using any of the standard techniques prescribed in a book of practical haematology or biochemistry with minimum laboratory requirement. The results of blood and urine analysis for various constituents can be compared with standard results age and sex-wise and nutritional status of an individual may be assessed in terms of levels of essential nutrients present or absent in the blood and urine. Inadequate levels of essential nutrients may indicate malnutrition. However, it may not be possible to find out whether this inadequacy of nutrients is due to inadequate diet or is due to poor absorption or defective metabolic utilization; but that really does not make any difference for in either case an individual is labelled as malnourished.

Another simple method of assessing nutritional status is the application of nutritional anthropometry. Since various physical dimensions of the body are considerably influenced by nutrition particularly in the rapidly growing periods of infancy and early childhood, any departure from normalcy can easily be detected. Some of the more sensitive body measurements such as weights, chest circumference, head circumference, upper-arm circumference and their ratios among themselves and with body length or stature together with subcutaneous fat and muscle development serve as useful indicators of nutritional status.

The need and the urgency for assessing nutritional status is governed by the vulnerability of an individual or a group towards nutritional needs. For example, expectant mothers, infants and children, adolescents, sick and the deprived have their own needs and therefore have their priorities.

Nutrition of expectant and lactating mothers and the newborn

Nutritional needs of expectant mothers and the new borns is of particular importance in the context of physical growth and development. The need for adequate and appropriate nutrition begins, even before the child is born. In this regard maternal nutrition is of importance since it is known to be one of the important environmental factors in the course of foetal growth. Expectant mother's nutritional needs increase progressively with the advancing pregnancy. Due to many profound metabolic alternations during pregnancy and also due to increase in the basal metabolic rate, the woman requires more calories, proteins, minerals and vitamins. Studies have shown that impaired material nutrition can increase the incidence of congenital malformations and intrauterine deaths and may result in reduction in birth weight.

Various surveys, Toverud et al. (1957), Burke et al. (1943), Sen (1954), Gopalan (1958), Belavady (1963), Ramachandran (1966) and Raman (1980) have revealed a close association between nutritional status and health of the pregnant woman and that of her offspring. Those mothers who had good diet, enjoyed superior physical conditions during pregnancy; their babies also enjoyed good health. While others who had poor diets had a higher number of complications of pregnancy such as miscarriage, premature birth, still birth, and toxemia and the babies who were born alive were in poor state of growth. It has been estimated by the WHO expert committee on nutrition (1962) that the increased energy cost is approximately 150 calories per day during the last half of pregnancy. The I.C.M.R. (1966) recommended daily allowance for calories for the last half of the pregnancy is 300 more calories than for the non-pregnant woman (Table 14.2). Besides calories, additional protein is also required in the mother's diet so as to provide for the growth and maintenance of the foetus. It has been estimated that an additional 900 to 950 grams of protein is needed for each pregnancy (WHO Report 1965). Similarly the need for minerals such as calcium, iron and iodine and vitamines A, B12, C and D are also increased during pregnancy.

During lactation, the nutritional needs of the mother are even greater than during pregnancy. The process of milk production is known to increase the need for all nutrients i.e., calories, proteins, minerals, vitamins and water. The extent of the increase depends to some extent on the mother's past diet, history. The stores of nutrients built up in her body during pregnancy her dietary pattern and the physical activity (Mc Divitt and Mudambi 1973). The energy need of the nursing mother is affected by the need for her daily work, the glandualar activity of milk production and the energy value of the milk secreted. It is estimated that 1000 food calories are required to produce 600 calories of human milk (WHO nutritional committee report 1957). Venkatachalam and Rebello (1966) have worked out the diets to meet the needs of pregnant women and nursing mothers. These are given in Table 14.2.

Average dietary intake of a woman belonging to a low income group is deficient in both quality and quantity. Table 14.2 gives the average intake of women in India as compared to recommended allowances of WHO and ICMR. Main deficit is seen in energy intake and important nutrients like calcium, vitamin A, iron and folic acid (Hytten and Leiteh 1972). The results of the deficient intake in the mothers are poor weight gain in pregnancy, anaemia and poor sense of being-well. These women are also prone to high incidence of complications during pregnancy such as toxemia, antepartum hemorrhage, premature delivery and infections (Raman 1980).

Anselmino (1954) has found that temporary condition of undernutrition which prevailed in European Countries during and after the second World War resulted in significant reduction in birth weight but a very slight shortening of the body length. He also found that undernutrition of mother leads to shortening of average duration of pregnancy. According to Anselmino (1954) it is the nutritional condition of the mother during the last three months of pregnancy which is of decisive importance in regard to the reduction of the weight of the new born, as during this priod the foetus gains over half of its weight. Halbrecht (1954) studied the importance of animal protein in the diet of pregnant mothers. He found that even when calorific requirements of the body are fully supplied, the reduction of animal protein during pregnancy, causes significant diminution in the birth weight. Burke et al. (1943) also arrived at a similar conclusion. According to them not only is the general growth of the foetuses is stunted but also they may be born with damaged liver caused by maternal protein deficiency. Ramachandran's studies conducted at the National Institute of Nutrition indicate that women from low-income group subsist on diets inadequate

TABLE 14.2
Actual Intake and recommended dietary allowances in Indian pregnant women

	Calories (K cal)	Protein (mg)	Calcium (mg)	Vitamin A (ug)	Ascorbic Acid (mg)	Iron (mg)	Folic Acidug
Actual Intake							
India*	1400-1800	38-42	300	304	30	18	-
Recommended allowance, WHO							
Pregnant	2200+350	55.5**	1000-1200	750	30	14-28	400
Lactating	2200+550	55+10**	1000-1200	1200	30	14-28	300
Recommended Allowances. ICMR (1977)							
Pregnant	2500	55**	1000	750	30	40	300
Lactating	2900	65**	1000	1100	50	30	150

* ICMR Bulletin, vol 7, 1977
** Protein with NPU of 70, caloric requirement fully met with (Source: Raman 1980)

to meet the nutritional needs even in the non-pregnant state. There was no significant increase in dietary intake of women during pregnancy and lactation. Diet surveys undertaken among women who had conceived during lactation indicate that there is no increment in their dietary intake either. The average dietary intake was below requirement and the diet was deficient with respect to all nutrients including vitamins and minerals (Ramachandran 1986). Dual stress of pregnancy and lactation has been found to further widen the already wide nutritional gap between actual dietary intake of nutrient requirements in women from low income groups. This may obviously leave expectant mothers more susceptible to infectious diseases and the outcome of pregnancy may have low birth weight.

Nutrition of Infants and Children

The period from birth to six months is a period of rapid growth of the infants and therefore a period of high nutritional requirement per unit body weight. During this period an infant requires more than twice as many calories per kg. of body weight as an adult man doing heavy work. A healthy well-fed infant, doubles its birth weight during the first six months. During the period between six months and tweleve months the rate of growth of body weight slows down so that by the end of one year the weight has increased to slightly less than three times the birth weight. First year of an infant's life is by far the most crucial period. Baby has not only to be provided with adequate and appropriate food but also has to be protected against infection to which a new born is most vulnerable. For this, breast feeding is by far the best means to provide, appropriate nutrition as well as protection against infection. During first three or four days mother does not secrete milk but instead a yellowish fluid called Colostrum which is the first baby food and contains certain vital nutrients and also provides valuable material which helps the baby to develop immunity against many infectious diseases. During the first four to six months the body's nutritional requirements can be met entirely through mother's milk, provided mother has normal lactation and remains free of disease. Nutritional value of mother's milk irrespective of socioeconomic groups is more or less identical. Gopalan (1957) has found that up to six months of age the growth rate of Indian babies, even those of poorly fed mothers is comparable to that of babies in countries where food is plentiful. However, any change from breast feeding to bottle feeding in early infancy can expose a child to both malnutrition and infection, even in affluent groups of people where the need for supplementary food (besides breast milk), after four to six months is not fully understood.

UNICEF's 1984 report on the condition of the world's children says that lack of food in early childhood is one reason for malnutrition, but there are other equally important causes. Intestinal parasites can cause malnutrition by consuming upto 25% of a child's calories intake. Changing from breast feeding to bottle feeding in early infancy can expose a baby to both malnutrition and infection at the same time. Ignorance about the supplementary foods (in addition to breast milk) from about the fourth to six months onwards, leads to almost certain malnutrition. And lack of knowledge about a child's special nutritional needs and how to meet them can cause malnutrition even in households where adequate food is always available. But the most important cause of all is infection which causes malnutrition by consuming the body's energy by reducing the body's absorption of food due to draining away of nutrients through diarrhoea or vomiting and by depressing the appetite so that the child does not want to eat at all. In fact the relative importance of infection and poor diet is less important than the truely deadly alliance between them if a child is malnourished, infection is both more likely and more severe. Children with even moderate malnutrition are three times as likely to get diarrhoeal infection and ten times more likely to die from an infection like measles. Conversly a child with an infection is also more likely to become malnourished. Frequent diarrhoeal infections can cut a child's growth rate to half and measles can take away upto 10% of a child's body weight. It is this vicious cycle of malnutrition and infection which is constantly assaulting the growth of such children. If such assaults are too frequent in early childhood then not only the growth slows down considerably but also the child is not able to achieve its full genetic potential of body and mind.

Since major part of growth of the brain takes place in the last few weeks of intra uterine period and the first year after birth, not only child cannot afford to suffer from any malnutrition or infection during this period but also steps should be taken well in advance to check its manifestation in any form which may ultimately affect the growth of the brain.

Head circumfrence has been used as a measure of brain growth during the first year of life. Normal brain growth has been studied by determining the increase in cell number (total organ DNA) and in weight protein and RNA per cell (weight/DNA, protein/DNA, RNA/DNA). Total weight protein and RNA increase linearly through the first year of life. DNA content begins to level off around birth and ceases to increase by six months (Wenik & Rosso 1969). Thus there is a very little increase in total number of brain cells after six months of age, with subsequent brain growth, explainable by an increase in weight, protein and RNA per cell. In children who died of malnutrition during first year of life, weight, protein, RNA and DNA were all proportinately reduced. Thus cell division is curtailed during severe early malnutrition and the resultant brain contains fewer cells than normal. The effect of moderate to severe malnutrition in infancy and early childhood have also been demonstrated by comparing the head circumference with chest circumference. In normal infants at birth head circumfrence is larger than the chest circumference. In well nourished infants in general chest circumference overtakes the head circumference much before they are one year old. In Indian population generally the crossing over of the graphs of chest circumfrence and head circumference takes place around one year of life. In undernourished and malnourished children from the rural and tribal areas and even those from the higher socio-economic groups of urban areas where children do not eat well despite availability of food and suffer from frequent infections, this crossing over is delayed by six months to two years or even more (Sharma 1982, 1935) depending upon the extent and duration of malnutrition. Sood and Kapil (1984) analysed the anthropometric data on pre-school children using different criteria of malnutrition such as weight for age, height for age, weight for height, body-mass index (BMI) (weight/height^2) and arm circumference/head circumference. They concluded that BMI had high sensitivity, specificity and predictability in detecting malnutrition in the children of a community (see table 14.3).

Weight for age or length for age tables are also useful to know whether a child has reached a right weight or length for age and whether the child is growing properly. Similarly one can know from the arm circumference, for age graphs, that a healthy well-fed child has bigger arm circumference than the one who is underfed or who does not want to eat despite plenty of food in the house. The level of malnutrition of a child or a group of children can be judged by comparison with the four 10% levels below the standards i.e., 90% - 81%, 80% - 71%, 70% - 61%, 60% & below. Gomez et al. (1955) have termed young children between 90% & 70% of the standards as falling in the first degree of malnutrition, between 75% & 60% as second degree and 60% and below as third degree. Ford (1964) has suggested that 66% of the standard weight should be regarded as malnutritional line. By following these classifications one can measure the nutritional status of children in a population. Downs (1964) has pointed out that children with nutritional dwarfing are light in weight and relatively of normal body proportions and are erroneously taken for healthy

TABLE 14.3

Various criteria used to define nutritional status in pre-school children

Index	Normal	Mild	Moderate	Severe
1. Weight for age Indian Academy of peditrics (1974)	80% & above	70-80%	60-70%	60%
2. Weight for height (Shakir 1972)	90% & above	80-90%	70-80%	70%
3. Height for age (Shakir 1972)	95% & above	90-95%	85-90%	85%
4. Midarm circumfrence (Shakir 1972)	13.5 & above	13.5 cm	12.5 cm	12.5cm.
5. Kanawati & Mclaren Index (1970) (Arm-circumfrence/Head circumfrence.	0.31 & above cms	0.280-0.310	0.250-0.279	0.250
6. Body mass Index (BMI) weight/height^2 (Rao 1920)	15.0 & above			15.0

Source : Sooc and Kapil (1984)

children. This condition has been observed in most of the Indian population in general but in economically weaker sections and the tribal populations in particular (Sharma 1982). That is why weight for height measurement, has little usefulness in judging the nutritional status of a community. Like body length, the head circumference has also been found to be least affected due to malnutrition, since major part of growth of head has already taken place by the first year of post natal life i.e., long before the crucial period of under-nutrition due to change over from breast feeding to semi-solid or solid diet begins in the life of the infants. However, head circumference has been found to be affected in severe malnutrition i.e., 3rd or 4th category of malnutrition with or without clinical signs of nutritional marasmus or kwashiorkor. It has been reported by several workers that malnutrition especially protein deficiency during the first six months of life leads to underweight of the brain and its low DNA contents. Thus the reduction in the head circumference in children due to malnutrition is indicative of under development of brain. Scientists have long suspected such a link between mental retardation and inadequate protein intake. This has now been confirmed and is amply visible not only in the poor growth of body but also in the form of general inertia and low intelligence even in the later life. Someshwara Rao et al. (1959) have studied the heights and weights of children from four South Indian States where protein malnutrition is highly prevalent. Comparison with Western children showed that even the lowest percentile for American children were considerably higher than the average curve for the South Indian children. Indian children derived from previleged communities and who enjoyed adequate nutrition on the other hand were found to be almost as tall and heavy as their American counterparts of the same age (N.I.N. 1970, Datta Banik et al. 1972). Slum dewellers of Chandigarh with low protein and low calorie diet and those children from high socio-economic group who did not eat well, throughout childhood were found to lie at or below third percentile of normal Chandigarh children for their height, weight, chest circumference and upper arm circumference (Sharma 1985.)

Malnutrition and undernutrition have also been found to affect the physical growth and sexual and skeletal maturity through adolescence. Tanner (1955) reported delay in appearance of growth spurt as a conseqence of under-nutrition brought about by famine associated with war. In Central Indian tribals where near famine conditions are chronic feature, the adolescent growth spurt is poorly defined and menarche is delayed (Sharma 1980). Satyanarayana and Naidu (1979) while reporting on nutrition and menarche in Rural Hyderabad also found that menarche in under-nourihsed girls was delayed. It was, however, not possible to find out whether this delay in the pubertal spurt and menarche was due to erstwhile or current nutritional status or both.

Reference List

Ankegowada K, Devi S (1976) Indian Pediatrics XII

Anselmino KJ (1954) Proc Internat Cong Obst & Gynaec, Geneva

Aykroyd WR, Gopalan C, Balasubramaniam SC (1966) ICMR special report series 42

Banik, Datta, Mayar S, Krishnan R, Raj L, Tasker AD (1972) Indian Pediatrics IX

Belavady B (1963) Studies on human lactation ICMR special report series 45

Burke BA, Harding VV, Sturt HC (1943) J Pediat 23

Downs EF (1964) Amer J Clin Nutr 15

Ford FJ (1964) J Trop Pediat 10

Gomez F, Galvan RR, Craviato J, Frenk S (1955) Advances in pediatrics in: Levine S (ed) Year Book Publishes. New York Vol 7

Gopalan C (1957) J Trop Pediat 3

Gopalan C (1961) National research council publication 843

Halbrecht I (1954) Proc Internet Cong Obst & Gynaec, Geneva

Hytten FE, Leitch I (1972) Physiology of juman pregnancy Blackwell Scientific Publication. Oxford

ICMR (1966) Special report series 41

Jelliffe DB (1966) The assessment of the nutritional status of community, WHO, Geneva

Kanavati, Mc Laven BS (1970) Nature 228

Mc Divitt ME, Mudambi SR (1973) Human nutrition principles and applications in India. Prentice Hall. New Delhi

NIN (1970) Annual report of national institute of nutrition

Raman L (1980) Indian Pediatrics 47

Ramachandran P (1986) Nutrition news national institute of nutrition, Hyderabad 7

Rao V, Singh SK (1970) J Clin Nutr 23

Satyanarayana K, Naidu N (1979) Ann Hum Biol 6

Sen NC (1956) J Ind Med Assoc 27

Shakir A (1972) Lancet II: 143-146

Sharma JC (1980) Proc Internet Symp Hum Biol. Ranchi

Sharma JC (1982) Bull Soci Bionet. Bhopal

Sharma JC (1985) Unpublished

Someshwara Rao K, Swaminathan MC, Swarup S, Patwardhan VN (1959) Bull Wld Hlth Org 20

Sood AK, Kapil U (1984) Indian Pediatrics 21

Tanner JM (1955) Growth at adolescence. Blackwell. Oxford

Toverud KU, Steams G, Macy IG (1957) Bull No 123. Nat Res Coun Nat Acd Sci. Washington

UNICEF (1980) Report on the condition of world children

Venkatachalam PA, Rebello LM (1966) Nutrition for mother and child. ICMR special report series 41

Villae Claude A (1977) Biology. W R Saunders Company. London

Warkany J (1944) (c f.Ankegowada, Devi S 1976)

WHO (1957) Nutrition ccmmittee report

WHO (1962) Report of expert committee on nutrition

WHO (1965) Expert Committee report on pregnancy and lactation. Wld Hlth Org Tech Rep Ser

Winik M, Rosso P (1969) J Pediat 74

FIFTEEN

PHYSIQUE AND BODY COMPOSITION OF INDIAN FEMALE PLAYERS

L. S. Sidhu, R. Mokha

Variations in the human body size, shape and body composition are of great significance in the field of sports. The morphological characteristics of athletes vary from one sport to another. The components of body composition i.e., the lean body mass and the body fat are also different in different games. Physical training generally produces an increase in lean body mass and a corresponding decrease in body fat, quite frequently without any appreciable change in body weight (Parizkova 1963, 1968; Dobeln and Eriksson 1972). The magnitude of change, however, varies with the intensity and duration of the training regimen.

Relationship between the physique and the components of body composition with the physical performance has been studied by many researchers (Malina and Shoup 1985; Wells et al. 1962, 1963; Malina and Rarick 1973; Godin 1920; Yuhasz, 1977, 1982, 1985; Tanner 1964; Eiben 1981; Conger and Macnab 1967; Gladden & Colacino 1978; Hosler et al. 1978; Malina 1983; Malina and Zavaleta 1976; Meleski et al. 1982; Morrow et al. 1979; Mokha and Sidhu, 1986; Sidhu et al. 1984; Sidhu and Grewal 1983, 1984; Grewal and Sidhu 1983). Changes in the aspects of physique and body composition, as a result of training, are usually most apparent in body parts specifically trained. Grewal(1983) studied the effects of participation in athletics training and reported the female throwers to be the biggest in size as compared with the other categories of players. They possess broadest shoulders and longest upper extremities relative to stature and they are the stoutest as indicated by the ponderal index. The jumpers possess most muscular calves and minimum amount of body fat. The runners are the lighest and the leanest among all the female athletes as indicated by the ponderal index. Eiben (1980) studied the Hungarian national female players of volleyball and reported them to be tall (174.8 cm) and 64.28 kg heavy with proportionally long lower extremities, wide trunks and muscular upper arms.

Several studies on national and olympic gymnasts have shown them to be exceptionally high in mesomorphy as compared with other groups of female athletes (Hirata 1966; Carter 1970; Sinning and Lindberg 1972). In addition, their percentage of body fat is very low. Female gymnasts have been described as basically small, neat ecto-mesomorphs (Plowman 1974).

In India, little research has been done on female players (Sidhu et al. 1984; De et al. 1980; Sidhu and Grewal 1980; Sidhu and Singhal 1981; Grewal and Sidhu 1983; Sidhu and Grewal 1982, 1983, 1984; Mokha and Sidhu 1986; Singh and Debnath 1986). In the present study an attempt has been made to study the physique and body composition of Indian female players of basketball, volleyball and hockey.

Materials and Method

The present study has been conducted on 121 Indian female players of basketball (25), volleyball (47) and hockey (49).

All the players were of the state level i.e., representatives of different states in the national level competition. The data have been collected from the various training camps held at Netaji Subhas National Institute of Sports, Punjabi University, Govt. College of Physical Education, Patiala and also from the All India Women Sports Festival, held at Calcutta. Nine anthropometric measurements were taken on each subject by following the standard techniques of Weiner & Lourie (1969). The antropometric measurements taken were: Body weight, stature, sitting height, upper extremity length, lower extremity length, biceps, triceps, subscapular and suprailiac skinfolds. Anthropometric somatotype method (Heath and Carter 1967)was applied for calculating the somatotype ratings of the subjects. The total body fat (%) was calculated by using the formula of Durnin and Womersley (1974).

Statistical parameters like mean and standard deviation were calculated and 't' test was applied to compare the magnitude of difference between the players of different games.

Results and Discussion

Table 15.1 gives the mean values of various parameters of

TABLE 15.1
Mean and Standard deviations of various parameters of the players of different games.

	Basketball		Volleyball		Hockey		Controls	
	Mean	S.D.	Mean	S.D.	Mean	S.D.	Mean	+S.D.
Weight (Kg)	52.48	5.54	53.21	5.39	52.15	7.04	46.31	5.89
Stature(cm)	161.64	5.92	162.14	5.64	158.25	4.68	156.64	5.23
Sitting height(cm)	85.58	2.99	83.53	2.15	82.87	2.23	82.37	2.87
Upper extremity length (cm)	71.09	3.06	70.82	3.86	70.07	2.73	69.01	2.77
Lower extremity length (cm)	76.06	4.57	78.61	4.76	75.37	3.28	74.27	3.19
Endomorphy	3.38	0.85	3.71	1.08	3.37	1.03	4.25	1.28
Mesomorphy	3.20	0.61	3.15	0.63	3.53	0.89	2.88	0.76
Ectomorphy	3.38	1.16	2.97	0.87	2.58	0.98	3.41	1.35
Body Fat (%)	22.46	3.18	22.76	3.82	21.95	3.92	24.81	4.27
Lean body mass (%)	77.54	3.18	77.24	3.82	78.05	3.92	75.19	4.27

the players of different games. It is observed from the table that the players of all the three games are taller and heavier than the controls. The former also possess bigger trunks, longer, upper and lower extremities than the latter. When we study these differences statistically it is observed that all the differences are significant for basketball players except for the lower extremity length; in volleyball players the differences are significant for weight, height and lower extremity length, whereas, the hockey players do not differ much from the controls as the difference is only significant for weight.

The players of all the games showed more mesomoprphic character than the controls. The controls, on the other hand showed more endomorphic and ectomorphic features. In statistical terms, the basketball players are significantly less endomorphic and more mesomorphic; the hockey players are less endomorphic, less ectomorphic and more mesomorphic than the controls, whereas the volleyball players do not differ statistically from the controls as far as these three components are concerned.

Players of all the categories possess less amount of body fat and more amount of lean tissue than the controls, however, the differences are significant for basketball and hockey players. The volleyball players do not differ significantly from their respective controls.

When we compare the players of different games among themselves, it is observed that the volleyball players are the tallest and heaviest, followed by the basketball players and the hockey players (Table 15.1). In statistical terms, the volleyball players are significantly heavier than basketball players, who are significantly heavier than hockey players. The basketball players and the volleyball players do not differ significantly as far as their height is concerned but both of them are significantly taller than the hockey players. The tall stature of volleyball players is mainly attributed to the longer, lower extremities whereas, in basketball players the trunk length is the main contributing factor. The basketball players possess longest upper extremities, followed by volleyball and hockey players. The basketball and volleyball players possess bigger trunks, longer, upper and lower extremities than the hockey players. Statistically speaking the basketball players possess significantly bigger trunks than the volleyball players and hockey players. The basketball players and the volleyballs possess significantly longer, lower extremities than the hockey players. The basketball players possess significantly longer upper extremities than the hockey players (Table 15.2).

TABLE 15.2

The values of 't' for the mean values of different measures of physique between the players of various games and their controls

	Basketball	Volleyball	Hockey
Weight	4.82*	4.71*	4.06*
Stature	3.80*	3.70*	1.57
Sitting height	4.79*	1.90	0.97
Upper extreity length	3.05*	1.83	1.83
Lower extremity length	1.84	3.82*	1.59
Endomophy	3.95*	1.83	3.73*
Mesomorphy	2.19*	1.57	3.63*
Ectomorphy	0.11	1.70	3.54
Body fat	2.47*	1.76	3.17*
Lean body mass	2.47*	1.76	3.17

* Significant at 5% level.

The players do not differ significantly among themselves as far as the endomorphic component is concerned. The hockey players are most mesomorphic and the difference is significant between volleyball and hockey players. The basketball players are most ectomorphic, followed by volleyball and hockey players and the differences are significant between the basketball/hockey and volleyball/hockey players(Table 15.3) .

TABLE 15.3

The values of 't' for the mean values of different meausres of physique between the players of different games.

	B'Ball/ V'ball	B'Ball/ Hockey	V'Ball/ Hockey
Weight	2.32*	2.19*	0.30
Stature	1.17	4.27*	3.69*
Sitting height	2.39*	3.79*	1.21
Upper extremity length	1.27	2.68*	1.51
Lower extremity length	0.14	3.35*	3.82*
Endomorphy	0.23	0.91	1.19
Mesomorphy	1.09	0.96	2.16
Ectomorphy	0.84	2.29*	3.32
Body Fat (%)	0.24	1.62	1.53
L.B.M. (%)	0.24	1.62	1.53

* significant at 5% level.

The hockey players possess minimum amount of body fat (21.95%) and maximum amount of lean tissue (78.05%), followed by basketball (22.46% & 77.54%) and volleyball (22.76% & 77.24%) players respectively; though the differences are statistically non-significant.

Thus it is concluded from the above discussion that the basketball players are tall, heavy with biggest trunks, longest upper extremities, long, lower extremities and most ectomorphic players. The volleyball players are the tallest, heaviest with bigger trunks, longer, upper extremities and longest, lower extremities. The hockey players are of medium height, smaller trunks, medium size upper and lower extremities, most mesomorphic and least endomorphic and ectomorphics.

Comparison with other studies

Basketball

The basketball players of the present study are taller and heavier as compared with the female basketball players studied by De et al. (1980). The latter are 160.5 cm tall and 49.6 kg heavy and represent Andhra Pradesh, Bihar, Goa, Maharashtra, Madhya Pradesh, Rajasthan and West Bengal; while the former are mainly from the Punjab state. However, Indian players are significantly shorter and lighter by 11.33 cm and 15.80 kg respectively than the top-level American women basketball players (Vaccaro et al. 1979) and 11.36 cm shorter and 18.72 kg lighter than the female USSR basketball players (Heath, 1970). Sinning & Adrian (1968), Mc Ardle et al. (1971) and Sinning (1973) examined College women basketball players and found their mean heights ranging from 165.3 cm to 169.1 cm and mean weights ranging from 62 kg to 65.2 kg, which is much more than those of our players.

Eiben (1980) reported a detailed anthropometric data for 30 members of the Hungarian national female basketball team. They are significantly taller (176.63 cm), heavier (67.18 kg) with bigger trunks (91.43 cm), longer, lower (99.80 cm) and upper extremities (75.80), as compared with our state level players.

Finally, when we compare the players of the present study with the Montreal Olympic basketball players who were 177.0 cm tall and 70.0 kg heavy (Hirata 1979), it is observed that our players are much shorter (15.36 cm) and lighter (17.52 kg) than their Olympic counterparts.

From the foregoing discussion, it is evident that the players at higher level of performance are tall, heavy with long trunks and upper extremities. As the level of competition goes on increasing from lower to higher levels the process of selection, with particular reference to the bodily characteristics, is also at work, with the result, those players who do not possess requisite physique are being eliminated at lower levels. This is perhaps one of the reasons why Indian team in basketball could not go up to Olympic level because our players are much below the standards of physique of their Olympic counterparts.

Volleyball

The volleyball players of the present study are significantly taller and heavier than the top-level female basketball players from Bihar, studied by De et al. (1979) who are 153.7cm tall and 40.8 kg heavy.

While comparing the national players of the present study with the American college women volleyball players (Hosler et al. 1978) and American national female volleyball players (Gladden and Colacino 1978), it is observed that the American female players are significantly taller (169.92 cm and 172.2 cm respectively) and heavier (65.06 kg and 65.80 kg respectively) than the Indian players.

Spense et al. (1980) reported data for heights and weights of 15 highly skilled members of the 1975 United States Women's Volleyball training team, most of them had performed in International competitions. The heights and weights of these players were 177.80 cm and 67.15 kg respectively which are significantly more than that of our national players.

Several other studies reporting mean ages, heights and weights for selected groups of American female volleyball players, are available. One of these groups was composed of 10 college women volleyball players; the comparative figures for this group were 166 cm and 59.8 kg (Conger and Macnab 1967). The second group included 335 players ranging from high school to open teams 169.11 cm and 61.75 kg. The third group was composed of 19 intercollegiate players: 172.2 cm and 64.1 kg. Indian players are much shorter and lighter than all the above groups of players.

Malina and Shoup (1985) studied anthropometric and physique characteristics of American female Volleyball players at three competitive levels i.e., high school varsity, University and Olympic levels. It is necessary to mention here that the Indian National players are significantly shorter and lighter with smaller trunks than even the American high school female players, which is the lower level of participation in their study. Eiben (1980) reported data for 25 members of the Hungarian National team who are significantly taller (174.75 cm), heavier (64.28 kg) with significantly bigger trunks (90.28 kg), longer, upper (76.58 cm) and lower (99.28 cm) extremities than our national players.

Finally, the comparison of our National players with Olympic female Volleyball players (Hirata 1979), reveals that the former are 8.66 cm shorter and 11.79 kg lighter than the Tokyo Olympic players, 10.86 cm shorter and 15.79 kg lighter than the Munich Olympic players and 12.86 cm shorter and 13.79 kg lighter than the Montreal Olympic women Volleyball players.

Hockey

There are no data available for female hockey Olympians for comparison with the players of the present study.

Reference List

Carter JEL (1970) The somatotypes of athlets a review. Hum Biol 42:535-569

Conger PR, Macnab RBJ (1967) Strength body composition and work capacity of participants and non participants in women's inter collegiate sports. Res Quart 38:104-192

De AK, Debnath PK, Nagchaudhuri J (1979) A comparison of physical efficiency between female volleyball and kabaddi players. SNIPES J 2:46-49

De AK, Debnath P, Debnath PK (1980) Few physiological parameters of the participants in the basketball competition of the IV National sports festival for women 1978-79. Proc of the IXth Annual conference of Indian association of sports medicine. Calcutta. India

Dobeln WV, Eriksson BO (1972) Physical training maximal oxygen uptake and dimensions of the oxygen transporting and metabolizing organs in boys 11-13 years of age. Acta paediatr Scand 61:635-660

Durnin JV, Womersley J (1974)Body fat assessed from total body density and its estimation from skinfold thickness measurements on 481 men & women aged 16-72 years. Brit J Nutr 32:77-97

Eiben OG (1980) Physique of female athlets anthropological and proportional analysis. Proceedings of the inter-national congress on women and sports. July 1980. Rome. Itly

Gladden LB, Colacino D (1978) Characteristics of volleyball

players and success in a national tournment. J Sports Med Phys Fit 18:57-64
Godin P (1920) Growth during school age (translated by SL Roy) Gorham Press. Boston
Grewal R (1983) Physique and body composition of Indian sportswomen with special reference to their level of participation. Thesis, Punjab University, Patiala
Grewal R, Sidhu LS (1983) the selection of female volleyball players with reference to ponderal index. Annali 1:107-112
Heath BH (1970)The somatotypes of athlets a review. Hum Biol 42:535-569
Heath BH, Carter JEL (1967) A modified somatotype method. Amer J Phys Anthrop 27:57-74
Hirata K (1966) Physique and age of Tokyo olympic champions. Sports Med Phys Fit 6:222
Hirata K (1979) Selection of olympic champions. Department of Physical Education, Chukyo University, Toyota, Nagoya, Japan
Hosler WW, Morrow JR, Jackson AS(1978) Strength anthropometric and speed characteristics of college women volleyball players. Res Quart 49:385-388
Malina RM, (1983) Menarche in athlets a synthesis and hypothesis. Ann Hum Biol 10:1-24
Malina RM Rarich GL (1973)Growth physique and motor performance. In : Rarick GL (ed) Physcial Activity: Human growth and development. Academic Press, New York pp125-153
Malina RM, Shoup RF(1985) Anthropometric and physique characteristics of female volleyball players at three competitive levels. In:Eiben OG (ed) Physique and body composition, Budapest, Hungary
Malina RM, A Zavaleta AN (1976) Androgyny of physique female track and field athlets. Ann Hum Biol 3:441-446
Mc Ardle WD, Magel JR, Kyvallos LC (1971) Aerobic capacity heart rate and estimated energy cost during women's competitive basket ball. Res Quat 42:178-186
Maleski BW, Shoup RF, Malina RM (1982) Size physique and body composition of competitive female swimmers 11-20 years of age. Hum Biol 54:609-620
Mokha R, Sidhu LS (1986) Body fat in various sporting groups. J sports Med Phys fit code no 1262
Morrow JR, Jackson AS, Hosler WW, Kachurik JK (1979) The importance of strength speed and body size for team success in women's inter collegiate volleyball. Res Quart 50:429-437
Muthiah CM, Sodhi HS (1980) The effect of training on some morphological parameters of top ranking Indian basketball players. J Sports med Phys Fit 20:405-412
Parizkova J (1963) The impact of age, diet and exercise on man's body composition. Ann N Y Acad Sci 110:661-674

Parizkova J (1968) Body composition and physical fitness. Cur Anthrop 9:273-287

Plowman S (1974) Physilogical characteristics of female athlets, Res Quart 45:349-362

Sidhu LS, Grewal R (1980) Age at menarche in various categories of Indian sportswomen. Brit J Sports Med 14:119-203

Sidhu LS, Grewal R (1982) Relationship of physique and body composition to the performance in the female basketball players. Proc of the International congress of Sports Sciences, NIS, Patiala, India

Sidhu LS, Grewal R (1983)Effect of training on subcutaneous and lean tissues of female volleyball players. Hung Rev Sports Med 25:85-89

Sidhu LS, Grewal R (1984) Effect of training on the cardio-vascular system of Indian women hockey players. J Sports Med Phys Fit 24:37-40

Sidhu LS, Grewal R, Verma SK (1984) Postional differences in physique and body composition among top level Indian women hockey players. J Sports Med Phys Fit 24:337-342

Sidhu LS, Singal P (1981) Relationship between age at menarche and adult morphology in sportswomen. J Sports Med Phys Fit 21:401-406

Sidhu LS, Sodhi HS (1979) Effect of training on subcutaneous tissue of top class Indian hockey players with respect to their field positions. J Sports Med Phys Fit 19:217-223

Singh G, Debnath K (1986) A Study of motor abilities and competitive performance of Indian female gymnasts. SNIPES J 9:1-6

Sinning WE (1973) Body composition cardiorespiratory function and rule changes in women's basketball. Res Quart 44:313-321

Sinning WE, Adrian MJ (1968) Cardiorespiratory changes in college women due to a season of competitive basketall. J Appl Physiol 25:720-724

Sinning WE, Lindberg GD(1972) Physical characteristcs of college age women gymnasts. Res Quart 43:226-234

Spence DW, Disch JG, Fred HL, Coleman AE (1980) Descriptive profiles of highly skilled women vollyball players. Med Sci Sports & Exer 12:299-302

Tanner JM (1964) The physique of the olympic athlete. George Allen & Unwin, London

Vaccaro P, Clarke DH, Wrenn JP (1979) Physiological profiles of elite women basketball players. J Sports Med Phys Fit 19:45-54

Weiner JS, Lourie JA (1969) Human biology a guide to field methods. Blackwell Scientific Publications. Oxford and Edinburg

Wells JB, Parizkova J, Jokl E (1962) The Kentucky physical fitness experiment. J Assoc Phys Ment Rehab 16:69-72

Wells JB, Parizkova J, Jokl E (1963) Growth body composition and physical efficiency. J Assoc Phys Ment Rehab 17:37-40

Yuhasz MS (1977) The body composition and body fat patterning of male and female athlets. In:Eiben OG (ed) growth and development; physique Biol Hung Symposium, Budapest 20:449-457

Yuhasz MS (1982) Body fat patterning of the subcutaneous adipose tissue. Anthrop Kozl 26:163-173

Yuhasz MS (1985) The subcutaneous adipose tissue patterning of olympic athlets in human biologia Budapestinensis. Physique & Body composition, Budapest 16:197-207

SIXTEEN

AUXOLOGICAL ANTHROPOMETRY IN MONITORING POPULATION HEALTH AND NUTRITION

S. Prakash

Health and nutrition are very intimately related aspects of an individual's biology. Both are under the influence of hereditary and environmental factors. Culture, the way of life, living conditions etc., influence them. Monitoring population health and nutrition is not merely a question of taking notice of prevalent diseases, quality and quantity of food but it is a matter of studying the whole ecology and adaptation. It involves the analysis of total parasitic load, total energy flow, reflected by resources, adaptive processes at work, space and the numbers that are to be supported in a particular ecosystem and much more.

Demographic characteristics such as birth rate, morbidity, mortality and life expectancy or longevity etc., are the indicators of population well-being and reflect the efficiency of adaptive mechanisms. These indices which are based on counting the numbers afflicted by sickness and diseases, births and deaths occu- rred and the average life span are undoubtedly strong demo- graphic indices. How much better it would be to find a method capable of issuing almost instantaneous warnings as to whatever is happening to the individuals' and the populations' health and nutrition so that proper remedial action can be initiated well in time. Auxological Anthropometry - the science of measuring the growth and development of human body, affords this possibility. It becomes the most efficient and powerful tool in the hands of an experienced anthropometrist for monitoring the nutrition and health of human populations. Many eminent scientists have written extensively on the application of anthropometry outlining the ways it is to be used for this purpose (Tanner 1976, 1978; Waterlow et al. 1977; Roche 1984; Roche et al. 1981; Zerfas 1975; Zerfas et al. 1977; Wolanski 1979; Bayer and Bayley 1976). Presently, it is attempted to reconsider of these views.

In a most inspiring lecture in our department couple of years ago, Prof. J.M. Tanner of the Institute of Child Health, London, outlined the following three main uses of auxological anthropometry: (a) Pure Science use (b) Medical use (c) Population health use. To these uses, we shall return a little later.

We may pause here briefly to consider simple, often taken for granted, but very important aspect of anthropometry. Osler about a century ago advised his students, "Observe, record, compare and communicate". According to him the art of measuring children is to be learnt by practice, it is not inherited. There is another very important element that in this practice of auxological anthropometry we are dealing with human material. We are not measuring the weight of a bagful of potatoes or we are not measuring the length and breadth of a log of wood - the inert material. In contrast, we deal with human children and adults who are very sensitive to a variety of stimulii to which they react. These reactions, however, may or may not come to surface, i.e., in expression of fear, anger, emotional upsets, withdrawals etc. The anthropometrist, therefore, has to be of amicable, understanding, charming and attractive personality, so that quickly a rapport of confidence is established between the measurer and the measured to be. Social and cultural factors are very important to take care when working in a community-setting. In hospitals, situation is entirely different.

The efficacy and utility of the anthropometric data rest solely on the foundation of methodological quality control, for, I totally agree with Zerfas (1977) that "a measurement poorly performed is usually not worthdoing". "Garbage in garbage out" is the motto of an anthropometrist. So we need to be aware of the problems and errors resulting from the following interactions:

1. Anthropometrist and the subject
2. Anthropometrist and the instrument
3. Subject and instrument

Actual calculation of the reliability of measurements in terms of within measurer error, between measurer error, error of the instrument, will allow correct interpretation of the data. Two other important errors i.e., systemic error and random error must also be minimised for enhancing the quality of measurement data. Systemic errors result from wrong definitions of measurements and incorrect identification of the landmarks. Random errors occur due to faulty positioning of the subject during measurement, wrong measurement technique, reading and recording errors etc. More detailed account of the quality control procedures in population anthropometric surveys can be had from the famous Cuban example (Jordan et al. 1975).

Anthropometry has a long history. It still continues to remain a very sensitive technique which can be utilised for different aims and purposes. Various measurements (Table 16.1) either alone or in combination provide useful information for specific aims, e.g., the study of the pattern and tempo of child growth or the screening for adult obesity. There are, of course, many other uses of anthropometric data.

TABLE 16.1
Anthropometric measurements

Lengths	Diameters	Circum-ferences	Fatfolds
Crown-rump	Biacromial	Head	Triceps
Crown-Heel	Biiliac	Upper arm	Biceps
Stature	Humerus-Biepicondylar	Thigh	Subscapular
Sitting ht.	Femur-Biepicondylar	Max. calf	Suprailiac
Limb lengths	Upper chest Bistyloid Bimalleolar	-	Medial calf

I wish to focuss our attention on the following three major areas where anthropometry contributes the most.

1. **Pure science**: It is the anthropological or human biological academic use of anthropometric data aimed at gaining insight into variation in growth process for greater understanding of important evolutionary aspects by comparing ontogenetic processes within the order Primates. It is now amply clear that at birth baby monkey is more ma-

ture than baby ape and the latter is more mature than the human newborn. Further, anthropometric data within and across geographically ranging human populations have been compared to understand human variations and to interpret the true nature of biological adaptations to varied ecological conditions. Although new and sophisticated technical and analytical procedures have been devised, still the two horned dilemma of genetic and environmental efforts has not yet become amenable to precise solution.

II. **Medical use**: Recording of height and weight in any general medical examination is essential for both children and adults. It is, however, important to recognise that when dealing with a single child patient, it is the growth velocity which gives most reliable information. In adults since normal growth has ceased we must have techniques to measure the hypertrophy—in most cases of overweight it is the hypertrophy of the adipose tissue. It is clear that for the diagnosis of several growth disorders* and to assess the effect of medical treatment longitudinal distance and velocity standards such as those devised by Tanner et al. (1976) are required. However, some children may be genetically short —a condition that can be diagnosed by family type standards (Tanner 1978). More or less for the same purpose slightly different standards with deviation charts are used in American Medical Schools (Bayer and Bayley 1976). I feel sad that there are no such standards available to our pediatricians, who need them most. Considering the importance of auxological anthropometry leading text books of pediatrics have an exhaustive opening chapter on child growth and development. (Jelliffe and Jelliffe 1979; Nelson 1983) There is a clear need to strengthen this part in Indian text books (Thaman 1984). Efforts of the Indian Council of Medical Research in this direction are praiseworthy and the data resulting from multicentric studies will be able to fill this gap only if quality control procedures are strictly adhered to throughout the programme—by no means an easy task.

About 30 diagnoses have been recognised e.g. HGH deficiency, Hypothroidism, Adrenal Hyperplasia, Hypochondroplasia, Kidney diseases, disease treated with cortisol, psychosocial short stature etc.

III. **Population health use**: This use of auxological anthropometry is in the area where scientists, health and social workers join hands with nutritionists and other government and voluntary organisations in improving the community health. These efforts are particularly directed to screening and identifying individual children or child population at risk for malnutrition - which in rural and poverty stricken sector is always the problem of undernutrition. Early dectection of these 'hungry' child populations will hopefully prevent full blown nutritional deficiency diseases as counselling and food supplementation programmes such as Anganwadis under the integrated child development scheme of Govt. of India, can be gainfully undertaken.

Screening of populations (both children & adults) for nutritional status is vastly different from assessing it in a clinic where in addition to recording the presence of certain signs and symptoms associated with various deficiencies, a detailed blood biochemistry and radiography of the joints can be easily employed. The attending physician might also go into the details of dietary history - either by recall or by actually measuring the intake.

Such a detailed medical examination is seldom possible in screening surveys in developing countries, primarily due to the lack of trained professional hands and also due to the paucity of resources. Indeed in a country like India. This is a mammoth task which can be achieved much faster and with less resource inputs by employing the auxological anthropometry as a population screening device, for growth of height, weight and other body measurements reflects the nutritional status of populations. Here growth means the size at given age (not the velocity) and incorporates the evidences from world wide observation of the secular trends and socio-economic class differences (Tanner 1976, 1978; Wolanski 1979; Van Wieringen 1978; ICMR 1984).

Since in population surveys individuals are measured only once, it is considered appropriate to use cross sectional data from the same or similar population as the reference standard, though different opinions have been expressed on this matter (Tanner 1978). Besides certain technical considerations, a universal reference standard might be misleading for the auxologically innocent. It should, therefore, be very clearly understood that a reference standard is only a reference and not the target for the population to achieve. Accepting the criticism of the WHO Expert Committee nutritional Surveillance has, under the compulsion of paucity of data from other populations, recommended the use of NCHS data upto the age of 10 years as reference for different countries (Waterlow et al. 1977).

Index Measurements: The problem in the developing countries is very different from the problem in the developed ones. So the WHO has recommended the use of only two simple measurements:

(a) **Weight for height:** which indicates present state of nutrition, and
(b) **Height for age:** which indicates the past condition of nutrition.

Although weight for age is an useful measurement but only in special situations e.g., serial measurement, or in neonates and infants of less than one year. It has been dropped and instead measurements at a & b, above recommended primarily because they distinguish between acute (a) and chronic (b) conditions of malnutrition. Weight for height is also nearly independent of age and ethnic group (Waterlow et al. 1977).

S.D. Scores : The reference data based on NCHS are presented in two ways: 1. Centile charts and 2. Standard deviation scores. Considering large number of children in developing nations remaining too far outside the range (lower) of reference, calculation of S.D. scores is recommended for classifying mild, moderate and severe degrees of undernutrition by using arbitrary cut off points, which give an additional advantage of looking at the deficit in weight for height (wasting) and deficit in height for age (stunting) simultaneously (Waterlow et al. 1977).

Notwithstanding small technical disagreements, it is often convenient to compare measurement data of different populations or trans-generational data of the same population by relating them to a single reference. Following criteria should be kept in view while developing anthropometric reference data.

1. Measurements should relate to a well-nurished population.
2. The sample should include at least 200 indiyidual in each age and sex group.
3. The sample should be cross-sectional, since the comparisons that will be made are of a cross-sectional nature.
4. Sampling procedures should be defined and re-producible.
5. Measurements should be carefully made and recorded by observers trained in anthropometric techniques, using

equipment 'of well tested design and calibrated at frequent intervals.

6. The measurements made on the sample should include all the anthropometric variables that will be used in the evaluation of nutritional status.
7. The data from which reference graphs and tables are prepared should be available for anyone wishing to use them, and the procedures used for smoothing curves and preparing tables should be adequately described and documented.

Although no estimates within and between observer errors are available for the ICMR standards, they fulfil most of these criteria in providing useful basic reference data (ICMR 1984). Also they were collected in the late 50's so there might be a need for revising them.

Based on anthropometric data as have been described, WHO has developed exceedingly simple devices requiring little training/skill in their use by often illiterate but actual health personnel at the grass root level in the villages. Two such devices are a bracelet - a ring of 4 cm inner diameter, which, if can be slid up the upper arm above the elbow indicates wasting. The other device is a simple arm band (shakir's tape) having green, yellow and red colour zones. On winding up the band around the arm, if the circumference remains in the red zone, it indicates severe wasting, yellow indicates border line and green indicates the normal range. There is yet another device called Arnold's Quack Stick, having 80% of expected mid upper arm circumference ploted against expected height. If actual height is less than the height indicated against the mid upper arm circumference, it indicates undernutrition. There are some other, more complicated indices, e.g., Rao's index and Kanawati's index, former using weight and height and the latter is a ratio of mid arm & head circumference. It is not clearly known whether these are more or less sensitive than other indices.

This approach of screening child populations for malnutrition is based on the fact that when for any reason a child becomes malnourished (undernutrition) first thing that happens to it is slowing down of growth. The signs and symptoms of various dietary deficiencies take much longer to appear.

Adult health monitoring: Let us now turn our attention from auxology to gerontology to see how anthropometry helps in monitoring the health of the adult population. Adult overweight or obesity is a growing health hazard of the well-off urban adults in Indian cities. Here I wish to refer to that form of overweight which takes place in the middle age and is related to affluence, plentiful rich food and sedentary habits. This is largely due to accumultion of extra heavy load of calories in the form of subcutaneous and deep body fat. In a modern city like Chandigarh its prevalence was very high—approximately every 3rd person over the age of 30 was found to be overweight by 10% or 20% or more (Prakash 1986). It is unlikely that its prevalence should be markedly different in Delhi or Bombay (Dastur 1977). Despite high level of conciousness in the industrially developed countries this problem is also very serious (National Centre for Health Statistics 1979; Russo 1978).

In view of its increasingly high prevalence, the adult overweight or simply obesity which has marked medical and social implications, needs to be diagnosed early enough and with easy methods. Obesity is commonly defined as excess of body fat in contrast to leanness represting a condition with very little body fat. Extreme leanness may be associated with emaciation as also with high degree of physical fitness, while high fat contents as reflected by percent body fat (% BF) and total body fat (TBF) could be related rather closely to gall bladder disease, gout and fatty infiltration of heart. Overweight might also exert additional increased mechanical load on the heart and bony joints, besides causing metabolic burden on the liver function.

It is clearly recognised that while anthropometry cannot replace the blood biochemistry, it provides a simple and eficient means for easy diagnosis and grading of body fatness (Roche et al. 1981).

The year 1963 is a landmark in the history of human body composition because Vol.110 of the Annals of New York Academy of Sciences was published in that year, under the expert editorial authority of Brozek (1963). Prior to 1963, effort to find methods to measure and grade aspects of body composition resulted in the pioneering researches involving predictive equations from skinfold thicknesses. (Matiegka 1921; Behnke et al. 1942; Brozek and keys 1951; Durnin and Taylor 1960; Parizkova 1961 a&b; Siri 1956) In the post 1963 era, both intensive and extensive reserches in this field have continued the world over. Considering the use and potential of anthropometric data as alternative to complex new emerging loboratory techniques e.g., densitometry, K^{40} and creatinine estimation, Computer Assisted Tomography, Ultrasonography and Nuclear Magnetic Resonance etc., the International Journal of Obesity, published a critical review of nearly 100 papers, titled "Anthropometric Methods: New and old, what they tell us" by Roche (1984).

Satisfactory equations and indices are now available for estimting body fat, grading body fatness and characterization of obesity in European (Durnin and Rchman 1967; Durnin and Womersley 1974; Durnin et al. 1974;), Americans (Roche 1984; ICMR 1954) and some information of the sort is also available for Indians (ICMR 1954; Singh and Raja 1980; Bhardwaj et al. 1977; Satwanti et al. 1977). However, much needs to be done in this area in India.

Now we may consider some of the more important anthropometric indices which have high correlation with and are useful in estimating % B.F. and TBF for describing, grading and characterisation of obesity. While anthropometry does not provide a very fine gradation of the degrees of obesity, in absence of direct measurements (e.g. CAT Scan is unlikely to be used commonly for population screening), anthropometry does provide a way how to define and describe the distribution of body fat. Subcutaneous fat distribution patterns may be (and are) associated with particular diseases, hence can be taken as useful risk factors; categorisation of obesity is only possible by anthropometry e.g., centripetal and centrifugal obesity. Discussing the limitations to the usefulness of anthropometry, Alex Roche has stressed that "a measurement may assist the meaningful categorization of obesity even if it is an inaccurate measure of what it purports to be. For example, the inaccuracy of typical measurements of upper arm fat area is of little consequence because they are useful" (Roche 1984).

Quetlet index (W/H) has long been used. More modern studies recommend body mass index (W/S^2 for men and W/S^{15} for women) as there are higher correlations with % fat & TBF which cannot be predicted simply by sum of the four skinfold measurements (t,b, ss & si), (Durnin and Womersley 1974) or even by a single skinfold (t) so as to avoid undressing in public view.

In conclusion, one might say that despite its limitations anthropometric monitoring of popultion health and nutrition is probably the best particularly in the developing countries. "This use of anthropometry" in the words of Tanner (1978) "actually monitors the efficiency of administration of a country and could be used as a criterion of a good government.

Rererence List

Advance data from vital & health statistics (1979) National Centre for health statistics 51

Bayer LM, Bayley N (1976) Growth diagnosis 2nd edn. Chicago University Press, London 2nd
Behnke AR, Feen BG, Welhoma WC (1942) J Am Med Ass 118 : 495
Bhardwaj H et al. (1977) Eur J Appl Physiol 36 : 141-150
Brozek J, Keys A (1951) Brit J Nutr 5 : 194
Brozek J (1963) Ann Ny Acad Sci 110 : 1-1013
Dastur RH (eds) (1977) Are you killing yourself Mr. Executive? All India Management, New Delhi
Durnin JVGA, Taylor A (1960) J Appl Physiol 15 : 142
Durnin JVGA, Rahaman MM (1967) Brit J Nutr 21 : 681
Durnin JVGA, Womersley (1974) Brit J Nutr 32:77
Durnin JVGA, Longergan ME, Good J, Ewan A (1974) Brit Nutr 32 : 169
ICMR (1954) Nutr Res Lab
ICMR (1984) Technical report series, 18
Jelliffe DB, Jelliffe EFP (1979) Nutrition and growth. In : (ed) Human Nutrition, Plenum Press, New York, vol 2
Jhayar WS (1919) Bull Johns Hopkins Hospital 30 : 198
Jordan J et al. (1975) Ann Hum Biol 2 : 153-171
Matiegka J (1921) Am J Phys Anthrop 4 : 223
Nelson WE (1983) Text book of Pediatrics, 12th edn. W.B. Saunders Company, Philadelphia, London
Parizkova J (1961a) Metabolism 10 : 794
Parizkova J (1961b) J Appl Physiol 16 : 173
Prakash S (1986) April 27, Sunday Reading, The Tribune
Roche AF, et al (1981) AM J Clin Nutr 34 : 2831-2838
Roche AF (1984) Intern J Obe 8 : 509-523
Russo P (1978) Aussierobics, Paul Hamlyn Ptg Limited, Sudney
Satwanti, Bhardwaj H, Singh IP (1977) Hum Biol 49 : 209-213
Singh R, Raja C (1980) Anthrop Kozl 24 : 223-234
Siri WE (1956) In: Lawrence JH, Tobias CA (ed) Advances in Biological and Medical Physics, Academic Press Inc, London
Tanner JM (1976) Proc Nutr Soc 35 : 315
Tanner JM, Whitehouse RH (1976) Arch Dis Child 51 : 170
Tanner JM (1978) Ekalgia Zywienia Ossolineum
Tanner JM (ed) (1978) Human Growth: postnatal growth, plenum Press, New York, p 445-470
Tanner JM (1978) Fetus into Man, p 45
Thaman OP (1984) Text Book of Paediatrics, Tata Mc Graw-Hill Publishing Company Ltd
Van Wieringen JC (1978) In : Falkner F
Waterlow JC et al. (1977) Bull World Health Organisation 55 : 489-498
Wolanski N (1979) Coll Antropol 3 : 275-280
Zerfas AJ (1975) AM J Clin Nutr 28 : 782-787
Zerfas AJ, Shorr IJ, Neumann CG (1977) Paediatrics Clinics of North America 24

SEVENTEEN

HEALTH CARE IN RURAL INDIA: PROBLEMS AND CHALLENGES

S. Srinivasan

Medical Anthropology as a special area of study is relatively new. It deals with the cultural component in the ecology of health and disease. It also refers to studies specially designed either help to solve problems in medical science or to provide knowledge about a practical problem in medical practice, the allocation of health resources or the operation of health facilities and services. It studies medicine as a system of behaviour. It is conceived as a discipline dealing with an interface between the providers and consumers of health and medical care services.

Health is a universally cherished goal. It is a state of complete physical, mental and social well-being and not merely the absence of disease or infirmity (WHO 1946). It is a positive attribute of life and therefore organisation of health services to all people is considered to be the key step towards development. It is an important input for the development of man and thereby to social and economic development of the country.

Health is widely linked with development. A rapid and equitable economic development is in itself a good health input; an adequate and equitable health care system stimulates development improving human productivity. That is why, investment in health is sometimes called an investment in human capital. It is regarded as an index of social development. Achievement of good health and its maintenance is one of the universal values accepted by humanity as expressed through W.H.O. definition of health.

Health is a social concept evolved and determined by the

perceptions of a group or community and therefore differs from one community to the other. Health is one aspect of culture. Change in one aspect of culture will change the other aspects of culture as well, since culture is an integrated whole. Health attitudes and practices of the people as also the prejudices are integrated with other aspects of culture and especially with religious aspects of culture. Attempts to change health atitudes of the people amount to attempts at culture-change. Health is one of the hardest cores of culture like religion where the people are change-resistant. For example, leprosy, the stigmatised disease naturally would be the lowest on the scale of acceptance-rejection in the field of health and there is no need to feel frustrated if people show the highest resistance to acceptance of the knowledge about the leprosy and change their attitudes and practices regarding the disease (Mutatkar 1979).

Health care is one of the most important of all human endeavours to improve the quality of life of the people. It implies the provision of conditions for normal, physical and mental development and functioning of human being individually and the group. It provides a wide spectrum of services including primary health care, integration of preventive and curative services, health education, the protection of mothers and children, family welfare and the control of environmental hazards and communicable diseases. A large proportion of the country's rural population has no access to health care at all and for many of the rest what they receive does not alleviate their problems, though there is a rising clamour to provide medical care to all the people in India by the year 2000 A.D.

DEFINITION OF HEALTH CARE SYSTEM

The Health Care System of India may be defined as the industry which provides health services (health activities) so as to meet the health needs and demands of individuals, the family and the community (Park and Park 1977). A Health Service system consists of an organisational structure which sustains a network of institutions for providing services, training, education, research and evaluation; which enables various types of personnel to make certain forms of medical technology available and accessible to a population (Banerji 1985). There are thus three major components of this system: the health institutions, a package of technology and manpower for its delivery and the organisational structure.

The Health Care System (HCS) of a society can also be broadly defined as a set of ideas, practices and organisations which have been developed to deal with problems of health and illness in the society (Lee 1982). A greater realisation is coming to the medical scientists that human being can no longer be treated as an anatomical and physiological entity but that his individuality should be understood in terms of his culture and belief system. A number of studies have been made in this direction to bring out the relationship between culture, society and disease (Carstairs 1955; Opler 1963; Hasan 1967; Kochar 1973; Mathews 1979). In every contemporary society, developed and developing, there has emerged more than a single medical tradition within the overall system of health care. More recent studies have shown that the dual system can and does exist side by side in India. Laslie (1976) and Udupa (1975) have shown that Ayurveda and Unani medicines in existence for centuries in India. Studies by anthropologists indicate that traditional medicines do persist even though the health consumer has access to western medicine which are deemed scientific (Laslie 1977). Laslie has shown ample evidence of integration of indigenous systems of medicine, namely, Ayurvedic and Unani with Western (allopathic) medicine. In India, both modern and traditional systems of medicine such as Ayurveda, Unani and Siddha coexist.

Health Care Delivery System in India

A three-tier system of health care delivery exists in India, i.e., provision of basic curative, preventive, promotional and rehabilitative serves to the rural areas through and upto Primary Health Centre level, the referral complex upto the taluk and district level and specialist service through medical colleges, teaching hospitals and other specialised institutions. Thus, comprehensive health care consists of health care delivery at the primary, secondary and tertiary levels.

Health Resources in Rural Areas

The primary goal of any health delivery system is to organise the health care services in such a manner as to optimally utilise the available resources, knowledge and technology with a view to prevent and alleviate diseases, disability and sufferings of the people. There are three types of health resources exist in the rural areas of India, namely, formal, informal and folk health care systems. The formal health system consists of the governmental network of primary health centres, subcentres and dispensaries (the P.H.C. Complex). This system is highly formalised and organised bureaucratically. The informal system consists of a network of private clinics of the full-time private medical practioners of various systems of medicine such as Ayurveda, Siddha, Unani and Homeopathy. The folk health care system consists of a variety of part-time health workers who function within the context of folk traditions and village organisation. All these systems fulfill the health needs of the rural population in India, to a varying degree.

Primary Health Care

Primary Health Care is an essential health care for all citizens easily accessible and at a cost that the citizens, and the community can afford (W.H.O. 1978). It embraces the main health problems in the community - curative, preventive, promotive and rehabilitative services. The care is based on practice scientifically sound and socially accepted methods and technology. The delivery of primary health care is the foundation of the rural health care system. Primary Health Care represents the first level of personal health services. It is the entry point to the health care system for most people. The organisation of primary health care takes care of family welfare, nutrition, communicable diseases and many other problems in a continuous manner. It is for the people but is above all, health by the people. This means, individual, family, community and national self-reliance in health. It is an approach shaped around the population it serves. It uses methods and techniques that are appropriate, inexpensive and acceptable to the community. It forms an integral part of the national health system. It is part of the overall social and eaconomic development of the community.

DEVELOPMENT OF RURAL HEALTH CARE SERVICES IN INDIA

The Rural Health Care Services have been developed broadly in line with the recommendations of the Bhore Committee (1946) relating to the establishment of Primary Health Centres (P.H.Cs.), for making medical and health services available to the rural people near their homes. Health care facilities in rural areas in India are provided through P.H.Cs. started as a part of a national rural development programme. The P.H.Cs. constitute the core of rural health services programme in the Country. The establishment of the first primary health centres in October, 1952 was the major landmark in the development of health care services in India (Dutt 1965).

The Primary Health Centre (PHC) concept implied delivery of integrated health services through an appropriate institutional framework to the smallest unit of population possible (Banerji 1985).

The P.H.Cs. function as the first anchor against disease and ill-health in rural areas. Medical relief in P.H.Cs. are the focal points for the delivery of health and medical care in rural areas. The P.H.C. in itself embodies an integrated approach to health services development - curative, preventive and promotive. Its major functions are: (1) Medical Care; (ii) control of communicable diseases; (iii) promotion of maternal and child health; (iv) collection of vital statistics; (v) protected water supply and promotion of environmental sanitation; (vi) conducting school-health programme; and also (vii) providing family welfare services. It is close to the people and offers adequate medical care services to meet the basic health needs of the people. Their operational responsibility is to cover medical care, M.C.H. services, family welfare, nutrition, control of communicable diseases, protected water-supply and environmental sanitation. In each health centre, there is one medical officer for curative and preventive work and one lady medical officer for M.C.H. and family planning work. Besides the doctors, the health team consists of (i) a dispenser; (ii) a male health assistant (sanitary inspector); (iii) two public health nurses or lady health visitors; (iv) 14 male multipurpose basic health workers including those for basic services and malaria surveillance; (v) 10 female multipurpose health workers including six for family planning work; (vi) a laboratory technician; (vii) an extension educator; (viii) a record keeper; (ix) a storekeeper; (x) a driver; (xi) two ancillary staff and (xii) about eight female attendants. There are some variations in the staff in different states, depending on the availability of staff and budgetary allocation (Ghai 1985). Primary Health Centres and sub-centres are designed to make primary health care available throughout the rural areas in the country.

In India, primary health care is privided through community development blocks. In each community development block, there is one primary health centre and six or eight sub-centres at present. An average, primary health centre in a community development block covers a geographic area of 400 to 500 sq.km. with a population of 1,00,000 to 1,20,000 persons living in about 100 to 125 villages. The block is taken as the base of the pyramid of the primary health care where the P.H.C. is located. The P.H.Cs. together with sub-centres haven been trying to do yeoman service to improve the health status of the rural populations.

There are 5120 community development blocks in the country. A total of 5,955 primary health centres (P.H.Cs.) and 65,643 sub-centres are functioning in the country (Health Statistics of India 1983), covering a rural population of 525 million (census of India 1981). Though P.H.Cs. have been established throughout the length and breadth of the country, yet they have not been able to cover effectively the whole population under their jurisdiction. The sphere of service of the P.H.C. has not, by and large, extended beyond 5 kms radius. About 70 per cent of the households came from the P.H.C. and sub-centre villages (Chuttani et al 1976; Srinivasan 1983).

The Primary Health Centres (P.H.Cs.) have not made as much impact as expected. The basic objectives of these health centres are to create a delivery of health service which reaches out to the grassroot level in rural areas. Thus, these health centres do not reach down adequately or uniformly and large areas and populations are really without even the most elementary health care. The curative aspect has received far more attention than the preventive and promotive aspects.

Health care delivery in rural India is impeded by the underutilisation of existing facilities. Earlier studies indicated that the health centres and the sub-centres were grossly underutilised (Datta and Kale 1969). However, the users of the rural health facilities were satisfied with the quality and the quantity of the services provided (Bose 1980).

Problems and challenges

The problems of health care services in rural areas are not as simple as they seem. They are clearly different from those of urban areas such as : (i) the concept of health and disease is rather traditional in rural areas (which results in their not seeking treatment at an early stage of physical maladjustment and frequent refusal of preventive measures) and their idea of medical care is some treatment easily accessible and available; In the rural culture, the people lack the motivation of availing medical care at the initial stage of the disease. The general apathy of rural people in seeking treatment from allopathic medical practitioners at a late stage is due to the fact that though the people accept the power of medical technology to cure the diseases, they do not accept the scientific theories of causation of diseases. (ii) limited paying capacity ; (iii) comparative inacccessibility of medical care services due to underdeveloped communication and transport facilities ; (ix) unqualified private medical pracititioners in villages and villages with small populations do not have even such practitioners ; and (v) qualified health workers and more particularly graduate professional medical and paramedical staff do not want to work in rural and tribal areas because of professional, personal and social reasons. These are some of the peculiar characteristics of the rural health services. Because of these characteristics of rural health services, the urban pattern of hospital based services manned by qualified physicians supported by paramedicals and equipped with sophisticated diagnostic and therageutic appliances is not suitable for rural situation.

A look into the pattern of rural health services in India shows that the scarcity of trained manpower for health is a major problem and this is an obstacle to the extension of health services to rural and tribal areas. Moreover, qualified health workers do not want to work in rural and tribal areas because of professional, personal and social reasosns.

The health problems of rural and tribal populations cannot automatically be overcome by establishing more primary health centres and sub-centres also imparting training to more health personnel. In order to develop the philosphy of providing integrated health care delivery system to the rural and tribal populations, our attempt in establishing P.H.Cs. in the countryside has not achieved desired results. Therefore, an integrated health service is absolutely necessary for the care of rurla areas whether the services are provided by a single authority or by a number of agencies. It will then be possible to ensure the provision of some limited service to the entire rural areas rather than providing more comprehensive servive for a small part of them. An integrated health service would be operated on a team work basis by division of labour so that the greatest possible use of professional skills could be made. While the physician is the central figure in the health centre complex, the efficiency and output health services would depend upon the supporting personnel consisting of nurses, various categories of paramedical and auxiliary staff. It is therefore that to extend health care to cover the entire rural areas, the exclusive use of auxiliaries is indispensable. The need for such supportive personnel is so great that the team work has become one of the paramount importance to health care services.

Rural Health Service is a hierarchical system in which all decision-making is confined to higher levels, namely, the state departments of healths in respect of general health services and the Central Ministry of Health and Family Welfare in respect of programmes relating to communicable diseases, family welfare, maternal and child health, nutrition and a part of child welfare services. There is, thus, a multiplicity of decision-making bodies at higher levels which creates difficulties in a coorinated development of what is necessarily a multi-dimensional health programme (Bose and Tyagi 1983). As a result, no streamlined organisation has emerged to serve the health centres and sub-centres located at the periphery of health services. This explaines the shortfalls and delays encountered by the P.H.Cs. and sub-centres in timely recruitment of staff, creation of new and maintenance of the existing components of their infrastructures including vehicles and procuring equipments, medicines, vaccines, etc.

With regard to the management of the services at the P.H.C. level, various problems have come to our notice, relating to suitability of the personnel, coordination of the work of different functionaries and the support received from health workers operating outside the services. These problems were further compounded by bureaucratic procedures and practices relating to postings and transfers of medical and paramedical personnel. It is thus evident that the rural health services suffer from a variety of limitations and shortcomings. Even when we judge from the point of view of government expectations, the performance of rural health services has been greatly wanting. So to say, the existing health infrastructure is capable of touching only a fringe of the health problems faced in the rural areas in which more than 70 per cent of the country's population live.

For increasing the accessibility of health services in rural areas and correcting regional disparities in the shortest possible time, the goals to be pursued are: (i) expanding the network of medical facilities and health services in the country; (ii) increasing the accessibility of health services in rural and tribal areas; (iii) correction of disparities in the provision of health services between urban and rural areas; (iv) intensification of national health programmes; (v) greater emphasis on protected water-supply; disposal of waste and improvement of environmental sanitation, (vi) improving the quality of health services, and (vii) providing a clear-cut referral system of medical services.

Keeping in view the experiences so far obtained and the difficulties in the provision of health services in rural and tribal areas, it has been realised that acceleration of the pace of health programmes is an urgent imperative and a much more concerted effort and substantially larger investment is vital for rapidly improving the health profile of the country.

In concluding remarks, we can therefore, only say that the problem of providing primary health care to the rural population of India is as difficult today as it has ever been in the past. Transport system and communication facilities have greatly improved the out reach of health delivery systems. In this process, the expectations of the rural people have greatly incrased leading to greater demands for hospitals, health centres etc. It is this context that lends great importance to the introduction of community health guides' scheme and multipurpose health workers' scheme which brought a ray of hope of the rural people. For making health care services more meaningful to the population of the country, it is necessary to bring about fundamental changes in focus and approach to the entire health care delivery system of the country in general and above all rural health services in particular.

Reference List

Banerji D (1985) Health and family planning services in India. Lok Parkash. New Delhi 53:253

Bose S (1980) Health situation and problems of village in West Bengal. ICSSR research abstract quarterly 11:83-90

Bose A, Tyagi RP (1983) Rural health services present status In: Bose A, Desai PB (ed) Studies in social dynamics of primary health care. Hindustan Publishing Corporation. India

Carstairs GM (1955) Medicine and health in rural Rajasthan. In: Paul BD (ed) Health culture and cummunity. Russal Sage Foundation. New York

Chuttani CS et al (1976) Factors responsible for underutilisation of primary health centres a community survey in three states of India. NIHAE 9:221-

Datta SP, Kale RV (1969) An operational research study in primary health care in Pondicherry. Ind J Prev Soc Med 65-72

Dutta PC (1955) Rural health and medical care in India. Army Education Press. Ambala

Dutt PR (1965) Rural health services in India. Primary health centres. Central Health Education Bureau. New Delhi ed 2nd

Ghai OP (1985) Management of primary health care. Interprint 40-41

Government of India (1946) Health survey and development committee. Bhore committee. Manager of publications. New Delhi Vol.4

Government of India (1983) Health statistics of India. Ministry of health and family welfare. New Delhi

Hasan KA (1967) The cultural frontier of health in village India. Manaktalas. Bombay

Kochar V (1973) Social organisation of health roles and resources in rural India. Unpublished paper presented at a seminar in the deptt of behavioural sciences. John Hopkins University. Baltimore. USA

Lee RPL (1982) Comparative studies of health care systems. Soc Sc & Med 16

Leslie CM (1976) The ambiguities of medical revitalism in modern India. In: Leslie CM (ed) Asian medical systems a comparative study. University of California Press. USA. 356-367

Leslie CM (1977) Pluralism and integration in the Indian and Chinese medical systems. In: Landy L (ed) Culture disease and healing studies in medical anthropology. Collier Macmillan. ISA. 503-510

Mathews CME (1979) Society and leprosy. Shubhada-Saraswat. Pune

Opler ME (1963) Cultural definition of illness in village India. Hum Org 22

Park JR, Park K (1977) Text book of preventive and social medicine. Banarsidas Bhnnot Publishers. Jabalpur

Srinivasan (1983) Medicare and health delivery systems in rural and tribal areas of Tamil Nadu. Research report. New Delhi

Udupa KM (1975) The ayurvedic system of medicine in India. In: Newell K (ed) Healthby the People. WHO. Geneva. 53-69

World Health Organsiation (1978) Primary health care report of the international conference on primary health care. Alma Ata. USSR. WHO. Geneva

World Health Organisation (1946) Constitution of the world health organisation. WHO.Geneva

EIGHTEEN

COMMUNAL HARMONY IN INDIA: REFLECTIONS IN A SECULAR CONTEXT

Shalina Mehta

Whenever we discuss the question of communal harmony in India, the debate invariably revolves around the eradication of communalism. In other words it implies if communalism is removed from the fence, communal amity awaits us. None of these forums evaluate communalism as a transitional process, a phase of emotive aggression or as a sense of insecurity (experienced by individuals but expressed through commune) which is only situational and not statutory. To most of the students of communalism, secularism is a negation of the former. Both of them can never co-exist and for one to survive the other must either die a natural death or be killed. It must be forewarned at the outset of analysis that regarding secularism as an antithesis of communalism amounts to misconstruing social reality. I have argued here that communalism, secularism and nationalism are all social processes which pass through various phases and their degrees of acceptance and rejection depends upon the need of a given social situation at a particular period of time in the history of a given society. Hence an analysis of communal harmony would aim at measuring the variation in the degree of acceptance of communal and secular elements in the existing socio-matrix.

Sociological interpretation of secularism

Social science literature frequently uses the term secular and the concept secularism but rarely attempts to ascribe any precise sociological meaning to its conceptualization. Dictionary of sociology interprets secularization (or the secularization process) as "the term popularly used to depict a situation in which the beliefs and sanctions of religion become or are in the process of becoming increasingly discounted in society as guides to conduct or decision-making."(p-170)[1]

M.N. Srinivas repeats the same when he attempts to define secularization as a process in which "what was previously regarded as religious is now ceasing to be such and it also implies a process of differentiation which results in the various aspects of society, economic, political legal and moral becoming increasingly discrete in relation to each other". (1966.119).[2] To him distinction between church and state in the west and the Indian concept of secular state, both assume the existence of such differentiation.

Social scientists writing on secularism regard rationalization as an essential component of the process of secularization. "Rationalism" is thus defined as "a comprehensive expression applied to various theoretical and practical tendencies which aim to interpret the universe purely in terms of thought, or which aim to regulate individual and social life in accordance with the principles of reason and to eliminate as far as possible or to relegate to the background everything irrational.[3]

At this juncture it is important to note that the process of secularization began as an unconscious endeavour to replace certain accepted traditions by scientific, pragmatic and modern values. Apparently, it attacked most established of the orthodoxies that is religion. Historically it can be argued that it developed almost as a parallel force to technological advancement and came to India as a ramification of westernization.[4] David Martin while developing a theory of secularization suggests that "...secularization initially occurs within the ambit of Christian societies ..... and was exported with modification to other societies"[5](1978:2).

Whatever may be the arena of origin of secularism, it all began within the gamut of religion as a slow mutational force initially broadening the spectrum of its bearer and gradually attempting to become an alternative to it. As suggested by David Martin "Coherent and massive secularism confronts coherent and massive religiosity, and to the extent that secularism is successful there is a partial tendency to erode institutional adherence and belief together. One ethos confronts an alternative ethos, particularly where the elite culture of the secular Enlightenment acquires a mass component and achieves a historicized ideology i.e., Marxism[6] (1978:6). Yinger also voices the same concern when he suggests that secular alternatives to religion were 'Positivism' with its faith in science, Marxicism with its faith in revolution and Freudianism (Science of religion) with its faith in psychoanalysis[7] (1916:190). Secularism like any other innovative process is supported by certain factors like industrialization, urbanization, universalization of education, mass communication, declining economic disparity and a broadening world view which perceives greater homogeneity of surrounding cultures; yet at the same time number of factors are operating to resist the universal acceptance of secularization. Most important of these factors are religious fanaticism, parochialisation, cultural identity crisis, political economic and ego-centric interests of individuals and groups.[8]

Religion, secularism and communalism

In the Indian sub-continent the most vital challenge posed to the process of secularization is religious fanaticism and orthodoxy which is wrongly interpreted as communalism. As Donald Smith argues, "it is by now well established by facts that religion as a socio-cultural pattern and the basis of ethical norms and metaphysical speculation, has been the most powerful single factor in India".[9] (1963). But then, religion is not community nor communal consciousness. At best defined it is "an acceptance of a level of reality beyond the observable world known to science, to which are ascribed meaning and purposes completing and transcending those of the purely human realm '(Martin : 13 : 78)'.[10] However, it is undeniable that it functions as one of the most important institutions of 'identity assertion.' Like Family and Kinship, religion also grows upon you and becomes an inseparable part of your being. Despite the pervasive effect of forces of rationalization which abhor your subservience to religion, religion continues to behold and beget most of us. Under the impact of logic, what one surrenders at the most is a section of rituals, a part of belief system but never the essence or the desire of achieving the ultimate.[11] But when this metaphysical transcends into physical then it becomes what Martin calls 'Experimental religion' which implies a "pragmatic experimental model of political activity."[12] It is this experimental religion which in the Indian context gives rise to what is erroneously called 'communalism' but which in reality means 'political segregation or politiking executed in the name of struggle for the survival of a religion". The term communalism is actually derived from the word 'communal' which in turn relates to a community[13] and when interpreted in terms of social relationships it implies sharing of common interests.[14] Thus per se it does not become negative nor an epicentre of conflict. An 'ism' becomes antagonistic only when it trespasses into the domain of other 'isms' and comes into open conflict with the interests of others which need not be religious but can be personal, economic or political.

Interpretational lacunae existing in the explanation of processes of secularism and communalism vis-a-vis religion are primarily because of social scientists inability to differentiate the 'colloquial' from the 'scientifc'. Invariably, social scientists writing on these processes have succumbed either to their personal community affiliations[15] or the political needs of the period in which they were writing.[16] Consequently, instead of becoming objective interpretors of existing empirical reality, they become champions of a cause which they very proudly sloganed as 'Achievement of Secularism'. P.C. Joshi substantiates my view when he writes, "A scientific treatment of the problem of communalism first requires clarification of the basic approach ..". In the past, the approach adopted by many scholars was dichotomous rather than dialectical, static rather than dynamic, partial rather than comprehensive.".... there has been bias for a 'single factor' or a 'basic factor' explanation which does not allow for dynamic interaction between all the relevant factors or for what Myrdal calls the process of 'cumulative causation'.[17]

Any generalizing theory of secularism and communalism must view 'religion' only as a mark of attestation and not as an abbrevationist or expansionist's strategy. A cumulative causation' approach will review both the multiplicity of the causes and the variety of effects that a single cause or a set of causes may have an effect or a set of effects. This would also determine the rate and growth of a transitional process in a given social situation and can possibly lead to engineering of a set of causes which may have the desired effects.

Scientific rationale and Indian social reality

In the Indian social context it is presumed both by the scientific community and the general masses that communalism minus religion is null and void and secularism minus religion and religious dogmas is all pervasive. With the help of our theoretical proposition we will try to show that religion consitutes a very small though significant cause in the processes of both secularism and communalism but its effect in both the processes differs depending on the nature of its coupling with other causes, namely economic, political and cultural.[18]

Let us review it in the context of Hindu, Muslim and Sikh interrelationships in India. These three communities distinguish themselves from each other on the basis of their adherence to different religions. If religion is to be regarded as the hall mark of communalism then relationship between these three communities should always remain hostile. A historical appraisal of the Indian social scene of the 39 years can rather simply be depicted as follows :

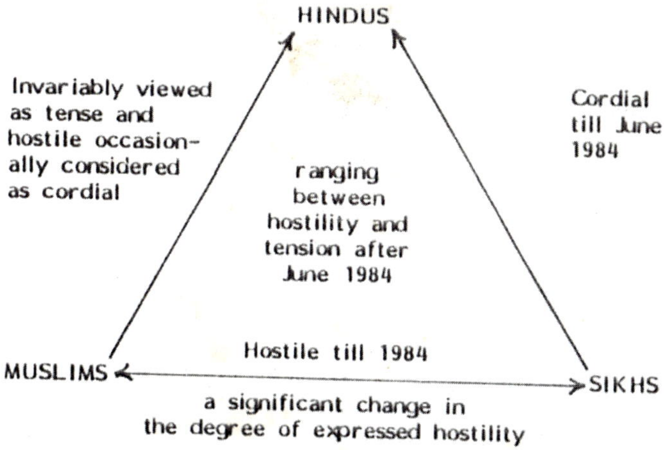

It may appear gross reductionism but if religion alone is the determining factor in inter-community relationships then the network of these relationships should have remained constant unless there was proselytization of direct interference in the religious affairs of one community by the other. But as has been clearly demonstrated by Martin, "Religion conceived as the source of sub-cultural identity tends to lack any direct ideological expression apart from basic consciousness of kind" (1978).[19] Therefore, religion becomes only a source of identification but the operational network of relations are regulated by factors other than religion. Inter-community relations within territories are determined by—

(a) structure of opportunities available to aspirants
(b) economic interdependence
(c) socio-economic lag between the members of the participating communities
(d) Political surroundings
(e) Nature of politiking and power structure

Nature of Inter-community relations will remain harmonious if the effects of the above mentioned causes are controlled in favour of all the participating communities. But once the balance is tilted in favour of one against the other the nexus of inter-community relations is bound to be disturbed. In this constantly viable network of relationships 'communalism' and 'secularism' become votary of individual and group interest. Whereas in reality both communalism and secularism are concomitant processes.[20] Predominance of one over the other in a given socio-political situation becomes apparent only when inter-community relations are tilted away from the apex either in favour or against political expectations. In this entire exercise religion becomes the 'key' symbol, whose rise and fall would indicate the rate of communalism and secularism respectively.

Inter-community relations in a secular state

When Independent Indis's constitution declared it a 'secular Democracy', the under-currents of the challenge posed by the neighbouring theocratic state clouded the judgement of the intelligentia involved in the construction of this historic document. Otherwise I do not understand the need for a nation who was laying the foundations of one of the biggest social democratic of this century to align itself with multiplicity of religions and their co-existence. India had always been a diversified pluralistic society in which relgion constituted only one criteria of sub-cultural indentification. Constitution[20] of such a democracy should have consciously avoided any reference to any of these sub-cultural identities and should have aimed at promoting an egalitarian structure of opportunities which did not recognise caste and creed but only acknowledged economic and social deprivation. By consenting to recognise categories based on caste and creed the founding fathers of Indian constitution inadvertently laid the foundations of present day social crisis experienced by one and all living in the Indian sub-continent. Nehru[21] was probably one of the first Indian leaders who sensed the consequences of policy of reservation, appeasement and protection by recognising the existing social conglomerates of pre-independence era, but his weak resistance and the needs of the 'political party' based democracy made him succumb to the pressures of his less rationalistic colleagues. This dilemma is apparent in the constitution itself. The article 26(B) recognises the sovereignty of all religions, article 51(A)[22] tries to dispel the relevance of religion in favour of developing a scientific temper. These inconsistencies have led to discrepancies and even misconstruction of empirical reality of eminent scholars. The concept of secular state which literally crawled into India's constitution as an apology to the pre-eminence of religion has been referred by the students of Indian polity as a "meaningless clause"[23] to its being parallel to a 'Hindu State'.[24]

It has been argued time and again that nationalism of Hindus is never questioned and as Srinivas also remarks, "nationalism, a secular phenomenon, became enmeshed with Hinduism at one stage" (1966:141)[25] but the nationalism of the religious and to an extent of the linguistic minorities is often questioned. Community consciousness of the numerically small communities in a pluralistic polity like India is commonly dubbed as communalism and the same consciousness of the majority though acknowledged as communalism is interpreted as nationalism by suggesting that they are more secular than their counterparts.

We must emphasize here once again that communalism, secularism and nationalism are merely transitional processes operating under the structure of 'cumulative causes' and their intermingling or juxtaposition is to be understood only with reference to the demands of modernization.

It may sound utopian but it is still not too late for Indian **socialistic** democracy and I underline socialistic to do away with offical patronage and recognition of categories based on sub-cultural affiliations. This and this alone can initiate the process of amalgamation in the melting pot of Indian diversities to produce an identity called Indian, distinctive and unique from any other sub-cultural identity.

Communal harmony and identity crisis in India

"Problem before Indian Muslims on the national scale is identical to the basic problem of international living itself, namely that of co-existence interse on a level of mutuality and reciprocity with other groups and sections of the people, united on the fundamentals of common objectives like democracy, secularism and the pursuit of socio-economic justice. But in effecting this reorientation the Muslims would have to transcend two inter-dependent emotional impediments namely their negative awareness of minority-status and their attachment to communal consciousness" (Rasheedudin Khan : 1977 : 152).[26]

"It is argued that integration is not threatened by the community assertion in politics but what is dangerous to it is the failure on the part of the ruling class and the state managers to evolve an imaginative and effective cultural policy. Maximisation of cultural differences should not bother any one so long as economic disparities are minimised and every form of cultural arrogance is curbed" (Moin Shakir : 1986 unpublished)[27].

"Religion, like castes, provide their followers with an identity and a set of values which profoundly influence their social attitude and behaviour. In India, religious and caste distinctions provide bases for political coherence as well as social competition since secondary organisations have not yet properly developed. It is here that traditional traits appear to be holding their own". (Jha : 1977 : 144).[28]

"A religious dominated country, possessing today a plural society, comprising diversified religious, linguistic, ethnic and cultural groupings it is but natural that homogenous entities consisting of just one religion, language, race or culture would exist based on narrow, yet not ultimately divisive loyalties"[29] (Smith Donald : 1963).

"The only chance of survival of the Sikhs as a separate Community is to create a state in which they form a separate group, where the teaching of Gurumukhi and the Sikh religion is compulsory and where there is an atomosphere of respect for the traditions of their Khalsa forefathers" (Khushwant Singh : 1966 : 305).

" . . .In a democracy each element has a claim and what is more important the right to preserve its identity . . .Minorities are thus essentially phenomenon of democracy" (Humayun Kabir: 1968)[30].

Without indulging into description, criticism or contradictions inherent in a comparative study of these statements which have been orated, by scholars, statesmen and politicians on different occasions, I want the readers to judge them as self explanatory. The three important questions dealt with in these statements relate to[31]

(a) communal harmony understood as national integration
(b) acceptance and assertion of different identities
(c) preservation and perseverence of these in a socialistic democracy without disturbing the existing political order.

The answers proposed invariably are -

(a) national integration or communal harmony as an end in itself
(b) necessity for recognising different identities both by the people and the state
(c) the need for promoting what Paul Brass succinctly labels 'consociational democracy'.[32]

It was in response to this socio-political model of Indian situation that Mrs. Gandhi time and again asserted that "secularism means neither irreligion nor indifference to religion - but equal respect for all religions - not mere tolerance, but positive respect . . . without it (secularism) there is no future for our nation".[33]

A policy statement like this plays truant with social theory and converts a transitional process into an ideology and admits presence of other ideologies and identities into whose functioning the state has avowed non-interference. This leads to ambiguity. Ambivalence of this kind render state, people and intelligentia confused and perplexed. Within this ambiguity lies the paradox which makes desired end of the individual and the state, of necessity alike. But in reality state is an agency and the individual a consumer. Consumer's loyalty to the agency would be determined by the benefits he draws from it and his attitude to his co-consumers would be proportional to his access to those benefits.

As Karl Manheim says, "in accord with the particular context of collective activity in which they participate, men always tend to see the world which surrounds them differently".[34] Same corollary applies to Indian polity and Indian social situation. The communal choreography has varied from discordant to harmonious depending upon the needs of the individuals and not that of the state. But then these individuals also include managers of the state who have occasionally manipulated their personal needs to become the needs of the state. Here the watch word for intelligentia is caution and not submission.

It is to be emphasized that if the state succumbs to pressures or needs of individuals or individual identities then it faces the threat of extinction but if individuals and individual identities opt to become secondary for the sustenance and promotion of state as an agency. Then by themselves they neither fear extinction nor subordination. Law of majority and minority operates only when numbers are regarded as greater than structure, and the structure adopts a policy of accomodation and not social expansion.

As for the graph of communal harmony and the fluctuating trends of Hindu-Muslim-Sikh relations are concerned it is an acknowledged fact that 'at certain times in its political history' a people chooses to remember different features of its past and to emphasize different elements of its culture"[35] and the trends in communal relations become open votaries of these changing world view. Inter-community relations (considered to be the crux of communal harmony) at various levels (personal, economic, political) may vary from intimacy to hostility within the same region at a particular period of time but then they do not become symbolic of national integration per se but remain only a fraction of a segment of a much greater organic reality.

Notes

1. Dictionary of Sociology. (p.170).
2. Srinivas, M.N. (1966). Social change in Modern India Bombay Allied Publishers. Srinivas is one of the few sociologists who has dwelled on the concept of secularization. Srinivas notes that Sanskritization and secularization are both gaining ground in modern India. However, secularization is a more general process whereas sanskritization effects only loweres castes among Hindus and some tribal populations whereas secularization is marked amongst the urban and the educated (p.118).
3. Encyclopedia of Social Sciences Vol.XIII P.113.
4. However, Srinivas subsumes secularization under westernization and regards it as 'reinterpreted Hinduism in which Sanskritic elements are predominant.
5. Martin David 1978. A general theory of secularization. Oxford : Basil Blackwell David Martin's book is one of the exclusive attempts at generalizing a theory of secularization, which he believes is quite close to realisation in sociology of religion and which will have important bearing on political sociology.
6. Ibid. p.6
7. Yinger, J.M. 1916.
8. Martin David (1978) M.N.Srinivas, S.C.Dube, all of them list one or more of these factors as determinants of rate of secularization in any society.
9. Donal E. Smith 1966. India as a Secular state New Jersey : Princeton University Press
10. Martin ibid.
11. David Martin suggests the same when he writes "...... religion has been a carrier of identity is axiomatic. The most resistant forms of relgion relate to just those rites de passage.
12. To this interpretaton of 'Experimental religion' Martin adds an interesting explanation of this political activity stating that politicians are judged by genuineness - and performance, not political dogmas. In so far as social alienation exists it can organize behind the mask of religion and when a stratum becomes newly self-conscious, it will politicize within a religious format.
13. P.N. Pimpley 1986. While delivering a lecture on "Communalism Approaches in the Social Sciences" at a workshop organised by CRRID on communalism, highlighted the need for differentiating colloquial interpretation of communalism from its scoiological meaning. To him 'communal has to do with community which is defined in terms of two criteria : first the common identity . . . and second the

basis of this community is some territorial unit. However, he asserts that in Indian context a community shares a common identity but not necessary a territory.

14. Max Weber in his famous analysis of social action and social relationship talks of two ideal typical relationships. He terms the first as Conflict relationships and the other he labels as Communal relationships.
15. Moin Shakir, Imtiaz Ahmed, Rasheedudin Khan, M.R.Baig, despite their excellent exposition have inadvertently fallen a prey to their inherent sense of identity. More recently Khushwant Singh's wavering stand on Punjab crisis is another example of the same.
16. Bipin Chandra's Work on 'communalism' and his approach to the issue in recent times is a classic example of a great scholar succumbing to political climate of the era.
17. Excerpts from a paper circulated at the workshop on communalism held at Chandigarh between June - July 1986. The paper is titled 'The Economic background of Communalism in India - A model of analysis (unpublished).
18. ibid. P.C. Joshi uses 'cumulative causation' theory to explain the rise of communalism in the pre-independence era..
19. Martin 1978.
20. Article 26 (B) of the Indian Constitution stipulates that the state cannot interfere in the exercise of the right of religious organizations to manage their own affairs in the matters of 'religion' unless they ran counter to public order, health or morality. It is though iinvoking moral-cum-religious authourity that religious institutions should administer their religious affairs rather than through drawing sanctions from Parliament, which is constitutionally committed to secularism.
21. Jawaharlal Nehru 1928. Selected Works Vol.3. P.52.
22. Article 51 (A) says that it shall be the duty of every citizen to develop a scientific temper. The development of scientific temper involves accepting the method of science for acquiring knowledge and recognising that a scientific attitude dispels dogmas, superstituion and obscurantism, which essentially, are propagated in the name of religion.
23. Khushwant Singh in his book 'A history of the Skhs Vol.II concludes "with the resurgence of Hinduism, the official commitment to secularism is being reduced to a meaningless clause in the constitution (1966 : PP 304-305).
24. Donald Smith writes in his book 'India as a secular state' that 'Hinduism is an ethnic religion . . . an Ethnic religion may easily become closely identified with nationalism . . . The promotion of national ideals thus tends to become the promotion of religion (1963 : 27). Even Srinivas raises the same issue when he writes that the state has become an im-

portant means of reinterpretation of Hinduism in the middle decades of the twentieth century, and this in spite of India's proclaimed policy of being a secular state" (1963 : 145).

25. Srinivas (1966 : 141) op. cited.
26. Khan Rasheedudin 1977. "The changing Role of Religious Minorities" in Tribe Caste and Religion ed. by Ramesh Thapar. Macmillan, Meerut.This article was originally published in Seminar (106) 1968.
27. Moin Shakir, 1986.
28. Jha, Chetkar 1977.
29. Smith, Donald, 1963 op. cited.
30. Khushwant Singh 1966 op. cit.
31. Kabir, Humayun, made this statement while delivering the Azad Memorial lecture at Usmania university reporduced from Akbar 1985 India the Siegé within London: Penguin books.
32. Brass, Paul 1975. Language, Religion and politics in North India. Delhi Vikas Publishing house.
33. Indira Gandhi Excerpts from a speech circulated at a political training camp organized by Congress in Delhi from 10th to 15th November, 1975.
34. Manheim, Karl 1936. Ideology and utopia: An Introduction to the Sociology of knolwedge (trans. by L.Wirth & E.A.Shills) Brace and Co., Harcourt, New York:
35. Nandy Ashis 1978. "The making and unmaking of political cultures" in " Challenges of society in transition". ed. by Manorama Barnabas et al. Madras : Macmillan Co. India. Ltd. (P.225).

NINETEEN

POLITICAL ANTHROPOLOGY OF DISPLACEMENT, RELOCATION AND FUTURE OF TRANSFER OF TECHNOLOGY: AN OVERVIEW AND ISSUES

B.K. Roy Burman

Types of displacement

In the contemporary world displacement of population can take place in different contexts, to wit, developmental, planned degradation of environment, prevention of environmental degradation, achieving viability of habitat for provision of social infrastructure, and security of the state.

Developmental context is generally provided by the establishment of major industrial mining complexes, like the new steel cities in India, or by the construction of dams for hydel power projects or irrigation projects in different parts of the world.

A case study of planned degradation of environment leading to large scale displacement of a population and deterioration of their economic and social life has been furnished by Kisle (1972) with reference to atmospheric nuclear testing in Micronesia.

Displacement for prevention of environmental degradation is best illustrated by the attempts of many governments in Asia and Africa, to settle the shifting cultivators and nomadic and seminomadic population away from their traditional habitats. Slum clearance and urban renewal schemes in different parts of the world also come under the same category.

There are also seemingly voluntary cases of diplacement of population so as to become viable in size for availing of the benefits of social infrastructure like drinking water, health care and education facilities. Grouping of villages through decision making at the local community level is an illustration.

Regrouping of villages as a counter-insurgency measure in several countries of South and South East Asia provides illustration of displacement for state security.

Types of issues

There are two types of issues involved in displacement, contextual and processual. Those who are concerned with the first aspect try to analytically examine the need and relevance of the factor of displacement in the particular historico-ecological context. Those who are concerned with the second, concentrate on the management and adaptive processes and on the viability of the survival system that emerges (Bartolome 1984).

While the two aspects are not mutually exclusive, in the present seminar which is being held as a part of inter-congress of IUAES, it is intended to concentrate on the second aspect. This will be preparatory to a comprehensive discussion which will take place in a seminar proposed to be organised by the Futurology Commission in 1988 as part of the XIIth International Congress of IUAES. However, a rapid appraisal of the first aspect will be made here, so that the issues in the second aspect can be seen in perspective.

Rapid overview of the contextual aspect

There is a fundamentalist orientation of doctrinaire relativists to the point of making living museums of isolated peoples in the name of sparing them the agonies of contact with 'modern' ways of living. But in today's world little heed is paid to the social scientist who "cries wolf at every turn and offers trivial solution to significant problems". (Bernard, Pelto 1972). There are others who consider problems of development and related dislocations in terms of alternative strategies. For instance in respect of Kano river project in Nigeria, Tina Wallace writes, "By introducing large scale, captial-intensive, technically complex, partly mechanised irrigation into the area, the government has accepted certain assumptions about 'rural deveiopment'. Alternative strategies such as improving rain-fed agriculture through increased use of fertilisers, feeder roads, improved access to remote areas, have been largely neglected. The introduction of the River Project shows that the F.M.G. believes that the best way to improve productivity and relieve poverty is to bring modern technology and skilled advisers into the rural areas. As Nigeria does not have the necessary manpower this means that they have to rely heavily on expatrate staff" (Wallace 1981). One may or may not agree with the merit of the plea made here for the particular alternative approach, but one has to appreciate that the basic orientation here is not anti-developmental. In a seminar organised by the Futurology Commission at Delhi (Futurology Commission 1983), it was pointed out that optimum utilisation of the irrigation potentials of the existing major hydel projects was thwarted by disharmonic co-existence of feudal and capitalist modes of maintenance and delivery systems. It was further suggested that going in for massive hydel projects without simultaneously resolving these contradictions through appropriate social action will mean "instransgience bonus" to the forces standing in the way of historical transformation. Another important point made in this seminar was that the scale and time schedule of implementation, should, as far as possible, be adjusted to the projected technological development and human resource formation within the country, so that relocation can be linked up with development rather than being a welfare or humanitarian measure or a political concession. The significance of the Delhi seminar is that it highlights the need of synthesis of technological and social planning. It is hoped that the present seminar at the international level, will lead to more intensive effort in this direction.

As regards displacement of population for prevention of environmental degradation, there is a growing demand from the concerned population like the shifting cultivators, that equally, if not more, deleterious practices like monoculture forestry to meet the needs of industrial and commercial establishments, should be stopped simultaneously. Unless they are convinced, their resistance to project relocations may be intensified in the future. Social scientists will have to interact more probingly with the bio-physical scientists and technocrats on such matters as well.

As regards displacement for state security and for creating more and more sophisticated machines of death, it is to be mentioned that in the contemporary phase of global communication, one cannot defend a territory; one can only defend a way of life. Social scientists will also have to assert as citizens, on wider platforms.

Voluntary grouping of settlements for having better access to productive and social infrastructure is of some interest for the present seminar with limited scope. At micro-level it is taking place in some parts of India. After the second world war, the shifting cultivators of five villages in North East India who were affected, voluntarily came together to set up one settlement so that they could establish education, health and social service institutions with their own resources. Along with this physical shift, they have struck upon a number of adaptive strategies in the social organisation and cultural realm. Within the common settlement, they have created jurisdictions of the original tribal villages and are by and large guided by their respective customary norms. Also they have made several bilateral covenants of mutual acceptance of selected cultural traits. Not that these arrangements have always worked satisfactorily; but the direction of the efforts, which appear to have been autogenous in origin, is worth mentioning. It is anticipated that technological development will make many uninhabitable parts of the world, like the deserts, the Polar region habitable. But man may not be able to take advantage of the same on a large scale, unless the issues of multi-national habitat planning are resolved not only in political terms, but also in social and cultural terms. Experiences at the micro-level, like the one cited, may provide insight, which can be drawn upon to face the future challenges of development in this sphere. Besides the experiences of voluntary relocation of settlements, set in motion through endogenous process, have relevance even for forced relocation. There is a growing realisation that by forced relocation even the economic goals cannot be fully achieved, unless the participation of the concerned population can be obtained in the long run through persuasion. It can be envisaged that once the relocation programmes harmonise with the adaptive processes of the communities, the cultural resources will be drawn upon in many innovative manners, as in the case of voluntary grouping, to reinforce the same.

Processual aspects of forced relocation

There is a growing literature on the processual aspects of forced relocation. On a comprehensive review of the same, Partridge (1983) has referred to four stages of resettlement process (a) Recruitment and planning, (b) Transition, (c) Economic and social development, and (d) Incorporation. These broadly tally with the processes observed by Roy Burman (1968) in the context of industrial displacement at Rourkela (India) in the mid 60's. An outline of the aspects and the processes observed by him will be presented here and these will be supplemented by the analytical statements and observations made by others.

A. Aspects studied

(i) Factors determining the choice of project site.

(ii) Attributes of the pre-displacement settlements.

(iii) Scheme for rehabilitation of displaced persons as originally formulated

(iv) Social processes on the eve of diplacement - (a) information circulation, (b) reaction of different sections of pople and developments immediately before displacement, (c) moves and counter moves, and (d) compromises and agreements about rehabilitation pattern in rehabilitation colonies in the fringe of the new industrial city as well as reclamation areas for continuation of cultivation.

(v) Extent and pattern of displacement and rehabilitation in resettlement colonies and reclamation areas with particular reference to (a) the factors determining the choice of particular colony by displaced persons with different antecedents and extent and reason of subsequent shift of choice, (b) manner of utilization of compensation and other facilities, and (c) extent of utilisation of facilities in reclamation areas and factors for non-utilisation.

(vi) Social processes in villages which continue to exist in spite of notice of evacuation, with particular reference to (a) circumstances of continuation, (b) changes in village layout and land utilisation pattern, (c) changes in ethnic composition and size of population, (d) changes in economic life of the population and in traditional patron-client relations, (e) changes in material equipment and food habit, and (f) changes in the membership of the household and in mutual relations among members.

(vii) Demographic pattern and social processes in reclamation areas - (a) demographic pattern with reference to caste and religion, age, sex and education, marriage age, marriage payment, and household structure, (b) economic life with reference to factors and processes determining the extent and intensity of utilisation of land and crop planning, (c) external relations with particular reference to categories of members staying outside, reasons and nature of contact, particulars of households that were separate in the old villages but were joined in the reclamation area and of households which constituted sections of joint family in the old villages and which became separated on settlement in the reclamation area, relation with the resettlement colonies, neighbouring villages and the industrial city, (d) social processes inside the reclamation area with particular reference to residential pattern and factors contributing to the same, segmentations based on village of origin, linkage with resettlement colonies, ethnic identity, religion, kinship, factions and leadership pattern in statutory body and/or functional setting of the reclamation area, and (e) administration of reclamation area.

(viii) Demographic pattern and social processes in a resettlement colony with particular reference to (a) demographic pattern, (b) household structure and changes in intra-family relations including nature of participation of women in economic activities, proportion of leisure time spent by the adult male members in and outside the home, changes among women in matters connected with leisure and recreation, in cleanliness and hygienic habits and in the nutritional value of food, (c) neighbourhood pattern including categories of neighbours with reference to caste/tribe, religious affiliation, village of origin, kinship, attitude towards neighbours, actual relations with neighbours, presents, help etc., given to others including neghbours, (d) role of ceremonial friendship, (e) economic resources, relationships and institutions including employment history of the households, and (f) community organisation and deviant behaviour.

(ix) Social processes in the industrial setting with particular reference to the displaced persons - (a) industries established at Rourkela and type and extent of employment of displaced persons, (b)social ramifications of job situation, and (c) industrial relations and role of displaced persons.

B. Synopsis of substantive observations at Rourkela

Apart from locational advantage of the presence of raw materials the Government of India decided to establish several major industries in more backward areas of the country, as a strategy of balanced regional development. It, however, appears that the exogenous intrusion has not always produced the multiplier effect. About 30 villages inhabited by 2500 households were affected by acquisition of lands for a steel plant and ancillary industries at Rourkela in the 1950's. Prior to acquisition a survey conducted in 1955 revealed that the high caste Hindus, untouchable castes, scheduled tribes and others constituted 20.6%, 9.6%, 45.3% and 18.5% respectively of the total population. In most villages, the people belonging to different communities used to live in separate clusters of their own. Even death could not bring them together. There were caste or community-wise separate places for the disposal of the dead bodies. In each village there was at least one sacred grove or sarna, dedicated to the tutelary deity of the village. On fixed occasions, the village priest used to offer sacrifices at the sacred grove, on behalf of the entire community. The village wasteland was under the control of ganjus or village headmen. Around 1951, however, with the establishment of statutory village council, the control of village waste-land, passed out of the hands of the Ganjus and the elected members of the village council tended to constitute alternative foci of power. In addition to the leaders at the village level there were leaders at the caste level. Sometimes the caste leadership covered a number of villages.

At the initial stage when the rumour about the project was floating about, the attitude of the people was that of accommodative indifference. They were not aware that they would be displaced on a large scale from their agricultural lands. They were prepared to accept a new economy in the region, but were not prepared to accept it as a substitute for the old economic base of their personal life. When it became clear that the agricultural lands would be taken over, the attitude of the people turned from accommodative indifference to bewildered confrontation. Through a number of village level meetings, convened by ganjus or traditional village heads, they began to register their protests. It is interesting that statutory village councils, which derived their authority from the government, failed to be the rallying points; and inter-village caste or community leaders also could not assume any special role. In fact a few attempts made to organise inter-village concerted effort failed. The villagers were having conflicting interests and ambivalent attitude in this matter, which could somehow be reconciled at the village level and not beyond that. The rich cultivators belonging to the higher castes wanted to have the best of both the worlds. They certainly wanted to retain their command over the traditional economy; but at the same time they aspired to enjoy the benefits of the growing industrial complex. The landless agricultural labourers also looked upon the project as a source of regular income. They had nothing to lose, except their familiar ancient world. It was the middle and small cultivators who felt disturbed at what was happening.

It is significant that when it was definitely known that a certain village was going to be dislodged, the solidarity of the village could assert itself in spite of the conflicting interests. It is quite possible that this solidarity reflected the moral order of the society at the village level. But perhaps the moral binding was not the solitary or even the most important factor. There were other factors as well which revolved round the questions of compensation for the immovable properties and facilities of resettlement. The landless cultivators for instance had no machinery of their own, which was organised on class basis and which could safeguard their interests. They, therefore, had to make common cause with the rest of the villagers - to safeguard their interests. Given their position in the power structure of the society, it is no wonder that their interest was hardly secured. It is, however, touching to see how on the verge of their dissolution, the village communities drew all their children under their failing arms.

It is at this stage, when the villages could attain in their internal unity that they could also serve as the bases for external unity. Gradually an organisation called Steel Plant Site People's Federation came into existence and persons with political contact at the district level came to the forefront. They, however, were local people and operated through the ganjus or traditional headmen of the villages. Thus an alliance between the traditional elite and the political elite at the district level took place. In several villages the resistance took the form of non-cooperation and steel authority found it difficult to recruit local labour. At last the then Chief Minister of the State had to personally come to the area and induce the people to give up resistance. This was a qualitative change both on the part of the Government and the people. The earlier approach was that of paying off the individual property owner; now the corporate entity of the village was partially recognised. The people on their part had to reconcile to the fact that their old world was irrevocably receding. The movement now developed two foci - one centering the question of compensation for the loss of their immovable property, the other centering the demand that they should get preference in employment and should have the facilities to settle near the plant site. The concept of children of the soil got mixed up with the second focus of the movement, but soon it fragmented into the genuine children of the soil and the spurious children of the soil.

After protracted negotiations it was decided that three colonies would be set up near Rourkela and lands would be provided in sixteen far flung forest areas for being reclaimed for agricultural purposes. Each married couple would be allotted one plot of land for construction of a residential house in the resettlement colony. Further, in the reclamation areas lands would be reclaimed and converted into wet lands of various classifications at government cost and would be given to the displaced persons in exchange of the lands acquired from them. Reclamation subsidy, free transport facility, transit camp facilities would also be provided.

The exercise of choice of residence after displacement brought certain interesting dimensions of the adaptive process. There was a tendency for the older people to shift to the reclamation centres and at the same time, there was a tendency for very old persons to stay in the resettlement colonies, as they were not physically fit to undertake the arduous tasks of reclaiming lands in the reclamation centres and carrying on cultivation in difficult conditions. On the other hand, people in early youth were more attracted towards the opportunity of industrial occupations near about Rourkela. Middle-aged persons who had less chance of getting regular employment in industrial establishments shifted to the reclamation centres in large number. Along with the middle aged persons, their wives and children also shifted to the reclamation centres. They had less scope of economic activity in the industrial setting, but in agriculture they could make substantial contributions. It seems that as a result of this pattern of physical split of households, education of the younger generation had suffered a setback. An analysis of the spread of literacy among the people of the different age-groups showed that there were comparatively more educated persons in the age-group 16-50 than in the lower age-group. It seems that the tomorrow of the coming generation had been mortgaged to the confused today of the present generation.

The physical break of the households had two types of repercussions. In about 50 per cent of the cases economic ties continued even after physical separation. But in some cases at least, economic unity did not necessarily mean harmonious interpersonal relationship. Frequently the members living in the industrial zone thought that those who were living in the reclamation centres were not doing their best to maximise the produce from the lands allotted to them. On the other hand those living in the reclamation centres felt that the members staying in the industrial areas had developed extravagant habits. In contrast, in many of those cases, where economic bonds had been discontinued there were less emotional tensions and mutual recrimination.

Out of the 30 displaced villages, households of only three villages were found in considerable numbers in more than one colony. These figures showed in a general way that the people of the old villages opted for rehabilitation with the village as the unit. In some cases, the people of a particular village who settled on block in a particular colony, had also established sacred groves, representing the tutelary deities of the old village.

Inside the colonies, kinship played an important role in

determining the immediate neighbourhood. In the matter of selection of reclamation centres, however, solidarity of caste or tribe played a more important role, though the solidarity of the village was subsumed under that.

No formal village panchayat or caste or community panchayat had come into existence in the reclamation centres. In matters of caste customs, sometimes the people joined the caste panchayats which were existing in the adjoining villages from before. In matters relating to common interests of the reclamation centres, they were guided by informal leaders. But factionalism based on old village loyalties continued to play some role. In one centre, two separate sacred groves had to be established because of such factionalism.

The atmosphere in the resettlement colonies was marked by free-floating tension. Some of the conflicts were carried over from old villages and others had grown around new situations in the colonies. But tension and factionalism at one level had facilitated integration at another level. Though there was a multiplicity of factions, the factions were not in a nesting pattern, in which one faction would have lied embedded in a larger faction. Taking an overview, the entire structure can be conceptualised as the outcome of a number of abortive social changes or as a mark of the failure of the new to cut-off from the umbilical cord of the past. For instance, in the changed context, the old village ties had become dysfunctional; but they were still continuing. The ties on the basis of caste and community affiliations had become irrelevant but they were also continuing. The ties on the basis of factionalism of the villages had lost their meaning; but still they were very much there. Taking separately, all these traits could be considered to be symptoms of cultural lethargy; but taken together, they served a very important function - the function of reducing the harmful effect of each of them in isolation. Hence though separately each of them was a symbol of the past, jointly they constituted the prop for the new.

The dynamics of evasion of change among the relocated persons of Rourkela, irrespective of whether they had moved to the rehabilitation colonies in the fringe of the industrial complex or to the reclamation centres in the agricultural interior, has discussed at some length to bring home the adaptive capacity of the survival system of the corporate groups when faced with the massive challenge of physical dislocation and economic disruption. Bartolome has discussed the issues both at the theoretical and empirical levels with reference to the forced resettlement and survival systems of the urban poor in the city of Posadas, Argentina, because of the Yacyreta Hydroelectric project (Roy Burban 1968). His paper focuses on the survival systems and adaptive strategies of affected population, about 20,000 in strength. "Adaptive strategies are the behaviour patterns manifested by the process of satisfying basic needs and coping with the pressures of the social system and physical environments". "Similarly, survival systems are the organized and interacting set formed by resources tapping strategies, behavioral and organizational patterns, and other components, that result in generalizing conditions for the survival of a social unit". Among the surviving strategies of the urban poor Bartolome makes a mention of the invisible economy. "The poor exploit residual and unwanted products, transforming these wastes into useful resources. Processing trash, industrial refuse, and discarded materials of all kinds are activities that are too costly or stigmatized to be part of the formal system. Within the invisible economy, everything is transformed into usable resources". Another adaptive strategy is "predicated on how the social captial of a household can be manipulated to secure a relatively steady inflow of resources". "This strategy imposes an adaptive value for large domestic groups. Large groups allow for an intensive use of free family labour and enhance the potential for expanding and diversifying the reciprocity network that supports the household. The overall objectives are to reduce the amount of uncertainty, in an otherwise unstable situation and to minimize the vulnerability of the group vis-a-vis the constant aggressions of its social and physical environments". If from this theoretical perspective the Rourkela materials are examined, the preference for village as a reference group in the choice of rehabilitation colony and of caste or community as the reference group in the choice of reclamation camp can be perceived as adaptive strategies. The adaptive strategies, however, came out in bold relief in the distribution of household members in dual residential units. There have been cases of both fusion and fission of families and even the rapid field observations suggest that each is adaptive in its unique configuration.

While understanding of these endogenous processes is important for the community leaders planning for social change at the level of the corporate group, knowledge about the "invisible economy" is important for them as well as for the exogenous agencies involved in large scale relocation of the population. In the tribal areas particularly, it is of considerable relevance. In the countries, which had been under colonial rule until recently, frequently there is a hiatus in the perceptions of the state and of the community about the right of ownership, control and management of the forests and forest based resources. The colonial rulers had transformed the homages and tributes received by tribal spokesmen and chiefs into rent towards the later phase of colonialism. In the post colonial period without vacating such usurpation of rights, the new states have frequently claimed proprietory rights over the resources covered by so-called rent, as a part of progressive land reform measures. This has led to 'legal' dispossession of the tribal communities from vast tracts of forest and other lands. But in actual practice these are still controlled and managed by the concerned communities. Apart from agricultural produce, the economic value of the forest products obtained by the tribal communities is not insignificant. An official document of the Government of India (1982) indicates that in the central tribal belt of the country, as much as 13-38 per cent of the income of the population is derived from forest. But such income is not taken into consideration while computing the compensation for the loss of immovable property of the project oustees. This seems to be a general feature in many countries.

The generally accepted principle is to pay compensation to the individual owners of immovable property for the loss suffered by them. Here the crucial question is the meaning of property. Hidayatullah (1983), Ex-chief Justice of India has put the issue in perspective - "In dealing with property in land always link political functions of a group with its social economy". "Thus property in land of the members of a clan or tribe had a dual meaning. While the devolution of property was from the community to the individual, the devolution was subject to the control of the community. It could then be said that it belonged simultaneously to the community and the individual either along or in a family group. Even in the family, there was always an overtone of communal interest, individual enjoyment notwithstanding". It is keeping this in view that Roy Burman (1981) had suggested that project oustees should be given rehabilitation subsidies in kind supplemented by cash rather than compensation. But they should be considered as equity shareholders of the projects and the value of their share should be computed after taking into consideration their visible and invisible income from various sources. He also argued that payment of compensation at existing market rate was highly inequitous, as the value of land and services escalated immediately on the introduction of the project and the compensation did not enable the oustee to get integrated in the new economy. Compensation was thus a negative instrument for the development of a people. Scudder and Colson (1972) have examined the issue of compensation in some detail and have observed that the total input probably did not pay people for what they lost in the way of permanent assets. Compensation payments were also offset by a loss of earnings from labour migration because persons who normally would have gone out to earn, stayed back to rebuild homesteads and clear new lands. Mahapatra has spoken about "the overnight pauperization of large populations of Swidden cultivators, hunters, food-gatherers or other subsistence seekers, who usually do not possess any legally enforcebale occupation or usufruct rights. Although they have occupied and utilized these territories for their sustenance for even thousands of years, through the stratagem of purely legalistic interpretation any compensation whatsoever may be ruled and usually is" (Mahapatra 1982).

Taking these and related issues in consideration a consensus was arrived at the Delhi seminar (referred to earlier), that a policy for relocation of the project oustees should particulary attend to :

(a) Physical and social environment as well as social composition and political economy of the area from where displaced;
(b) Participaton of the different sections of the population in the catchment area in deciding the pattern of rehabilitation; and
(c) Policy decisions about rehabilitation of the oustees with particular reference to (i) compensation versus rehabilitation subsidy and quantum of each (ii) factors and processes determining the site of rehabilitation, (iii) unit of rehabilitation: individual vs community and criteria for the identification of the community in case of the latter being considered as the unit, (iv) optimum population size in a settlement and socio-cultural, political-economic and ecological determinants of the same, (v) infrastructure and unities, (vi) interplay of endogenous and exogenous factors, (vii) dynamics of stabilisation of settlements, and (viii) integrated development of catchment and command areas of projects.

The review paper of Partridge (Mahapatra 1983) has brought out several issues not covered by the Delhi seminar. These include problems of health and nutrition related to project dislocation; alternative models of integration of the relocated population, other migrant population and pre-existing population in the command areas of the project. While it is expected that the various aspects mentioned here would be considered in the seminar as distinct items, an attempt will be made towards a synthesis through recognition of the emerging dimensions ofhuman needs and human potentials in the catchment and command areas.

Reference List

Bartolome LJ (1984) Forced resettlement and the survival systems of the urban poor, Ethnology XXIII

Bernard HR, Pelto J (1972) introduction technology and social change, In: Bernard HR, Pelto PJ (ed) The Macmillan Company, New York

Futurology Commission (1983) Seminar on Oustee relocation. Council for Social Development, New Delhi

Government of India (1982) Report of the committee on forest and tribals of India p 21

Hidayatualah M (1983) Right to property and the Indian constitution. Arnold Heinemann, New Delhi p 22

Kisler (1972) Relocation and technological change in Micronesia in technology and social change. In: Bernard HR, Pelto PJ (ed) The Macmillan Company, New York

Mahapatra LM (1983) Development for whom symposium E-040-00 XIth International Congress of anthropological and Ethnological Sciences, Vancouver

Partridge WL (1983) Stages of resetlement programme in the development of hydroelectric enterprises. Paper presented to seminar Efectos Sociales de las Grandes Represas de America Latin orgnaised by the CIDES Buenos Aires, Argentina

Roy Burman BK (1968) Social processes in the industrialisation of Rourkela (with reference to displacement and rehabilitation of tribal and other backward people. Mimeography Series, Office of the Registrar General of India, New Delhi Vol I

Roy Burman BK (1981) Transfer and alienation of tribal land. In: Choudhury B (ed) Tribal development in India. Inter-India Publications, New Delhi

Scudder T, Colson EF (1972) Kariba dam project. In: Bernard HR, Pelto PJ (ed) Technology and social change. Macmillan & Co, New York

Wallace T (1981) The Kano river project, Nigeria: the impact of an irrigation scheme on productivity and welfare. In: Heyer J, et al.(ed) Rural development in tropical Africa. Macmillan Press, p 283

TWENTY

ANTHROPOLOGY OF THE DISPLACED: PROBLEMS OF RESETTLEMENT AND DEVELOPMENT ALTERNATIVES

P.K. Nayak

It has been intended in this paper to envisage the competence of anthropology in bringing to the fore the ensemble of facts of human society and culture most accurately and in making scientific interpretation and analysis of group and institutional life for further application. Keeping in view such an objective, adaptability of anthropology to problems of contemporary societies and cultures and to the issues of the modern world has been reiterated. The emphasis "anthropology of the displaced" connote a study of the organizational behaviour of man in society under conditions of forcible displacement and the emerging pattern of relations and interactions with a motto to help solve the human problems arising thereof. The anthropologist in this context makes scientific approach towards the problem and at the same time feels the obligation to do something in the humanistic way so that he is not divested from the ethics of his discipline. For this, he has to understand the problems in the right earnest and prescribe solutions in the right perspective being aware of the blame that would come to the anthropology community incase his endeavour goes invain.

In the backdrop of the above assertions, the problems of resettlement due to the Rengali Dam Project in Orissa has been studied and development alternatives have been suggested which, it is hoped, not only will contribute to the applied nature of the discipline of anthropology to be put to practice by the anthropologists themselves, but also will add a new dimension to anthropology under the rubric of "anthropology of the displaced".

Widening Horizons of Anthropology Today

Anthropologists are in the march of studying phenomena of the order with which they were not acquainted earlier. They have been stimulated to investigate problems which are noval to anthropological tradition. World War II marked a major turning point in the development of anthropological concern for contemporary human problems. Researches were undertaken to help solve the administrative and human problems. Attention was given to problems of social and cultural change among living peoples, adjustment of indigenous people to modernization, problems of both administrative, human and social consequences in resettlement communities and above all to industrial organizational behaviour and business administration, a new branch of scientific investigation being labelled "interaction analysis". Of late, anthrrpologically based scientific reserch in policy formulation and implementation reflects the maturation of anthropology. Thus, a variety of human problems has drwan the attention of the anthropologists.

There has been a discernible shift from the study of ancient societies and pastcultures to the study of contemporary ones. Anthropologists have been enthusiastic rather to select topics on the basis of their relevance to current issues, contemporary problems and issues. Consequently anthropology has been developed as a systematic, comparative and holistic science of man. It balances the scientific and humanistic approaches and keeps pace with changes in the conditions of human life. More particularly anthropologists' intellectual concern to practical issues bring it into the main stream of social sciences. Application of holistic view to the understanding of human problems, and the anlaysis of social systems in terms of their interdependence, are unique contributions to the new types of organizational problems which confront all of us (Voget 1975).

Anthropologists derive strength from their holisitc approach towards the study of society and culture. Most of them still view the study of "primitive cultures as a key to comprehending modern societies. Anthropology's chief concern with the primitive cultures has undeniably set its theoretical and methodological perspectives. The dedication to empirical data collection distinguishes the anthropologists from other social scientists. Coupled with this they develop knowledge necessary to understand society and culture through micro-observations. The encounter with varieties of primitive cultures has made the anthropologists to realize of the cultural values of the respective cultures and societies. They study unwritten languages, oral tradtions, primitive and archaic customs-thus they value what others undervalue. They are the champions of the dispossessed, defenders of the despised and the neglected and pleaders of wider view and greater tolerance (Eddy and Patridge 1978). As essayist-scientists, anthropologists maintain caution in reporting practices of the people under study. The trained anthropologists develop awareness by the enthics of their discipline and while reporting their findings respect the beliefs and practices of the people.

Concern for applied anthropology has remained quite secondary, despite the ostensible commitment to make anthropology serve the interests of human welfare. Being guided by the ideal image of science anthropological investigators concentrated more on increasing the store of knowledge through objective observation and impartial analysis. Application of scientific knowledge and insights into the social problems has been felt to the administrators who control and make major decisions. Therefore, demand of anthropologists have only remained primarily at the pursuit of knowledge. Participation of the anthropologists in organized efforts to alleviate the conditions of peoples has been largely causal and private. At the level of critical policy decisions and implementation of welfare and development programmes it can' be said that there is only adhoc involvement of the anthropologists. Even while implementing development programmes in the tribal areas and while proposing to alleviate the pressing problems, counsel of the anthropologist is only accepted as an interpreter of primitive man (Mead, 1978).

Government shows little readiness for utilization of the knowledge of the anthropologist. It is observed that at some level under some circumstances the point of view of the aged anthroplogist is given more weightage irrespective of his specialization. The young and the fit are deprived fo their due. Close collaboration between professional administrator and the anthropologist is not permitted. Their roles have been restricted to that of a technical officer providing data analysis. Anthropologist's counselling is not the end but his participation is warranted. His neutrality is an essential factor in his effectiveness as a scientist.

What anthropologists can bring to planned change is not a methodological schema that could be applied with predictive confidence, but a perspective. The perspective is people-oriented, enunciating a principle of respect for ethnocultural differences and the right of minorities by self-choice to achieve their own life style. Whatever the people wish would prevail and not the action anthropologists themselves might consider a better choice.

The application of anthropological theory, method and perspective to community development is governed by the principle that a subject's life-style possesses an intrinsic worth and is directly relevant to a solution of his disturbance. The people need to be encouraged to participate in decisions and to build on the traditional strengths of their cultures (Nayak 1985). Anthropologists need to be allowed considerable latitude in formulation of the research problem and on the basis of their findings should be given the oppurtunity of pusuing action programmes. Their development programmes should not take on a more narrowed set of political objectives.

The anthropological reviews and evaluation of projects uniformly uncover the lack of success in coming to grips with the complexities of the local social and cultural context at every phase of the programme. Planned and controlled change obviously requires a sound set of theoretical and practical instruments if success is to be achieved (Nayak 1986). There are no set rules that can give part anwers; but there is now a considerable body of helpful information that has been gathered by social scientists and development specialists. The cultural factor which influence the acceptance and rejection of new idea can be considered either as obstacle or as stimulants according to the attitude of the change agents.

Problems of resttlement : Field findings

On request from OXFAM, Bhubaneswar, I had the opportunity of conducting one month field work in the resettlement areas around the Rengali Multipurpose Dam Project, Orissa, during July-August 1986.There investigators were engaged to fill out the detailed household schedules in 6 resettlement sample villages and detailed village schedules of 22 sample villages chosen on the basis of this regional distribution and strategic location with irrigation and without irrigation facilities. The major emphasis of the fieldwork was to assess the magnitude of problems faced by the resettled villagers.

Construction of Dam across river Brahmani in Dhenkanal district of Orissa State for flood control, irrigation and power generation purposes created a reservoir spread over 414 sq. k. affecting 9585 families in 265 villages. Out of 265 villages 44 were fully submerged, 70 were partly submerged and in the rest 151 villages only cultivable lands were submerged partially without affecting houses. In all 2972 famililities were displaced from the 114 villages, who have been allotted land for homestead land and land for cultivation besides having given the compensation. Whereas in the other 151 villages the people whose agricultural land was submerged were only given compensation and no rehabilitation facilities.

The important public institutions submerged were 6 High Schools, 20 M.E. Schools, 88 Primary Schools, 2, Public Health Centres, 11 recognized Temples and 1 Police Station.

2972 displaced families were resettled in 61 new resettlement villages set up in vacant Government land out of which 25 were set up in command area of Gohira irrigation Project. These villages were provided with (1) earthen road inside the habitation site with cross drainage work; (2) 3 wells for every 100 families with an additonal tube well for school and club; (3) 1 tank for each 100 families, (4) 1 primary school for each village upto 100 families; and (5) 1 club for each village upto 100 families (Superintending Engineer Rangali Dam 1986).

Another 4114 families were resettled in groups in vacant Government land of their choice in 92 different localities in existing old villages known as Individual Settlement Clusters. These 92 individual clusters were provided with (1) 1 well for every 15 families; (2) 1 tank for 30 families; (3) 1 two-roomed Upper Primary School for 30 families and apprach road where there is no approach to nearby P.W.D./Panchayat road.

The balance 2499 families opted for cash in lieu of land for their settlement (Superintending Engineer Rangali Dam 1986).

The displaced persons who were resettled in villages were provided with 0.5 acre of homestead land free of cost in which the people built their houses at their own expense. Timber required for building about 2 rooms were provided to each family through Forest Department on payment of nominal charges at concessional rate. Six acres of unirrigated land/3 acres of irrigated land were given to each family in resettlement villages for agricultural purposes on payment of nominal charges of Rs. 300/- per acre to Government. Landless displaced persons were exempted from payment of charges. The land was at Government cost and reclamation work included jungle clearance, uprooting of stumps, and field bunding to demarcate the plot only.

The displaced persons who opted for resettlement in individual clusters were also provided with agricultural land and homestead land as in the case of resettlement villages but reclamation was done by people themselves for which they were given Rs. 600/- per acre (Rs. 1000/- per acre of irrigated land).

The Government realized that shifting of persons from their ancestral home land to new areas involved massive problems which were predominantly humanitarian in nature and therefore provided facilities which were understood in liberal terms. However, our investigation shows that in the rrsettlement villages the problems faced by the people are zigantic in nature contributing to their present predicament. Some of these probles are highlighted below.

Problems of land, labour and cultivation

In the submerged villages, mainly paddy was exchanged for goods and services. The labourers were being paid in kind than cash. The services of barbers, blacksmiths, washermen, carpenters, potters and basket-makers were also exchanged for paddy. It shows that in the old villages they had some marketable surplus which enabled them to have command over other goods and services. However, due to resettlement the transition occurred from kind to cash as people had the compensation money with them and the yield from land diminished to 67.8%; which hardly left any farmer with some surplus to make various payments in terms of paddy. Monetary transactions are being made in every sphere of economic activity in the new settlement which has posed grave dangers for people having no other source of income except agriculture. Compensation money got 6/7 years before (paid in 1978-79) were spent towards meeting their daily consumption. Consequent upon more cash coming to them at a time, many oustee families spent the amount prodigiously in marriages and feasts which had remained unsettled and were being deferred earlier due to want of such an accumulated wealth. They did it so being propelled by the motivation and worldview characteristic of a group of unprogressive peasants. Under the circumstances lending something to a needy fellowman has been checked and the lender expresses his inability and helplessness.

The Government waste land and forest land alloted to the displaced families were more a liability than an asset. They are unprocessed and unproductive. In some plots big trees have been cut down and stumps have not been removed. Removing stumps, stones, and morrums from the fields have taken away lot of their time and energy. Neither lands have been levelled nor properly reclaimed. Especially lands allotted in the foot hills are full of forest growth and big trees. Because of these difficulties many individual households have not been able to cultivate the total amount of 3 acres/6 acres of land. In the 6 villages under intensive household survey it has been found out that only 59.3% of the allotted land have been made cultivable by the people. The allotted lands by and large belong to the type, such as, laterite, forest, sandy, and full of gravels. The quality of soil is poor due to low fertility. The per acre yield is abysmally low 1.84 quintals in the new settlements against 5.72 quintals in the old villages. The farmers find it difficult to go in for extensive cultivation as production is not commensurate with cost. The geographical conditions are not congenial or favourable to grow cereals and pulses.

Except a microscopically small number of villages adequate irrigation for lands has not been made effective till August 1986. As such farmers could ill afford to adopt HYV seeds let alone other methods of scientific cultivation. Discernible diminution in yield has caused people to wallow in poverty. This resulted in majority of villagers become indigent.

Multiple cropping was the pattern of agriculture in the old villages. In the new allotted land of 6 acres/3 acres the disadvantages of cropping are innumerable, viz. i. the land has not been brought under plough for obvious reasons of forest growth and foothill terrain and the reclamation cost being prohibitive, ii. the rain water during rainy season come flowing down torrentially causing soil erosion, sand casting and thus unsuitable for manuring and consequently low fertility. One important change has taken place with regard to cultivation of paddy. Here most of them grow **Guda dhan** (short term paddy of the upland variety) in which case the yield is less than 50% and this paddy was not frequently cultivated in the old village.

The economy in the old villages was characterized by "hand to mouth" concept. Many families were below the poverty line (Acharya and Das 1986). The people used to cultivate major cereals and pulses, many types of vegetables, oil seeds, tobacco and other cash crops basically for their own consumption. After moving to the new settlements they tried to resume their cultivation in the same old pattern but failed miserably due to the significant change in the geographical conditions. While in the old villages the varieties of crops grown were mostly for their consumption as well as small-scale commercial purposes. These varieties are yet to be grown to supplement their economy.

The landholder and the landless, rich and poor have been equalized in terms of allotment of land (6 acres/3 acres). Pride in one's status prevents the rich to labour in the paddy field. In the old village the system of relationship was such that labourers were being employed on annual, biennial end triennial contract and were paid in kind. No longer this has been the practice in the new settlements. The alternative is that only one can employ daily labourers on payment of cash which the relatively rich cannot afford. And even if some of them could afford it for sometime more they are not sure of the yield from the undependable land. Some of them apprehend that thereby they would lose the last money. They were economically more secured with their valuable possession, that is land. Their wealth was cattle. Prospect of cattle raising in the new environment is not encouraging.

Structural and cultural poblems

The people of the resettlement villages are living like individual families. The individual families have been compensated and resettled in scattered homestead land. Each family has its own way of presenting the problems and the problems of the community is rarely emphasized. "Individualism" has been more expressed than "collectivism". The "group based tie" or joint tie which is the ideal feeling tone of the family in Indian Society has been thoroughly overtaken by wants and deprivations at the level of each individual family.

The basis of selection of individual families taking into consideration the married couple and their unmarried children has posed a problem in the process of resettlement. It has been seen that it some cases after 1971 (the threshold year upto which the composition of family has been taken into account by the Government) the unmarried son has got married and has not been considered as forming a separate family and therefore not given land who, as such shares with the land allotted to his father and therefore the burden on family. In some other cases the father having received the compensation money has not given each son his legitimate share and the discrepancies maintained by the father has upset the rules of inheritance, for the son could have demanded his legitimate due had it been land. But since the father receives cash and he is the authority, sons could not challenge this officially. Altercations between father and married son and between married brothers breeds anomie in the family life. Consequent upon this estrangement in the family it has been seen that father and son and also joint brothers have chosen to resettle in separate villages. Frailty in the authority of the family has reversed the interpersonal role relationship which does not seem to be a happy trend.

The 'biradari' group relationship and the lineage tie at the level of 'caste group' has been broken off for the families have been spread out in different resettlement sites. At the time of the life-cycle rituals the unity has fallen behind. The service caste members, such as, barbers, washermen, and scavengers have been disturbed from the patron families. These services of the pople are conisdered quintessential for the maintenance of relative ritual status of the caste group on the line of purity and pollution. But as now the displaced persons are not being properly served by the traditional service caste men, they have been relegated to lower social status positions. The neighbouring villagers label them and refer to them as "budi loka", which means not merely the "people of the submerged area" but conveys an inferior status. Because of the low estimation of the social status of the oustees by the neighbours, getting brides for their boys has become a problem and getting groms for their daughters costs them more because of the trend of heavy demand of dowry. There has developed a trend of endogamy confined to the resettlement villages only.

The denizens of big villages have been dispersed far and wide and have been living in small groups in hamlet like structures. The section of the denizens having 'decisive dominance' have weilded power and have manipulated at the level of the Government officers, incharge of rehabilitation to take away with them a major share of the communal property and have succeeded in establishing schools, health centres and other amenities according to their own convenience in the new settlements. As a result the weaker section being dispatched to interior and far off areas has been denied and deprived for these facilities.

The village level unity has been eroded and socio-culturally the most prominent villages have lost their past glory, for these villages were forming the nucleus of a host of other villages. Thus, the "Unity and extension" which was being permeated at the inter village level has come to null and void. The displaced denizens hardly afford to foster a spirit of welfare and development for the "whole" and hence the inaction. Except on the occasion of religious ceremonies the village leadership, especially in developmental matters is defunct now.

Psychological problems

Leaving one's birth place and resettling in new surroundings amidst all odds and all the time fighting against these odds have made the people psychologically upset. The precarious living condition in the new settlements, insufficient food stuff, scarcity of water, threat of malaria and other uncommon diseases, and lack of facilities to give their children education, have been construed to persist long. All these have weakened their moral strength and courage. People are still brooding over the past issue of displacement and curse the multipurpose Dam project which has damned their life. In case of resettlement of groups of individual households, the neighbouring old villagers do not accept them well and treat them nicely for which there is growing frustration among them. In the new settlements everybody, irrespective to rich and poor, money-lender and debtor, the problem is same and of similar stretch. Under the circumstances one becomes helpless even to extend helping hands when he discovers his fellow neighbour in distress and remains in the brink as a mute spectator. At the sight of the Government officers visting their village they scramble over and lose temper on them, for they have not provided the required minimum facilities. The growing dissatisfaction among them has retarded their day to day progress and they feel as if they have been pushed back to the past four-five generations.

The uncongenial forest clad environment, the unsupportive community life and the struggle for eking out a living amidst the burden of the family have contributed to their growing frustration and dissatisfaction. Added to these, disruption in the cultural set up and anomaly in the social-structural makeup has rendered the individual oustees irrespective of young children and the elderly men and women, very much concerned and consequently the reign of inaction.

The quality of life has deteriorated to such an extent that people complain about the quality of drinking water, its use in food preparation and in taking bath. Skin diseases, particularly scabbies are rampantly found among young and the old. Children suffer the worst from ill health. People in general suffer from inferiority complex and express the view that they have been made destitute and feel as if they have been outcasted hanging onto the fringe of community life. Women in particular do not feel homely in the new settlements and suffer from mental isolation. Women in such peasant communities used to share with the activities of men but their spheres of activities have been squeezed. All the time they lament over the artificial life situation here in the new settlements.

Displacement and development alternatives

The Government policy enunciated in liberal terms for the displaced denizens of Rengali and the steps and measures taken at their end are not totally unconvincing. The survey of the resettlement areas and the empirical observations into the multiple and complex problems of the diplaced bring to light the lacunae in the rehabilitation policy as well as the major drawbacks in the implementation of the resettlement measures. In keeping with the tradition, culture and habits of the denizens nothing has been clearly spelt out at the stage of policy formulation and nothing concrete has been envisaged and pursued either during implementation or resettlement messures to satiate the felt needs of the people. It has never been envisioned that forceful displacement of people could be christened as a "crisis situation" and hence the need for "followup action".

It has been only construed that the people of the submerged villages are poor and therefore needed to be extended facilities in liberal terms by way of providing each family half acres of homestead land and 6 acres/3 acres of land for cultivation irrespective of the landless and the landholder. But never has it been conceptualized that these people represent a segment of rural peasants having mutual interdependence on one another and do have a culture of their own within the framework of which they interact and behave. Irrespective of the differences in the caste identity, most of them pursue agricultural occupation and derive nourishment from it at the same time being served by a few service-caste households who are indispensable to their very life and living.

Much before the completion of infrastrucutural work in the resettlement villages the people were evacuated, just when water submerged their native area. Although people were served the notice to vacate the villages as and when they were disbursed compensation money, due to lack of prior altertness, decisive planning and timely execution, the evacuees were digressed and rambled, and being scared of their life, shifted to the allocated area in haste, and in the process, suffered from untold miseries. This could have been avoided less humanistically but more realistically and pragmatically.

There is a note of satisfaction among the general public as well as among the officers in charge of rehabilitation that the relatively rich in terms of more landholding have got more compensation money to support and maintain their respective standard of living. But paradoxically enough, all this amount has gone into wasteful expenditure like having been spent in marriages long deferred, and in building fire-proof pucca houses in the new settlements from which return for their living is nill. Instead, the alternative would have been more economic and enterprising had the money been spent in renovating the land given to them for agricultural purposes under the direct supervision of field technicians and the affected people themselves.

Being constituted of a group of "unprogressive peasants" (crude technology with literacy approximately being 44%) and having the ideology of seeing future in their present most of the displaced denizens lacked the knowledge of the investment value of money and in few exceptions only understood its storage value. Only sparingly money has been used in renovating land. As a result, 59.3% of land, somehow has been brought under one-crop cultivation and the rest has been left untouched. In addition to this, the land has low fertility value, yet be developed, and domesticated, for which vigorous agricultural work has not been resumed. Without understanding the field constraints, the settler families are being castigated as lethargic and indolent, who do not have the mind to cultivate more and grow varieites of crops to help themselves. However, it would have been proper had the expertize of a team of agricultural scientists, soil analysts and environment scientists (anthropologists included) been sought from the beginning till the resumption of normal agricultural activities by the people in the new settlements. They would have been helpful in assessing suitability of land for settlement as well as for cultivation, in creating viable conditions for living in mutual consultation with the displaced, and above all, in providing expertize in solving their emergent and in situ problems in the beginning, and in furthering the interests of the people by pursuing follow-up action programmes with the spirit of a team of "development scientists."

Construction of Dams for the wider interest of the State and the Nation is as much warranting as resettlement of the displaced denizens who sacrified for the cause. Logically, further as security and maintenance of the Dam is the responsibility of the Government so also is taking care of the displaced, and their future development. Just having seen the people resettled somehow, should not be misconstrued as the end in itself (Nayak 1979).

In view of the foregoing delineation of facts and discussions of the complex problem of resettlement, the development alternatives for the displaced could be more precisely put in abstract terms as follows :

1. Problem of displacement is not merely the problem of the people concerned but of the State, the Nation and the wider society as a whole.

2. Wisdom of rehabilitation officers need to be guided and supported by the ingenuity and expertize of the "development scientists", for certain human problems are to be comprehended realistically and tackled more pragmatically. Under the circumstance, these issues become technical and need to be technically handled.

3. "Displacement" and "resettlement" are complex problems, for it involves real life situations of human beings. At the level of identification, problems are to be seen in reality - abstraction continuum. For tackling the problems of real life situations, the problems are to be comprehended from a wider angle than from a narrow and limited point of view.

4. Since the problem refers to groups of interacting human beings, development actions need to be people - oriented. The displaced community should be encouraged to formulate its own goals and organize human and technical resources for the attainment of community objectives. Through suggesting and providing opportunities (within the limits of the resources) the people should be presented with alternatives for decision and should be left free to formulate and implement their own goals with dignity and self respect.

Reference List

Acharya P K, Das M (1986) Rehabilitation of people displaced due to construction of Rengali dam, procee of the 53rd annual research and development No 148, New Delhi

Mead M (1978) the evolving ethics of applied anthropology. In : Eddy, Patridge (ed) Applied Anthropology in America, Columbia University Press. New York

Nayak P K (1979) Foreseeable problems of displacement a study of the Denizens of Indravati dam project, procee of the research seminar, Department of Anthropology, Utkal University, India

Nayak P K (1985) Tradition and development in tribal Orissa. Directorate of Harijan and tribal welfare, Government of Orissa, News Magazine II : 1-11

Nayak P K (1986) Welfare and economic development in Bhuiyan Pirh, Keonjhar need for scientific understanding and implementation, procee of the national seminar on monitoring and evaluation of tribal development programmes, Bhubaneshwar, Orissa

Patridge, Eddy (1978) the development of applied anthropology. In : Eddy and Patridge (ed). Applied anthropology in America, Columbia University Press, New York

Superintending Engineer Rengali Dam (1986) Rengali multipurpose project note on rehabilitation work

Voget F W (1975) Applied anthropology. In : Rinchart H, Winstron (ed) A History of Ethnology, New York pp 773-777

TWENTY ONE

ECOLOGY, ENVIRONMENT AND POPULATION: SOME BASIC ISSUES

M.R. Chakravartti

As we near the end of the 20th century, we have begun to discern the beginning of environmental crisis, which is characterized by the unprecedented growth and development of human society. Over-utilisation of natural resources and harnessing the forces of nature for the benefit of a growing human population and concurrent apathy towards environmental degradation and conservation have begun to boomerang on the hitherto unsuspecting world population. An ever-increasing population with aspiration for a quality of life hitherto unknown is placing a tremendous stress on all that the environment can provide; so much so, in parts, the environment has started to give way. Evidence of these phenomena can be seen in the spread of desertification, soil maladies, floods and droughts, urban congestion, extinction of/or threat to countless species of plants and animals that make the ecosystem and the ubiquitous pollution of land, water and air. The situation calis for a new approach to development. Faced with such environmental and ecological concerns, the International Union of Anthropological and Ethnological Sciences (IUAES) has rigntly set up a Commission of Human Ecology (CHE)[1] in Februrary 1986. The interdisciplinary approach of CHE will aim at minimising the impact of human activities on the physical and ecological environment. The Commission will make a sincere endeavour to monitor the overuse misuse and abuse of the environment through rational implementation in various frontiers with the active cooperation with a number of working groups.[2] The working group proposes to endorse the theme 'Development without Destuction' as launched by the World Conservation strategy. The concept of protecting ecosystems while providing a base for sustained development will also be maintained by the working group.

The ecological crisis

Human being imposes changes on natural ecosystems and increasing control of his environment often creates conflicts between his goals and natural processes. In the present economic system of free exchange takes place between the natural ecosystem and the socioecosytem, which is increasing in an unidirection. This has caused the ecological crisis. The human exploitation of natural resources at a greater rate than it can be regenerated, and putting back inputs into the natural ecosystem is responsible for environmental maladies. One of the consequences of this one-sided exchange system has been the failure of the established geobiological balance of an ecosystem in which human being too has evolved and found a niche (Khoshoo 1984). This mis-allocation of resources thereby leading to over-production of wastes eventually poses a threat to to the survival of mankind.

The people of our contry must realize that the future of mankind is intimately interwoven with ecology. They must use natural sources rationally and must take immediate steps to repair the damage already done to the ecosystem. Our immediate need is to ensure ecology and ecodevelopment in a manner that these have self-rectifying capacity so that our life support system is not strained beyond measure. Unless ecology becomes a people's movement we cannot achieve results. The initiative for drawing attention to the important task of protecting our natural resources from degradation must come from the general public. The edited version of Gadgil-Malhotra (1983) report is a case in point. The shortfall between consumption and production results in undue pressure on our plant cover which has been reduced progressively. As a result of the reduction of plant cover as also the three major environmental ills, population, poverty and pollution, we are indeed at cross road. All this is the result of development and progress which reflected on the importance of environment and ecology.

The government of India has set up a Department of Environment at the centre with the overall responsibilities of ensuring environmental protection nd conservation. Environment is the resource comprising land and all that it contains on the surface and beneath, water and the life it suports with air. The department has started deploying these resource components of the environment, for efficient development for optimum benefits to all, and for enhanced quality of life and the environment.

Enhancing quality of life : Environmental management

It is essential to assess the potential of the environment for supporting life processes and for providing the resources for development. This is vital for the continued progress of manking. To put this in another way, the carrying capacity, which implies the ability of the environment to supply the inputs for man, animal and plant must be evaluated as precisely as possible.

Population regulatio is a concomitant necessity for environmental management. It is quality of life that people aspire to which may set the environmental goals. Graves (1983) stated that at the basic level the quality of life is concerned with the conditions which make survival possible. Yoong (1985) while discussing the environmental component related to the quality of life, raised the two components of the environment which are directly connected with the quality of life.

The environment consists of (a) the natural environment and (b) the human environment. The natural environment includes the natural resources of the country. Much of quality of life is influenced by one's attitudes towards the environment and how we perceive we ought to relate with. In general, the quality of life will be severely reduced if the natural environment is excessively exploited and abused in the interest of economic progress. Air and water pollution is largely the result of man's activities and of technological industrialisation and which have become the main factors to affect the quality of life. Quality of life also depend on society's efforts to preserve its natural heritage and life forms and quality of life will utlimately depend on the balance achieved between the society, its economic well being and the environment. The human environment comprises the socialization process and the relationship among members of the society within the environment. Quality of life has criteria which related to friendship and to how close people are interacting with each other in the community or society at large. The close the relationship and cooperation among people, the higher is the quality of life. Environmental management needs an integrated planning approach, which is aimed at managing human activities in order to maintain an acceptable balance between the qualities of the human and natural environments.

Envrionment Management

For management of a system, there is a need for system status evaluation. In the case of a complex dynamic system like the environment, one possible approach would be to attempt evaluation of status of subsystems. Khoshoo (1984) presents conceivable subsystem of the environment.

Subsystem	Index of status
Air	Air quality
Water	Water quality
Land	Soil characteristics/ Productivity
Flora and Fauna	Population size; Population Dynamics, Genetic Diversity

Even so, it is readily apparent, the difficulties of quantitative evaluation are not resolved. Especially with regards to flora and fauna, we enter into a complex, interlinked web of living systems, which even by themselves are inherently complex. On a macro-scale, it has been suggested that the health of a population is an index of the health of its habitat. Human health as reflected by the mortality rates can possibly measure the effect of overall environmental situation in which the population lives. Another possible macro-index of the environmental status could be derived from indices based on resource measurements. Estimates of avilable resources, and economically exploitable natural resources are routinely made for the purpose of assessing potential for development. The answer to a reasonably accurate measure of the environmental status must come from ecology, which provides a perceptive on the relationship of an organism to the environment.

One of the primary tools to date for bringing out the potential effects of human activities on environmental systems is the Environmental Impact Assessment. In some cases, such as pollution impacts, a certain measure of quantification is possible, but in respect of long term ecological and social impacts, the desired degree of quantification is not achieved. To be fully effective, the Environmental Impact Assessment must identify, measure and evaluate both the beneficial and adverse environmental impacts of the development project. In order to undertake environmental management practice, the following support systems are necessary :

(a) Environmental Management and Information system
(b) Environmental Monitoring and Surveillance System
(c) Environmental Research

We need to know the status of environment before we can attempt to manage it. An adequate environmental information system is an indispensable adjunct to the environmental management system. Similarly, environmental monitoring systems are equally important for successful environmental management. Khoshoo (1984) mentions three subsystems for monitoring enironmental change. These three subsystems involve the periodical evaluation of the status of the environment and its components and includes the health status of the people, population dynamics of human being and sensitive species, the yield of plants and animals, the productivity of soil and so on. One must search for sensitive biological indicators of environmental degradation and monitor their status in the prevalent ecosystem. In so far as environment is concerned, there are a host of interacting interlinks between environmental media, ecosystems and species. Research is urgently needed into the methodology of invironmental appraisal, improved techniques for monitoring environmental change, finding solutions for imminent environmental problems, controlling environmental degradation and reversing environmental trends and restoring the health of the environment. Enumeration of these tasks serves to illustrate how much research yet to be undertaken and how little has been the research inputs so far. We have hardly established an adequate research base for environmental management. A systemwise linkup of scientists, technologists, anthropologists, social scientists and others concerned, is therefore absolutely essential for penetrating the complex system we know as our environment and evolving the optimum approaches to management of the system.

Environment management policy has to define how much environmental protection society can afford to insist on, without grossly compromising other equally relevant but often conflicting social aspirations for imporved quality of life, enhanced development opportunity, stable economic climate, equaitable income distribution, availability of needed energy, gainful employment and leisure time activites. This concept of integrated physical, socio-economic and environmental planning and management is therefore the only comprehensive and multi-goal strategy for environmentally sound resource utilisation for attaining desirable quality of life.

Population perspective

There have been a number of discussions on the subject : Population, environment and natural resources and development are indeed interrelated. The International Conference on Population held in Mexico in 1984 recommended that 'population distribution goals should be pursued to the extent that they help to achieve broader Societal goals, such as protecting the environment and improving quality of life.'

Population of India, according to 1981 census was 685 million with 354 and 331 million males and females respectively. In India, contrast to developed world, age-wise population distribution has a pyramidal pattern. Children constitute 39.7%, youth 32.6%, middle-aged persons 21.5% and old 6.2%. While such a structure of population on the one hand is a big asset, on the other hand it is conducive to further population growth. With the predominance (73%) of young people (upto 34 years of age) the momentum of our population is such that it would grow at a faster rate because the number of couples entering reproductive age would be far greater than those who will move out of this age group. An aspect needing investigation in depth is the motivation of child-bearing in a country like India which is over 76% rural and agricultural in character. In 1980, the birth rate in India was around 34/1000. The rate will come down from over 30/1000 people to about 21/1000 and nearly 11/1000 by 2020 AD with a death rate to 9/1000. This itself indicates that the family planning coverage should be increased to 60% couples. There is a particular need for spreading education and literacy, providing vocations and enhancing income levels and earning capabilities among women. There appears to be a direct correlation between this and the falling birth rates. The crux of the matter is that future population growth has to be related to the resource base in order to have sustainable development. The interaction between societal needs and life support system combined with aspirations needs a closer study. The size of population is governed by :

(a) resources needed by population
(b) existing environmental conditions
(c) limits of tolerance to various environmental conditions

The maximum populatio size that an ecosystem can support indifintely under particular environmental conditions is called the carrying capacity of that ecosystem. If the population size overshoots the carrying capacity by a wide margin, it undergoes a population crash which can occur when there is a change in environmental conditions that lower the level of carrying capacity. In essence it implies that only a certain number of people can be supported by the resources of a country. Zero population growth holds the key to our prosperity and to achieve this there should be a close cooperation between the government and the public at large. In fact the policy on population should be a movement in concert with the whole spectrum of government and the public.

Ecology and human settlements

India's population has grown in three decades, steadily over the years from 361 million in 1951 to 685 million in 1981. This has been the result of improvement in health standards as also a measure of socio-economic transformation. Average population density jumped from 77/km^2 in 1901 221/km^2 in 1981. This amounts to 300% increase. Due to influx of rural people in urban areas in search of livelihood population has increased from 11% in 1901 to 25% in 1981 and projections are that by turn of century the population in urban areas would not be less than 70%. Over 40% of India's population in rural areas is below the poverty line. For them agro-climatic factors are critical and their energy needs (about 90%) are met from non-commercial fuels like firewood, vegetable waste, dung, etc. of this 85% is collected free of cost. The per captia land area in the country was 0.82 ha in 1951 and under impact of growing popultion and land availablity has declined to 0.48 ha in 1981. However, only 62%of our land is suited for human settlements and real per capita land for human use is only 0.27 ha. Nearly 17.8 million ha is under non-agricultural use of which only 1.8 million ha accounts for land used for 3215 urban settlements. The man-land ratio in India is one of the lowest in the world. (UNEP, 1985).

Human settlements cannot be treated in isolation. Housing is a felt-need both in urban, slum and rural situations. Currently, there is shortage of 21 million houses (16 million in rural and 5 million in urban areas) (Khoshoo 1986), in our country. The populatio of slums is likely to go up from 28 million to 53.2 million by 1990. Commensurate with this is ill planned or unplanned or even absence of water supply and sanitation systems. Furthermore, in any programme on drinking water, sewerage has been constantly ignored. The refuse, therefore, affects water-bodies and in turn causes problems of environmental sanitation and health. Coupled with this is the fact that 80% of the diseases are water-related. The vulnerable sections of our society and among them women and children suffer the most.

There has been a tendency to accuse the rural people as also the slum dwellers for environmental degradation, but it is actually the urban-high-energy and high-consumptive life styles which put pressure to improve the living conditions of the weaker sections of our society, it is important that the life styles of urban people becomes less energy demanding and less consumptive in character. The country is facing acute shortage of at least 21 million houses of which 76% (16 million) are needed in rural and 24% (5 million) inurban areas. Nearly 91% and 92% in Bihar and Assam respectively is needed in the rural sector (MWH, 1984) To provide housing of this magnitude, future expansion and growth of settlements will depend on theseveral socio-economic, ethnic, cultual and other considera-tion including agricultural productivity in relation to avialability of goods and services from the ecosystems. The negative impacts of the absence of housing are indeed the cause of a lot of human misery with consequent degradation in physical health, economic and socio-cultural environment.

According to a survey of National Building Organisation, there are merely 25 million people in slum settlements of which 40% live in metoroplitan cities. About 67% of population in Cal-cutta and 45% in Bombay are slum dwellers. Jawaharlal Nehru once remarked that 'if you cannot provide buildings for those dwelling in slums, give them open space to live and give them at least some social services like good sanitation and water supply. The rest will follow.'

Thus the slums need basic amenities which may be looked as minimum needs like drinking water, sewerage, storm water drainage, paved lanes, street lighting, community latrines and bath rooms and above all education. If these become available, slum dwellers will undergo a sea change. the need to accelerate the provision of houses to homeless has been stressed time and again. The UN has declared 1987 as the International year of shelter for the HOuseless (MWH, 1984). It is not only a means of providing shelter but also an instrument of social policy and ensuring social justice for this economically weaker section. Other aspects of the programme include, provision of drinking water, sanitation, water disposal etc. which are directly related to the quality of the environment that would emanate in a par-ticular human settlement.

According to TCPO (1985), there are about 28 million people in the slums to day and in 1990 this figure is likely to go up to 55.2 million. Roughly, 38.8% of the slum dwellers will be located in the 12 metropolitan cities. A scheme for Environ-mental Improvement of Urban Slums (EIUS) was launched in 1972 which envisaged one tap per 150 persons, one lavatory seat for 20-50 persons and one community bath for 20-50 persons. On November 10, 1980 an 'International Drinking water supply and Sanitation Decade' was launched to supply clean water and dis-posal of night soil as also dirty water. The programme assumes added importance because 80% of the diseases are connected, in one or the other way, with water. The cost of lost production to India on account of these diseases has been estimated as Rs.4,500 million per year (Agarwal et al 1983). According to MWH (1984) out of 3800 cities and towns in the country, over 2100 towns were provided with water supply but 200 of these have sewerage system and that too partially.

The picture in the next two decades would be that India would become increasingly industrial and there would be more people (about 70%) in urban areas. The urban planning has, therefore, to be based on the needs of the poor. The strategy has to be, to plan settlements on the basis of environmental considerations and on land-use rather than land economics. Environmental impact assessment of land use has to be worked out together with a strategy aimed at minimising environmental stress on settlements. Furthermore, a policy on population distribution and settlement development in relation to ecological functions and landscapes of the regions need to be chalked out on a location specifica basis. The industrial location policy and relevant employment need to be assessed for environmental impacts. A thorough understanding of physical, economic, health and social impacts on the life of the under-privileged needs to be obtained.

Environmental education

The year 1985 was declared by the UN as the year of the youth and by FAO as the year of forests. More than any other country, for India both these programmes were most relevant. With more than 58% of its population in age-group of 5 to 34% years, there is an urgent need for utilising this work force for cleaning, greening and grassing of our country. The Tiwari Committee Report (1980) which has already been accepted by government of India, however, states °the need to cultivate sound, well organised interest in environment and incorporate environmental education at all levels'. On the occasion of the first International Conference on Environmental Education held at New Delhi in 1981, late Prime Minister Mrs. Indira Gandhi observed that the environmental education is to help 'arouse social consciousness and make Community aware of the fact that the good of the individual and that of the community are both harmed by ecological disruptions'.

The importance of environmental education cannot be over emphasised, because environment is a common heritage. It is essentially a partnership programme in which an individual plays a pivotal role. If individuals are enviromentally educated; the society and the government are automatically educated because the latter two are only an extension of an individual. The Chinese perception about education is thus quite significant in this respect :

> 'If you plan for one year, plant rice
> If you plan for ten years, plant trees
> But, if you plan for one hundred years, educate the people'

Recommendation of the working group on resources, population and technology

The VII Plan has assumed that, on the present reckoning, the net reproductive rate (NRR) will be reduced to one only by the year 2011. There is need for a reappraisal of this target, and that every possible effort should be made to achieve NRR 1 by year 2000, as recommended by the Working Group on Population Policy set up by the Planing Commission. In a seminar on exploring India's development perspectives for the year 2000 AD held recently in New Delhi under the auspices of IASSI, the recommendations of the Working group are stated below. The group recognised the hard core of the problem as in the case of universalization of elementary education, involving the economically and socially deprived sectors of the population, and that the younger age of the target couples called for a major structural change in the mix of contraceptive methods, and correspondingly in the delivery system. Also, a special major effort was needed in the States of Bihar, Rajasthan and Uttar Pradesh, where among other things, female literacy was very low, female age at marriage was also low, and the infant mortality very high. Special efforts therefore would include additional resources for various socio-economic programmes such as elementary education, expansion of PHC and hospital facilities, rural water supply, nutrition, women's welfare, etc., which have an influence over fertility behaviour.

The group noted that reduction of women's drudgery, in particular with regard to collection of firewood and drinking water, emphasis on female education, and the ehancement of the Status of women in society, would also have an important bearing on fertility behaviour.

Even if NRR 1 could be reached by year 2000, the country would have a population of approximately 100 million. The development process is therefore going to have a very considerable impact on the land, water and forest resources of the country. The planning and execution of many projects, the pattern of land and water use, and the thoughtless deforestation that has been going on, have been a cause of considerable concern. There is an urgent need to prevent any further degradation of the country's basic natural and life-support systems of land, water and vegetation, and to counter the damage already done by vigrous efforts to replenish forests, to conserve soil, to restore water tables, and to desalinate lands lost to cultivation. Conservation of available water resources, development and use of water resources with watershed as a unit, careful husbanding of ground water resources including steps to recharge depleted ground water reservoirs, cropping patterns which do not overuse available water and allow for an equitable sharing of water and an optimal use of the land, are some of the measures that were recommended. Environmental concern has also to extend to preservation of genetic diversity.

The group was concerned about the exploitation pattern of some of the minerals in the country, leading to the rapid depletion of some of these non-renewable resources. It was of the view that the exports of raw ores must be replaced by exports of value-added products.

The group noted that the entire field of environmentally sound natural resource management, involving as it does questions of the land use patterns in villages, deforestation by vested interests versus need for reforestation by, and for the community, the pattern of sharing of water within a basin or between basins, will call for the exercise of an extra-ordinary degree of political understanding and will, coupled with financial and administrative inputs.

The group was concerned about the adverse impact on the ecology of the Himalyan region due to the many development projects including hydro-electric projects, road construction, tourism and associated activites, exploitation of forest and other resources, etc. While the region had to be developed economically, it was necessary to adopt a systematic approach, with co-ordination of the various agencies involved, so as to ensure that the adverse environmental impact is minimal.

The group was conerned about the increasing consumerism in the society, and especially about the fact that the mass media were being exploited for promoting consumerism rather than for education and for projecting new values and a vision of the kind of society that one would like to see emerge by year 2000.

The group recognized the importance of substantial and sustained R & D efforts in the areas of energy-conserving technologies, new energy source, and biotechnologies for agriculture and health.

Notes

1. The Commission is headed by Dr. N. Wolanski (Warsaw, Poland) with Dr. M.R. Chakravartti as one of the members from India. The secretariat of the CHE is situated in France.
2. The working group on 'Social and Biological problems of

human environment' has been set up under the Chairmanship of Dr. M.R. Chakravartti.

Reference List

Agarwal A, Kimondo J, Moreno G, Tinker J (1983) Water sanitation health for all ? Earthscan publ Int Inst for environment and development. London

Gadgil M, Malhotra K (1983) A people's view of eco-development ESG publ 7. New Delhi

Graves NJ (1983) Geography and the quality of life. ICSU. London

Khoshoo TN (1984) Environmental concerns and strategies. Ind Envt Soc New Delhi

Khoshoo TN (1986) Environment priorities in India and sustainable development. Presidential address 73 session of Indian Sc Cong association. Delhi

MWH (1984) International year of shelter for the homeless. Ministry of works and housing. Govt. of India. New Delhi

TCPO (1985) Indian slumps town and country planning orgn Govt of India. New Delhi

Tiwari committee report (1980) vide ref Khoshoo TN (1986)

UNEP (1985) The state of environment 1985. UNEP. Nairobi

Yoong CS (1985) Biology education for improving quality of life ICSU/CTS paper number food and and agriculture 18. London

TWENTY TWO

MAN - TREE RELATIONSHIP IN AN URBAN SETTING: A SOCIO-ECOLOGICAL STUDY

Kailash C. Malhotra, M.Vijaya Kumar

INTRODUCTION

The last decade has witnessed a growing concern among the academicians, politicians, planners and the masses regarding forests and forestry practices in the country. The crucial role played by the forests in maintaining the life support systems is being increasingly realized.

It is, however, highly noteworthy that practically no attention has been paid regarding the tree cover and man-tree relationship in urban areas. No systematic studies are available for any of the urban centers in the country in terms of the tree densities, the types of tree species planted, the role trees play in the lives of the city dwellers and the wild life. An understanding of these aspects is indeed very necessary for formulating a national policy on trees in urban centers.

With this in view, a pilot study was undertaken on a 4.6 km stretch on Barrackpore Trunk Road. The specific object of the investigation was to estimate the density of avenue trees, the type of trees planted and the role played by the trees in the life of city dwellers and wild life. The study demonstrates that the trees not only play important ecological role but also provide a specialized subsistence niche to a large section of the city population in general and poor people in particular.

Method and Materials

For the present pilot study a 4.6 km stretch on Barrackpore Trunk Road (B.T.Road) from Hemanta Setu in the south to Dunlop Bridge Crossing in the north was selected (Fig 22.1) A

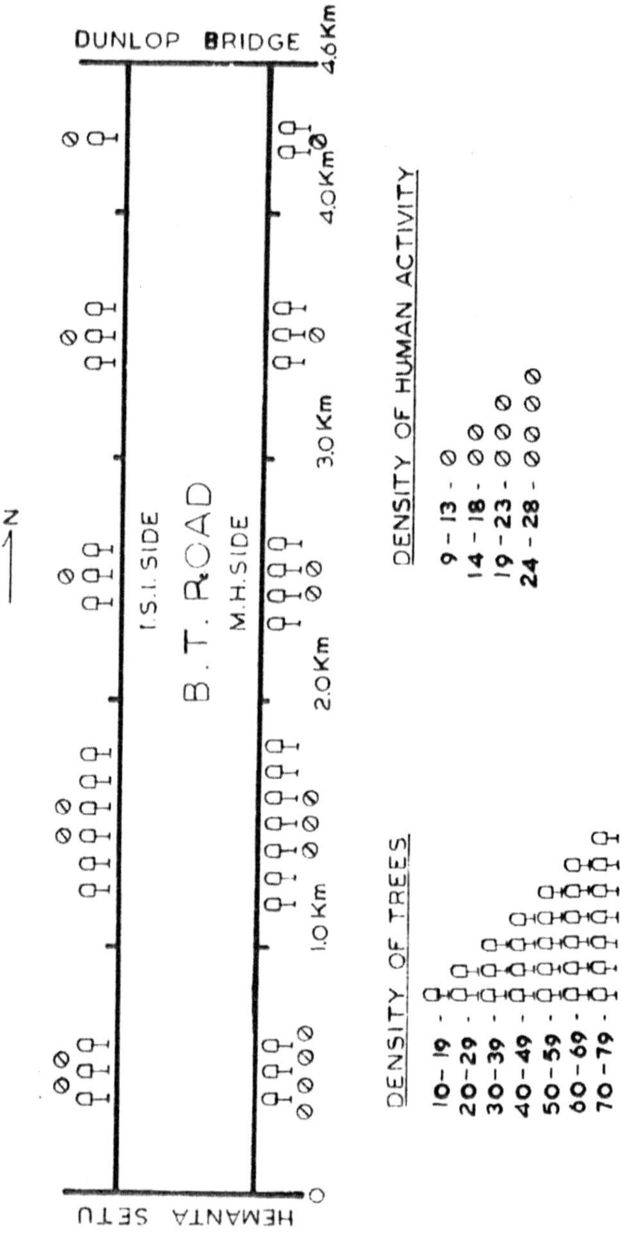

FIGURE 22.1 : SCHEMATIC MAP OF THE DENSITIES OF TREES AND ASSOCIATED HUMAN ACTIVITY ON B.T. ROAD

complete census of all the planted trees, separately for each side of the road, was made. For each tree the associated human acitivity was recorded. The survey was conducted between 9 am and 1 pm in March 1986. A number of photographs, representing various human activities associated with avenue trees, the species diversity and other relevant ecological features, were taken.

In order to get details about the history of plantation efforts, it was necessary to have obtained the exact age of each tree. Unfortunately such information was not readily available and the local residents could provide accurate information only about the trees planted during the last 5 years. We have, therefore, classified the trees into two categories: (i) those planted during the last 5 years are referred to as 'Young' and (ii) those planted before 5 years are desginated as 'Mature'.

Dr. Sunanda Chanda of the Leaf Protein Research Unit, Indian Statistical Indstitute, kindly identified and provided the scientific names of the various plant species encountered in the survey.

Results

Density of Avenue trees

Table 22.1 gives the number of young and mature trees observed on each side of the B.T.Road. The two sides of the road, for the sake of clarity and convenience, are designated as Indian Statistical Institute side (ISI side) and Milan Hotel side (MH side). In order to comprehend the probable variation in densities along the B.T. Road, the 4.6 km stretch under consideration has been treated seperately under five sections (for details see table 22.1). Except for the stretch between Bonhooghly to Dunlop Bridge which is 0.6 km, the remaining four stretches are 1 km long each.

Altogether 400 trees, 186 on the ISI side and 214 on the MH side, were observed at the time of the survey. There is a marked variation in the densities of trees between the 5 stretches of the road. On the ISI side the densities vary from a minimum of 20 trees/km (weighted for 1 km) to 63 trees/km with an average of 38.8 trees/km. The densities of trees on the MH side vary between 35/km to 74/km, averaging 45.6 trees/km. The best stretch, on both sides of the road is between Sinthee More and Police HQ where 137 out of the total 400 trees i.e., 34.25% have been observed. The trees on the MH side are slightly more (53.5%) compared to ISI side (46.5%).

Thus, the average densities works out to be only 42.2 trees per km on each side of the road.

TABLE 22.1
Tree densities along the 4.6 km strech of the Barrackpore Trunk Road

Stretch (south to north)		Side MH	ISI	Total
Hemanta Setu to Police HQ (1 km)	M	15	14	29
	Y	23	23	46
	T	38	37	75
Police HQ to Sinthee More (1 km)	M	10	16	26
	Y	64	47	111
	T	74	63	137
Sinthec More to Tobin Road (1 km)	M	16	13	29
	Y	29	22	51
	T	45	35	80
Tebin Road to Bonhoogly (1 km)	M	23	12	35
	Y	13	27	40
	T	36	39	75
Benhoogly to Dunlop (0.6 km)	M	11	8	19
	Y	10	4	14
	T	21	12	33
TOTAL (4.6 km)	M	75	63	138
	Y	139	123	262
	T	214	186	400

MH = Milan Hotel side; ISI = Indian Statistical Insitute side; M = Mature trees; Y = Young trees; T = Total.

It is observed that the proportion of young trees is nearly double (65.5%) then the, mature trees (34.5%). The proportion between young and mature trees, however, varies considerably between the 5 stretches of the road. Except for the stretch between Bonhoogly to Dunlop Bridge, the frequency of young trees is higher than the mature ones in all the other stretches;

the maximum difference is observed between Sinthee More and Police HQ (26 mature, III young).

Species diversity

In tables 22.2 and 22.3 are given the local as well botanical names and the number of various plant species obeserved on each side of the road. Altogether 17 species were noted. Irrespective of the side, three spcies, namely, Bat (Banyan) (Ficus benghalensis L.) Aswath (Peepal) (Ficus releqiosa L.) and Krishnachuda (Caesalpinia pulcherimma SW.) were the most dominant ones. These three constitute 74 per cent (296/400) of all the species encountered. The percent occurence of these three species Bat, Aswath and Krishnachuda is 37.75%, 13.75% and 22.50%, respectively. The other species occuring in appreciable number are Neem (Azadirachta indica Adv. Juss.) (20/400, 5%), Kadam (Anthocephalus Kadamba Mieq.) (5.75%) and Radhachuda (Delonix reqia Raf.) (3%). The remaining species occur only sporadically and none exceeds 1.25%.

An inspection of tables 22.2 and 22.3 reveal highly interesting result in terms of the proportion of young and mature trees. The proportion for Aswath and Bat more or less remains same, mature being 98 and young ones 108. However, in the case of Krishnachuda the difference between the frequency of young and mature trees is highly marked; of the total 90 trees only 3 are mature while 87 are young. The other species occuring sporadically are mostly represented by young trees.

It is thus clear that the species preferred earlier for plantation were primarily Bat and Aswath with occassional Neem as reflected by the proportion of mature trees. In recent years the most preferred species has been Krishnachuda, as compared to other spcies. Earlier mature trees of Krishnachuda were only 3 while that of Bat and Aswath were 98, but in the plantations undertaken during the last 5 years 87 of Krishnachuda and 108 of Bat and Aswath were planted.

Human activities associated with Avenue trees

In table 22.4 are listed the different types of human activities that have been observed associated with the avenue trees on B.T.Road. It is noted that 142 trees (35.5%) of the total 400 trees were associated with some kind of human activity. The proportion of such activities was associated more with the mature trees than with the young trees. Of the 138 mature trees 88 (63.8%) and of the 262 young trees 54 (20.6%) were associated with human activity. Since the propor-

TABLE 22.2
Distribution of tree species on the ISI side of the B.T.Road

B.T. Road Tree species	0.6 km M	0.6 km Y	1.6 km M	1.6 km Y	2.6 km M	2.6 km Y	3.6 km M	3.6 km Y	4.6 km M	4.6 km Y	TOTAL M	TOTAL Y	M+Y
Aswath Ficus religiosa L.	0	1	2	0	0	1	5	5	5	8	12	15	27
Bat Ficus benghalensis L.	7	2	7	1	10	4	8	6	7	7	39	20	59
Neem Azadreachta indica Adv.Juss.	1	0	0	1	1	2	1	0	2	2	5	5	10
Mango Mangifera indica L.	0	0	0	0	0	0	0	0	0	0	0	0	0
Kadam Anthocephalus Kadamba miq.	0	0	0	1	1	1	0	5	0	1	1	8	9
Krishnachuda Caesalpinta Pulcherrima Sw.	0	1	1	15	0	9	0	16	0	4	1	45	46
Radhachuda Delonix regia Ref.	0	0	1	3	0	0	0	3	0	0	1	6	7
Causurina Causurina equsitifolia Forst.	0	0	0	0	0	2	0	0	0	0	0	2	2
Eucalyptus Eucalyptus globaers Labil	0	0	0	0	0	2	0	0	0	0	0	2	2
Chatim Alstonia Scholaris R.Bv.	0	0	0	0	0	0	1	1	0	0	1	1	2
Tamarind Tamarindus indica L.	0	0	0	0	0	0	0	0	0	0	0	0	0
Kat Badam Anacardium occidentale L.	0	0	0	0	0	0	0	0	0	0	0	0	0
Bakul Mimosa elangii L.	0	0	0	0	0	0	0	1	0	0	0	1	1
Akashpati	0	0	0	0	0	0	0	0	0	0	0	0	0
Meghagani Salmalia malabarica	0	0	0	0	0	0	0	0	0	0	0	0	0
Guava Fsidium guyava	0	0	0	0	0	0	0	0	0	0	0	0	0
Teak Tectona grandis L.f.	0	0	0	0	0	0	0	1	0	1	0	2	2
OTHERS	0	0	1	6	1	1	1	9	0	0	3	16	19
	8	4	12	27	13	22	16	47	14	23	63	123	186

M = Mature tree; Y = Young tree

TABLE 22.3
Distribution of tree species on the MH side of the B.T. Road

B.T. Road	0.6 km		1.6 km		2.6 km		3.6 km		4.6 km		TOTAL		
Tree species	M	Y	M	Y	M	Y	M	Y	M	Y	M	Y	M+Y
ASWATH Ficus relegiosa L.	0	1	2	0	1	4	4	6	6	3	11	17	28
BAT Ficus benhalensis L.	9	6	10	2	9	9	3	23	5	16	36	56	92
NEEM Azadirchta indica Adv. Juss.	1	1	1	0	3	1	1	1	0	1	6	4	10
MANGO Mangifera indica L.	1	0	0	0	0	1	0	0	0	1	1	2	3
KADAM Anthocephalus Kadamba miq.	0	0	6	2	0	1	1	3	0	1	7	7	14
KRISHNACUDA Caesalpinia pulcherrima Sw.	0	0	2	6	0	6	0	30	0	0	2	42	44
RADHACHUDA Delonix regia Raf.	0	0	1	1	1	1	0	1	0	0	2	3	5
CAUSURINA Causurina equistifolia Font.	0	0	0	0	0	1	0	0	2	0	2	1	3
EUCALYPTUS Eucalyptus globosus Labil.	0	1	0	0	0	0	0	0	2	0	2	1	3
CHATIM Alstonia scholaris R.Br.	0	0	2	0	0	0	0	0	0	0	2	0	2
TAMARIND Tamarindus indica L.	0	0	0	0	1	0	1	0	0	0	2	0	2
KAT BADAM Anacardium occidentale L.	0	0	0	0	1	0	0	0	0	0	1	0	1
BAKUL Mimosa alangii L.	0	0	0	0	0	2	0	0	0	1	0	3	3
AKASHATI	0	0	0	0	0	1	0	0	0	0	0	1	1
MEGHAGANI Salmalia malaberica	0	0	0	0	0	1	0	0	0	0	0	1	1
GUAVA Psidium guyava	0	0	0	0	0	1	0	0	0	0	0	1	1
TEAK Tectonia grandis L.f.	0	0	0	0	0	0	0	0	0	0	0	0	0
OTHERS	0	0	1	0	0	0	0	0	0	0	1	0	1
	11	10	23	13	16	29	10	64	15	23	75	139	214

M = Mature tree; Y = Young tree

tion of mature and young trees as well as the total densities considerably vary in the 5 different stretches of the road (table 22.1), it is expected that the proportion of trees used by the people will also vary. Thus, in the stretch between Tobin Road and Bonhooghly only 26.7 per cent of the trees were used while between Bon Hooghly and Dunlop 54.5 trees were used (table 22.5). On an average, thus, about 31 trees per km show some associated human activity.

TABLE 22.4

A list of the observed human activities associated with trees on B.T. Road

Human activity		Frequency ISI	MH	Total
I	**Religious purposes**			
1.	Temple/religous use	25	27	52
II	**Public Utilities**			
2.	Police assistance booth	1	0	1
3.	Notice boards/ advertisements	8	2	10
4.	Platform - bench for rest	7	7	14
5.	Rikshaw stand	1	1	2
6.	Tempo Stand	1	0	1
7.	Recreation (card playing)	1	0	1
8.	Bus stop	2	5	7
9.	Memorial plaque	0	2	2
10.	Residence/shelter	0	2	2
11.	Statue	0	1	1
12.	Swing for children	0	2	2
13.	For fencing	0	1	1
14.	Hand cart parking	0	1	1
15.	Clothes hanger for bath	1	4	5
16.	Bus association cabin	0	1	1
17.	Used as a tent - pole	1	0	1
18.	Water hole	2	0	2
	TOTAL	25	29	54
III	**Economic purposes**			
19.	Cobbler	3	1	4
20.	Pan shop	4	9	13
21.	Bamboo shop	1	2	3
22.	Flower shop	1	0	1

23.	Fruit shop	1	1	2
24.	Vegetable shop	4	2	6
25.	Tea shop	2	12	14
26.	Motorcycle workshop	3	1	4
27.	Book shop	1	0	1
28.	Steel vessel shop	1	2	3
29.	Lottery ticket shop	1	2	3
30.	Tobacco (Khaini) and lime shop	2	0	2
31.	Egg shop	1	0	1
32.	Sugar cane juice shop	2	0	2
33.	Cycle repair	1	1	2
34.	Tea-cum-cigarette shop	1	0	1
35.	Muri (puffed rice) shop	1	0	1
36.	Cucumber shop	2	1	3
37.	Coconut (tender) water shop	1	1	2
38.	Bamboo store	0	1	1
39.	Tyre shop	2	4°	6
40.	Automobile works	1	1	2
41.	Palmist	1	0	1
42.	Iron scrape shop	1	0	1
43.	Meals hotel	1	0	1
44.	Ladder storage	1	0	1
45.	Begger	1	0	1
46.	Rice shop	1	0	1
47.	Sweet shop	1	0	1
48.	Kulfi shop	1	0	1
49.	Second hand clothes	2	0	2
50.	Art dyer	1	0	1
51.	Barber shop	6	3	9
52.	Tile storage	1	0	1
53.	Steel works	2	1	3
	TOTAL	56	43	99
	GRAND TOTAL I+II+III	106	99	205

Interestingly, it was observed that some trees were associated with more than one activity. The results sepearately for each side of the road are presented in tables 6 and 7. It is seen that of the 142 trees 97 (68.3%) were associated with only one activity whereas 30 (21.1%) showed two activities and only 15 (10.6%) displayed 3 or more activities. The maximum number of activities observed were associated with a Bat tree. As expected more than one activity was primarily associated with mature trees. Of 45 such instances 36 (80%) were seen associated with mature trees while only 9 (20%) representing mostly two activities (8 out of nine) with young trees.

TABLE 22.5
Distribution of Human Activities associated with avenue trees on the B.T. Road

Stretch (South to north)		Associated human activities			
		MH side		ISI side	
		P	A	P	A
Hemanta Setu to Police HQ (1 km)	M	8	7	10	4
	Y	17	6	5	18
	T	25	13	15	22
Police HQ to Sinthee More (1 km)	M	8	2	13	3
	Y	15	49	2	45
	T	23	51	15	48
Sinthee More to Tobin Road (1 km)	M	11	5	7	6
	Y	5	24	3	19
	T	16	29	10	25
Tobin Road Bonhoogly (1 km)	M	11	12	8	4
	Y	0	13	1	26
	T	11	25	9	30
Bonhoogly to Dunlop (0.6 km)	M	7	4	5	3
	Y	4	6	2	2
	T	11	10	7	5
TOTAL	M	45	30	43	20
	Y	41	98	13	110
	T	86	128	56	130

P = Present; A = Absent

Thus, counting each activity separately it is obeserved that while the number of trees involved is 142, the number of activities total to 205 (93 on the ISI side and 112 on the MH side).

For the sake of convenience, the observed 205 activities have been grouped under three categories: (i) Religious, (ii) Public utilities and (iii) Economic.

Religious activities

A total of 52 trees (13%), 25 on the ISI side and 27 on the MH side, were found associated with some religious activity in the form of places of worship like temples - open or covered structures. Three trees, namely, Bat, Aswath, and Neem were associated with religious activities; one Kadam tree was also found associated with this activity. Of the 52 trees, however, a majority were Bat (73.1%) amd Aswath (21.2%). It is thus highly noteworthy that at the time of survey 25.2% of Bat and 20% of Aswath trees along the B.T.Road were worshipped by the local residents.

Public Utiliies

It is observed that about 17 kinds (though not necessarily totally different) of public utilities are provided by the avenue trees. These were found associated with 54 trees and constitute 26.3% of all the activities observed. Details of the activities are listed in table 4. The trees provide place for parking cycle riskshaws, tempos, and hand carts. In absence of built-in bus stands, it is seen that several avenue trees provide shade from sun and protection from rain to passengers waiting for Buses and are thus used as Bus stops. Trees also provide a shady and cool place for rest and recreation. Small traders even use the trees for putting up advertisements and notice boards, and some trees are also used for drying clothes.

Economic activities

A wide range of economic activities were observed associated with the trees. A total of 99 (48.3%) activities out of 205 belonged to this category. These pertain to 34 different kinds of pursuits. For details see table 4. A majority of the activities relate to selling of vegetable, fruits, eggs, cereals, cigarettes, betel leaf (Pan), tobacco etc. Some were engaged in repair activities like cobbler, cycle and motorcycle workshops, etc., and yet others provided services like barber. Notably the largest number of shops were serving tea. In a majority of the cases the persons simply prepared a small platform without cover and performed the activity. In some cases, however, small, mostly bamboo made, covered structures were also seen. Others mostly selling cigarettes and pan, had small stalls but located under the trees. For a select number of activities the frequency occurence is as follows: tea shops (14), pan shops (13), barber (9), vegetble shops (6), cobbler (4).

In short, the avenue trees provide space to a large number of poor people who can not afford to pay the exorbitant rents and have a place to operate in the organized city markets. These persons sell and/or provide services at a much cheaper rates compared to their counterparts who operate in the organized markets. Thus, these people cater to the needs of the weaker section of the city dwellers.

Discussion: Table - 22.5, Table - 22.6, Table - 23.7

The observed density of trees on the 4.6 km stretch of B.T.Road is 43.5 trees per km on each side of the road or 87 trees per km. This density, as will be seen below, falls markedly short of the attainable density.

TABLE 22.6
Distribution of number of Activities under a single tree on the ISIS side of B.T. Road

Stretch (south to north)	Activity Single		Double		Three and more		Total	
	M	Y	M	Y	M	Y	M	Y
Hemanta Setu to Police HQ (1 km)	6	5	2	0	2	0	10	5
Police HQ to Sinthee More (1 km)	7	2	2	0	4	0	13	2
Sinthee More to Tobin Road (1 km)	2	2	2	1	3	0	7	3
Tobin Road to Bonhoogly (1 km)	6	1	2	0	0	0	8	1
Bonhoogly to Dunlop (0.6 km)	2	2	3	0	0	0	5	2
Total	23	12	11	1	9	0	43	13

The density of trees on a given road depends on a number of factors, such as the quantity of space available on both sides of the road, the nature of physical constraints like road crossings and entrance to establishments, electric and telephone connections and the tree species to be planted. The density and the choice of tree species, therefore, will vary from one road to another.

The available space on B.T.Road, in most parts, is sufficient to have a single row of trees; in patches even double rows can be planted. If, for whatever reasons, trees like Bat, Aswath or Neem which develop large canopy, are to be planted, as has been done in earlier times, then 140-180 trees per km or 70-90 on each side of the B.T.Road can easily be planted. On the other hand, if trees like Krishnachuda or Kadam or a mix of these two are planted on the B.T.Road. In such a mix species model, 200 trees per km (100 on each side) can be sustained.

TABLE 22.7
Distribution of number of Activities under a single tree on the MH side of B.T. Road

Stretch (south to north)	Activity Single		Double		Three and more		Total	
	M	Y	M	Y	M	Y	M	Y
Hemanta setu to police HQ (1 km)	4	14	4	2	0	1	8	17
Police HQ to Sinthee More (1 km)	6	10	1	5	1	0	8	15
Sinthee More to Tobin Road (1 km)	8	5	3	0	0	0	11	5
Tobin Road to Bonhoogly (1 km)	8	0	2	0	1	0	11	0
Bonmoogly to Dunlop (0.6 km)	3	4	1	0	3	0	7	4
Total	29	33	11	7	5	1	45	41

It is thus obvious that the observed density of 87 trees per km is markedly less then what can be sustained. In otherwords, as against 920 trees, presently only 400 trees exist on the B.T.Road.

It is a matter of great concern that so much of land suitable for plantation has not been utilized so far. There is, therefore, an urgent need for the concerned authorities to take up immediate steps to put these areas under tree cover.

As noted earlier, a number of tree species have been planted along the B.T.Road. The predominant ones, however, are Bat, Aswath, Neem and Krishnachuda. It is also seen that there has been a significant shift in the choice of the species in recent years. Earlier, as witnessed by surviving nature trees, the preferred species were Bat, Aswath and Neem. However, the plantations undertaken during the last 5 years comprise mostly of Krishnachuda and Kadam.

We shall now consider whether the species planted earlier and recently on the B.T.Road are the most appropriate ones. The appropriateness of a species clearly depends upon the anticipated function(s) that is expected to be performed by the trees.

Till recently, the avenue trees in the cities have been viewed largely from the beautification or aesthetic point of view. Therefore, in general, the choice has been for ornamental or the so called exotic species. It is now well established that for the proper maintenance of ecological balance about 33 per cent of the total city area should be put under tree cover. It is known that trees help in regulating temperature, moisture and wind speeds. Trees also play vital role in maintain the balance between oxygen and carbon dioxide and help in reducing sound and dust pollution levels. Trees are also known not only to restore the soil and prevent soil erosion but also build ground water table. Trees in cities also support wild life particularly insects and birds.

The present study, for the first time, has demonstrated unequivocally that avenue trees play a very vital role in the lives of city dwellers in general and the weaker sections in particular. The trees provide place for recreation, leisure, livelihood, a number of public conviniences and religious functions. The single most important aspect that people make use of the trees is the shade provided by the canopy.

This important aspect has hitherto remained totally unnoticed. In short, thus, our choice of the species should be such that the above three functions, namely, socio-economic and religious, ecological and aesthetic, are maximized.

Before we delibrate further on this point, it would be appropriate to recall that the densities in different stretches of the road under consideration showed a wide variation. A careful examination of the patches with high or low densities revealed an interesting fact. We observed that wherever there were some shops or other establishments along the sides of the road the trees came up very well, while in their absence the number of trees was rather low. In otherwords, whereever the density was high it were the local people who protected and nourished the trees. It is thus clear that if the trees along the road sides have to survive, involvement of the local people, wherever possible, is absolutely necessary, otherwise there will be high martality of the trees. It was further observed that if the people worshipped a particular tree its chances of survival are almost 100 per cent.

The local climatic conditions should also be given due consideration in the choice of trees. The city of calcutta before and during monsoon experiences several rather high speed storms. The trees should be able to withstand these storms, otherwise we may lose a large number of mature trees every year.

It is, thus, evident from the above discussion that the specie(s) to be planted along the B.T.Road should be evergreen, native and fast growing (this will ensure shade throughout the year); should be sturdy enough to withstand storms; should have high probability of survival; and should be able to provide furits and nesting facilities to the birds.

The species that has all the above characteristics is indeed the native evergreen fast growing Banyan (Bat). Some ecologists suggest that a mixed species plantation will serve ecological functions better than mono species plantation. It is, therefore, suggested that a mix of Banyan, Peepal and Neem in the proportion of 60:20:20 respectively, would be most ideal. All these three species are worshipped by the Hindus. All of these bear edible fruits for the birds and provide excellent nesting facilities. However, it may be noted that Peepal and Neem are not evergreen species, but a mix plantation would ensure good patches of shade throughout the year.

Lastly, we woulsd like to stress that the nature and extent of associations as detailed earlier between avenue trees and city dwellers, particularly the poorer sections, is in fact an excellent indicator of the prevailing socio-economic conditions in a city and/or country. Knowing the economic conditions in other parts of the country we predict that similar associations (the extent will however vary) will be observed in other cities/towns as well. Although no quantitative data are available in respect of other cities, on of us (KCM) has observed similar pattern in several cities like Patna, Ranchi, Bhagalpur, Pune, Ahmednagar, Kolhapur, Delhi, Rajkot. We further predict that while similar relationships will also be observed in cities of other developing countries like Bangladesh, Pakistan, Nepal etc., the situation will be quite the opposite in developed countries.

This brings us to another important point. That is, should we allow the self employed poor people of the cities to use the space under avenue trees?. Of course, the law prohibits construction of permanent structures. In fact while we had just finished the survey of B.T.Road, one fine morning the city authorities forced all the hawkers to dismentle their shops/hotels etc. Clearly we can not allow people to establish permanent structures under the avenue trees since this will hamper smooth running of the traffic. But in our opinion those who just use the space without building any permanent structure and those with small moveable stalls(the dimensions can be worked out and specified) should be allowed to persue their livelihood. There is, therefore, an urgent need to review the policies related to the use of space under avenue trees keeping in view the prevailing socioeconomic conditions in the cities.

Summary and Conclusion

An exploratory survey was undertaken in March 1986 on a 4.6 km stretch from Hemanta Setu in the south to Dunlop Bridge Crossing in the north on the Barrackpore Trunk Road in Calcutta to understand various social, economic, religious and ecological problems and issues associated with avenue trees in urban centers. A complete census of all the trees was made and aspects like species, age of the tree, associated human activity etc. were noted for each tree. Following are the main findings of the study:

Tree density

The observed density of trees is only 43.5 trees per km on each side of the road or 87 trees per km. We estimate that about 200 trees per km can easily be sustained on a long term basis. The observed density thus falls short by 113 trees per km.

There is a marked variation in the densities of trees between different stretches of the road; the minimum and maximum are 20 and 60 trees per km, respectively.

The proportion of young trees (aged 5 years or less) is nearly double (65.5 per cent) compared to the mature trees (more than 5 years old; 34.5%).

Species diversity

Altogether about 17 trwee species were planted along the stretch of the B.T.Road under consideration. The predominant species were, however, Banyan (37.7 per cent), Krishnachuda (22.5 per cent), Peepal (13.7 per cent), Kadam (5.7 per cent) and Neem (5 per cent); these 5 species constitute 84.6 per cent of all the species encountered.

It is observed that earlier the preferred species were Banyan, Peepal and Neem. However, in plantations undertaken in the last five years there has been a major shift in the choice of species as revealed by the presence of a large number of young Krishnachuda trees. Among the mature trees there were only 3 Krishnachuda, but among the young trees there were 87 Krishnachuda.

Associated human activities

Of the total 400 trees, 142 (35.5 per cent) were found associated with social economic and religious human activities.

52 trees of Banyan, Peepal and Neem were found associated with religious activities; the people worship these trees.

54 trees provided various kinds of public conveniences to the people such as parking place for rickshaws, hand carts, tempos, shady place for recreation, leisure, bus passengers.

A wide variety of economic activities were found associated with the avenue trees. A total of 99 activities (48.3 per cent) of all the 205 activities observed belonged to this category. 34 different kinds of persuits such as selling of vegetables, fruits, eggs, cereals, cobbler, cycle and motorcycle repair shops, etc. were observed under the trees.

It was observed that whereever the tree density was high it was because of the fact that local residents protected and nourished the trees.

The study indicates that the nature and extent of use of avnue trees is an excellent indicator of prevailing socio-economic conditions in various cities and/or countries.

This study, for the first time, demonstrates that the avenue trees in urban centers not only perform important ecological role but also play significant socio-economic and religious role in the lives of the urban dwellers, particularly the weaker sections.

The choice of the species to be planted on a given road in urban areas should be guided by the above considerations. In general, we recommend that the species should be evergreen (to provide shade through out the year), native, fast growing, sturdy to withstand local climatic conditions, and should provide fruits and nesting facilities to the birds.

The species that has all the above characteristics is indeed the native Banyan. For ecological reasons, however, a mix of

Banyan, Peepal and Neem would be most ideal. These species, however, can not be recommended for all the roads.

For successful implimentation of road-side plantation programmes it is absolutely necessary to involve local residents and voluntary organizations.

In view of the lack of systematic data it is suggested that immediate efforts should be made to undertake extensive studies of trees along all the roads not only in Calcutta but other cities as well.

There is an urgent need to undertake extensive plantations whereever vacant space is available along the road-sides.

There is also an urgent need to formulate a comprehensive national policy in regard to the use of space under the avenue trees.